Discursive Constructions of Corporate Identities by Chinese Banks on Sina Weibo

Wei Feng

Discursive Constructions of Corporate Identities by Chinese Banks on Sina Weibo

An Integrated Sociolinguistics Approach

Springer

Wei Feng
School of Foreign Languages
Shanxi University
Taiyuan, Shanxi Province
P. R. China

ISBN 978-981-10-4468-7 ISBN 978-981-10-4469-4 (eBook)
DOI 10.1007/978-981-10-4469-4

Library of Congress Control Number: 2017939537

Printed on acid-free paper

This Springer imprint is published by Springer Nature
The registered company is Springer Nature Singapore Pte Ltd.
The registered company address is: 152 Beach Road, #21-01/04 Gateway East, Singapore 189721, Singapore

About the Book

This monograph belongs to the outcome of "Research Project Supported by Shanxi Scholarship Council of China".

Contents

List of Figures

List of Tables

Abstract

Given the speedy development of social media in revolutionising the way corporate communications used to be undertaken, the present monograph attempts to address one pressing yet somehow neglected issue: the discursive construction of corporate identities on social media by Chinese corporations. Representative of numerous corporations actively engaged in their social media accounts with diverse economic ownership, two Chinese banks—the state-owned Bank of China (BOC) and the joint-equity China Merchants Bank (CMB)—were compared and contrasted in the present study in terms of identity construction and interaction with their followers. The entire microblogging updates by these two corporations during a time span of approximately three years (from 1 September 2013 to 30 September 2016) were collected for the present investigation.

A two-way dialogic framework of corporate identity construction on social media was conceptualised to consist of two pairs of discourse initiations and responses: company's initiation and followers' corresponding responses, and followers' initiation and company's corresponding responses. In regard to the methodology, an integrated sociolinguistics approach drawing upon thematic analysis, interactional analysis and in-depth insider interviews was employed to shed light on the BOC and the CMB's shared and varied means of identity construction and interaction with followers.

The findings illuminated differential multifaceted identities of the selected corporations on Sina Weibo. Amongst a number of humanised identities constructed on the corporate social media, the CMB primarily projected itself as an intimate companion to its millions of followers (59.5%, 825 items), whereas the most noticeable identity of the BOC is the specialist identity (40.1%, 573 items), followed by the companion identity (25.8%, 368 items). In addition, two overarching impression management strategies were discovered: humanising and popularising the corporate self and persuading followers into trusting (and eventually trading with) the corporate self.

Furthermore, a careful examination of the firm–follower interaction patterns on Sina Weibo revealed a handful of dialogic patterns with its relevant linguistic realisations that are used in the process of followers' co-construction of corporate identity: storytelling/praise-acknowledgement and question-raillery between the BOC and its followers versus question-raillery, storytelling-raillery, storytelling/praise-acknowledgement, question-answer and raillery-counter-raillery between the CMB and its followers. Finally, the variations in corporate identities between the two corporations are both statistically elucidated and qualitatively discussed vis-a-vis the in-depth interview data.

The present study bears special significance to the theoretical and methodological development of studying corporate identity by developing a dialogic framework of analysis, which illuminates and explicates the multiplicity and fluidity of corporate identity construction on social media such as Sina Weibo. Furthermore, it bears significant practical implications for both practitioners and teachers or trainers in corporate communication who are faced with the challenges in managing public relations and corporate images in the age of social media.

Chapter 1
Introduction

1.1 The Construction of Corporate Identity in Public Relations

Over the past half-century or so, identity, its construction and corporate identity construction have emerged and flourished as a vibrant and inspiring realm of research not only attracting continuous scholarly devotions (e.g., Erikson 1964, 1968; Tajfel and Turner 1979; Peverelli 2006) but also pertaining to the daily practice of practitioners' and the interest of the general public.

The construction of corporate identity has, in one way or another, been verified to resemble the process of individual identity formation (e.g. Hatch and Schulz 2002; Johansson 2007). Nonetheless, the construction of corporate identity seems to be mostly "man-made" and under control of the corporation (Topalian 1984), evolving from the initial stage of logo to the later stage of corporate reputation. Sometimes interchangeably used as a corporate image, the corporate identities, underlying the corporations' distinguishing traits, are always in the making and are never fully made (Balmer 2008). Scholars have furthermore revealed the dynamics and multi-faceted nature of corporate identity. According to Balmer (2001), the focus on the identity traits of the corporation entails that corporate identity is characterised by their complexity (they are multi-faceted and multi-dimensional in nature in that they are informed by various spatial/temporal dimensions), variability (they are immutable but evolutionary in character) and heterogeneous (they are informed by multidisciplinary perspectives in terms of comprehension and management).

Central to external corporate communication strategies, however, is the designing and implementation of corporate identity, as an unavoidable step, during

W. Feng, *Discursive Constructions of Corporate Identities by Chinese Banks on Sina Weibo*, DOI 10.1007/978-981-10-4469-4_1

which corporations define and present "who are we?" as corporations and position themselves to stakeholders "where are we going?" Basically these two questions summarise the essential elements shared by many definitions of corporate identity. As Balmer (2008) proposed, corporate identity has a more overt external, customer/stakeholder and enjoys a hegemonic profile/usage in marketing scholarship and in management. As such, up-to-date methods and modes of communication of corporate identity serve as a long-standing notable issue in corporate communication and management (Boggio 2010).

Unlike personal identity formation, another major uniqueness of the construction of corporate identity lies in the efforts corporations constantly make to differentiate themselves from their rival companies (Abdullah et al. 2013). In business practices, the design and communication of corporate identity accord with the "persona" of organisations in their self-presentations and point to the ultimate attainment of a variety of corporate objectives, such as impression management and profit-making. Although largely being confined to corporate culture and values, the construction of corporate identity, i.e., the projected corporate self is subject to the management arts and the expertise of the marketing team. That is, it is a key task of the management specialists to build a desired and favorable corporate identity for the sake of the interests of all the stakeholders. The centrality and significance of corporate identity are manifested in numerous scholarly endeavors dedicated to exploring many aspects of this issue, e.g., the definitions of corporate identity (Balmer 1998, 2001; Peverelli 2006), theories of corporate identity (He and Balmer 2013), its relationships to marketing (Balmer 1998, 2001), the entities incorporated in an integrated corporate identity (Melewar and Karaosmanoglu 2005; Balmer 2008) and its variations in the new modes of communications (Abdullah et al. 2013; Lillqvist and Louhiala-Salminen 2014).

Contextualising corporate identity as the research focus, the present research resides in two prominent and distinct contexts: the flourishing social media era that human societies are currently confronted with and a transitioning, emerging "superpower": China and one of its pillar industries: the banking sector.

1.2 The Rise and Flourish of Social Media

In his New York Times bestseller of 2016 *The Inevitable: Understanding 12 Technological Forces that Will Shape Our Future*, the futurist Kevin Kelly divided the evolution of human being into three distinct epochs, in accordance with the interdependence between mankind and the medium of information, namely: (1) the epoch of people of the word, when word-of-the-mouth is the primary means of information dissemination; (2) the epoch of people of the book, when paper is the primary means of information dissemination; and (3) the epoch of people of the screen, when electronic screen becomes the primary means of information dissemination. According to Kelly (2016), we are currently living in the epoch of electronic screen where social media play an irreplaceable role in the information dissemination, interpersonal interaction and public relations, shaping the next 30 years and transforming our lives.

The advent of social media that has sprung up since the first decade of the new millennium has redefined and reshaped both message contents and mode of communication in an unprecedented way in places wherever it is accessible (cf. Tannen and Trester 2013; Thurlow and Mroczek 2011). Friedman's (2006) bestseller The World is Flat has innovatively depicted and conceptualised today's world as flat, alluding to the perceptual shift required for countries, companies and individuals to retain competitiveness in a global market where historical and geographical divisions are becoming increasingly less relevant. Notwithstanding this brilliant insight, this bestselling book had been written and published shortly before new media[1] was widely accessible to the general public. In other words, in just a few years since 2006, the world has transformed to become even flatter due to the sheer fact that the new media has absolutely revolutionised the way present-day communication works. A consensus has been achieved that new media has ushered in a brand-new age of human communication (Tannen and Trester 2013) and it is even claimed that the advent of social media represents the most significant paradigm shift since the Industrial Revolution, i.e., the so-called Social Media Revolution (Pacea 2011).

New media, also known as social media, made its initial presence in 2004, and was later referred to as "websites and applications that enable users to create and share content or to participate in social networking" in the Oxford English Dictionary. The American Merriam-Webster dictionary, defines social media as "forms of electronic communication (as websites for social networking and microblogging) through which users create online communities to share information, ideas, personal messages, and other content (as videos)". A pioneering and more scholarly definition of social media is as follows: a group of Internet-based applications that build on the ideological and technological foundations of Web 2.0, and that allow the creation and exchange of user-generated content (Kaplan and Haenlein 2010). A classification scheme is also created, with seven different types of social media: collaborative projects (e.g. Wikipedia); blogs and microblogs (e.g. Twitter); social news networking sites (e.g. Digg and Leakernet); content communities (e.g. YouTube and DailyMotion); social networking sites (e.g., Facebook); virtual game-worlds (e.g. World of Warcraft); virtual social worlds (e.g. Second Life) (ibid).

[1]"New media" in this monograph is entirely meant social media, or social networking site.

Social media is regarded as an imperative component in shifting contemporary communication landscape (Hopkins 2009). As such, waves of movements worldwide, political, economic or social, are taking advantage of social media in public engagement. In the wake of the newer, smarter and more interactive social media tools, the former U.S. President Barack Obama wisely and skillfully won the poll in his election of 2008 and 2012 with his active updates and interaction with millions of followers in his Twitter and Facebook account (Vaccari 2010; Conway et al. 2013). This popular case has imaginably contributed in countless public relations and new media lectures as legendary teaching material. More importantly the list of similar successes with the help of social media is endless. As noted, terms such as "Twitter revolution" and "Facebook revolution" have been used widely to conceptualise the notions of "dynamic media" or "Web 2.0" as "potentially radical, disruptive and socially transformative" (Cheong et al. 2012, p. 1).

Up until now, the best-known global brands of social media are bound to be the US photo-sharing network Facebook and the US microblogging network Twitter. In other parts of the world where censorship is causing Facebook and Twitter to be inaccessible, e.g., China, the same wave of social media battle to fight for users is being waged fiercely. According to the official statistics from the China Internet Network Information Center (CNNIC), by the end of 2015, Internet users of the People's Republic of China have exceeded 688 million (over half of its total population) with an annual increase of users amounting to 395 million, ranking as the world's No. 1 with the largest number of social media users. The figure is expected to grow rapidly over the next decade. The focal point is not only that there are enormous Internet users in China, but also that they are better-off consumers as evidenced that China passed Japan as the world's second largest economy by GDP in 2011.

There is no denying that social media has posed sufficient uncertainties and challenges to public relations managers in the field of external corporate communication (e.g., DiStaso et al. 2011; Briones et al. 2011). In the absence of editorship, unverified and unfavorable news against corporate reputation might cause widespread and uncontrollable public misunderstandings, confusion and anger, leading to an intensified difficulty of crisis communication. To cope with social media risks and to take full advantage of it, research attempts (e.g. Waters and Jamal 2011) have been made mostly in the English-speaking context or in countries and regions using English as a lingua franca, thus neglecting other emerging economies, such as China.

From a microeconomic viewpoint, given this enormous market of a relatively younger generation, coupled with a presumably positive foresight of Chinese economic growth, no enterprises, domestic and international, can afford to overlook its effective communication with wealthier Chinese consumers on the Internet (i.e. the netizens), especially on social networking sites, as their customers or potential customers. In fact, a growing number of companies worldwide are either becoming fully aware of social media or are actively involved in using it, as research suggested that the new form of electronic word of mouth is approximately two times more effective than marketing events and thirty times more effective than traditional media appearances (Trusov et al. 2009).

1.3 The Emerging, Transforming China and Its Banking Industry

Some light needs to be shed on the second key research context, a transforming, emerging China as the geographic location of the present study and its banking industry as the research focus. China under the rule of the Chinese Communist Party (hereinafter referred to as CCP) had practiced a completely collective economic ownership until 1978 (Hou 2011). The year of 1978, when the third Plenary Session of the Eleventh Congress of the Chinese Communist Party took place, was historically remarkable and epoch-making due to both its official farewell to the outdated ideology of class struggle, and more importantly, for its reemphasis on economic development (Feng 2008). This milestone switch to a market economy from a highly centralised and planned economy has resulted in long-standing impacts on both the Chinese economic landscape and on the Chinese people's mindset. China's entry to the WTO in 2001 has caused even greater transformations of in the economic and social landscapes. To make a long story shorter, on one hand, having long been hungry for the vast Chinese markets, multinational corporations were flooding China, aided by market entry limitations being unprecedentedly lifted since 2001. The management, operations as well as discourse practices of the multinationals in the host country were examined from various perspectives, among which for example, globalisation is one of the realms of research that raised much attention (Liu and Wu 2015; Wu 2008; Wu and Ng 2011). On the other hand, the globalisation of China is by no means a one-way street. Chinese companies are investing heavily on a global scale, as evidenced most prominently in the banking and manufacturing industries typified by multinationals such as Haier, Lenovo, Huawei and Bank of China, among which accomplished investors are not confined to large and medium-sized Chinese SOEs but also comprise as well as a fast-growing, fully-fledged troop of private businesses (c.f. Gilmore and Dumont 2003).

Drastic reforms in the economy and society has taken place in China in the past three decades, leading to the all-rounded evolution from the completely planned, centralised economy to the infancy of a market economy. This long-standing reformation of the economic base has resulted in fundamental changes in the underlying ideological and various aspects of social life in the past three decades or so (Feng and Wu 2009). It has been confirmed that China is changing from a poor and very isolated nation into a world superpower (Streissguth 2008). Although this opinion may be critiqued and subject to contention, transformations in China since the reform and opening up policy in the late 1970s have been indeed drastic. The truth is that China's annual economic growth over the past three decades peaked at a historical high of a little less than 10%[2] on average according to the IMF report in 2011.

The transition of the China's communism-centred economic structure to capitalism and privatization has been systematic, consistent and ongoing (Garnaut and Song 2004; Mantzopoulos and Shen 2011). It is claimed that a growing share of private sectors in the total national output is self-evident and in some eastern coastal provinces such as Guangdong, Zhejiang and Fujian, private-owned enterprises have in fact replaced the state-owned enterprises as the primary contributor to government financial revenue (cf. Zeng 2013). The privatization of China has been widely reported and studied (e.g. Peverelli 2006), leading to both well-noticed prosperity and problems in public spheres of politics, culture, education and environmental protection. Parallel with the rise of private ownership, since the 1990s, a large wave of state-owned manufacturing industries across the nation, have unprecedentedly lost their government subsidization for market competition and struggled for survival in 国企改制 (State-owned enterprises or SOEs reforms or restructuring), resulting in the large-scale bankruptcy, privatization, public offering, or debit-equity swap of state-owned enterprises (Garnaut et al. 2006). In the year of 1995, the State Council of China issued an overarching policy of SOEs reforms and resturcturing, nicknamed as 抓大放小. This entails that the Chinese government would protect and help existing large or super large SOEs to elevate their management skills and overall competitiveness and stop funding the rest of the small and medium-sized enterprises (SMEs) for fair market competitions on their own in order to eliminate some unsatisfactory players and save governmental funds. Those state-owned SMEs with undesirable and unsatisfactory market performance were encouraged to go bankrupt or restructure through mergers and acquisitions. Consequently, a nation-wide restructuring reform of SOEs led to tens of millions of laid-off SOE workers in China since the 1990s. Peverelli (2006) vividly summarised the socio-economic turn of China since the 1980s, from a *danwei* (SOEs as social intuitions) based society which used to provide a whole package of social welfare—salary, housing, schooling of employees' children, medical care and so forth—to all *danwei* employees, to a economically diversified and modernised society, incorporating all sorts of enterprises.

[2]For more information refer to http://www.imf.org/external/pubs/ft/weo/2011/02/.

In view of the target industry of the present study, an overview of the recent history of China's banking sector indicates that although the progress and development in regards to its financial service types and service standards have been remarkable since the late 1970s, problems and embarrassments caused by tight governmental control and deficiencies of the state-of-the-art management and professionals are prominent (Peng 2007).

China's full-fledged banking sector hitherto may be categorised into the following stratifications: state-owned commercial banks (nicknamed as the Big Four), policy banks, other (regional, city, national) merchant banks, rural credit cooperative, urban credit cooperative; postal savings, asset management company, trust and investment company as well as foreign banks or its branches (see Franklin et al. 2008). It was estimated that by 2014, the total numbers of banks amounted to approximately 3000, among which however private banks including joint-equity banks were less than ten. Of more significant importance than industry size is the stirring annual reports of the banking sector. The most powerful domestic key players are undoubtably the "Big Four", namely the Industrial and Commercial Bank of China (ICBC), the Agricultural Bank of China (ABC), the Bank of China (BOC) and the China Construction Bank (CCB), all of which are entirely state-owned. Over the decades, banks in China have substantially profited from the nation's overall economic growth and a deepening reform of the industry. According to the statistics from the China Banking Regulatory Commission, the average annual revenue of banks in China increased by 39.3% in 2012. Steady reforms of the China banking industry have deepened under a general direction of being free from government control. Nonetheless, despite the formal guidelines stipulated in the Commercial Banking Law, the government still wields a heavy influence on the operations of the commercial banks in China as the State Council maintains purview over credit allocated by the banks (Werner and Chung 2010).

As an exception of the vast majority of industries (e.g., manufacturing) that exploited various preferential policies against the backdrop of economic boom and privatization initiated in the early 1980s, the reforms of the banking sector undertook rather prudent and circumspect procedures, resulting in the de facto situation of the monopoly of the "Big Four" super giant banks (Tan 2014). As a matter of fact, the "Big Four" phenomenon in the nation's banking sector may be interpreted as an excellent demonstration of the well-acknowledged theory of "too big to fail" in the financial studies originated in the United States commencing in the mid 1980s (Lin 2010). As per Lin's (2010) definition, the 'too big to fail' theory asserts that certain financial institutions are so large and so interconnected that their failure would be disastrous to the economy as a whole, and they therefore must be supported by government in face of difficulty and crisis. The monopoly of the "Big

Four" was not challenged until the rising wave of a number of newcomers starting in the 1980s, including a school of foreign banks. From the 1990s onwards, a loosening market entry in the banking industry has been witnessed. As a milestone, the emergence of China's first private bank, China MinSheng Bank did not come into being until 1996. Thanks to China's fast economic growth in recent decades, banks at large are profiting substantially, as evidenced by the fact that six national banks in China are being listed in the Fortune 500.[3]

Competition among banks in China did not accelerate until the late 1980s, with a step-by-step steering of the industry upgrade for an evolution of improved financial service (Liu et al. 2009). For decades, the rigid planned economy of China granted neatly differentiated roles for each of the "Big Four" banks to play a role in one specific sector of the national economy, as their names hint, i.e., the Agricultural Bank of China specialising in rural agriculture; the China Construction Bank specialising in construction, the Bank of China specialising in foreign exchange and the Industrial and Commercial Bank of China specialising in the manufacturing and commerce. The wider gate-opening of the banking industry to foreign banks induced by China's access into WTO in 2001 stirred even ferocious market competition. The WTO membership stipulated that foreign banks would be allowed to offer the Chinese currency Renminbi business to local corporate clients within two years after 2001 and can conduct full domestic currency operations five years since 2001 (Cinar and Tang 2003).

The economic transition of China's banking industry, perhaps inevitably, has laid a foundation where Western consumerism flourishes. Sennett (2006) noted the prevalence of New Capitalism or New Economy across developed nations, which suggesting an economic transition from manufacturing-based economy to service-based economy and massive colonisation of consumer culture in each domains of social life. Consistent with the flourishing consumer culture in China's banking industry, which certainly applies to other sectors, is a consensus that the key to success resides in the ever-increasingly emphasised role of customers and corporations' quality of service to their customers, underpinning the desirably brother-like identities banks aspire to establish and maintain in dealing with their customers. Overall, notwithstanding too big to fail, state-owned banks in China is increasingly pressurised and desirous of better financial statements and being more skillful in dealing communications with their stakeholders as listed companies, in comparison with just one or two decades ago.

In such an industry background in the transforming China, the present-day market positioning of the BOC and the CMB is briefed. Founded in 1912 and as the oldest bank in China still in existence, the Bank of China is the fifth largest bank in the world by capitalisation value, ranking as the 35th in the Fortune 500 global corporations in 2016. By the end of 2015, the Bank of China operates businesses in 46 nations and regions through its 644 branches overseas. The Bank of China has

[3]http://money.cnn.com/magazines/fortune/global500/2012/countries/China.html.

long been reputed in taking the lead in handling financial businesses regarding foreign exchange and international settlement, given the glorious century-old history of its foreign exchange operations, which also justifies its columns on foreign exchange on the Sina Weibo that characterise its identity as an authoritative industry specialist and commentator.

Debuted in 1987 as the ever first non 100% state-owned banking corporation, the setup of the CMB is labeled a watershed in the water-testing reform of China's banking industry. The newborn CMB has drawn the curtains of fierce domestic competitions in banking industry, posing expanding challenges to the monopoly of the "Big Four" (Cinar and Tang 2003). The biggest shareholder of the CMB, a state-owned corporation China Merchants Group, which is headquartered in Hong Kong, holds only 18.7% of its total shares, indicating a wide mix-up of the shareholders of the CMB. In this sense, truly a joint-equity bank is the CMB, specialising in personal banking, credit card businesses and loans granted to small-and-medium-sized enterprises (SMEs) (announced in the official website of the CMB). This smart market positioning is fully manifested through its brand ambassador Mr. Lang Lang, a world-renowned Chinese-immigrated Hong Kong pianist, to cater for upper-middle-class individual clients with artistic tastes and elite educational background.

1.4 Scope of Research and Research Objectives

The present research addresses one pressing issue of general concern, to which devoted attentions are far less adequate across disciplines, e.g., discourse analysis, corporate communication studies as well as identity studies, namely, the presentation of corporate self on social media, which is rather likely to be an imperative concern of universal corporations in the incoming decades in their daily external corporate communication with stakeholders. Given the new birth of social media, despite several attempts in only a few limited developed nations, e.g. Denmark, there is still a global dearth of empirical research on the discursive construction of corporate identity in social media settings. In addition to a timely contribution to the literature of corporate communication and identity construction, the present research is equally inspiring to both office buildings and classrooms. In selecting China as the research context, the research findings prove to be meaningful and significant, as they not only shall be applicable to other (developing) nations, but also offer insights to millions of multinationals which have either selected China to invest and outsource or have targeted at China as their marketing destinations. This is especially realistic for the international banking industry whose presence in China is still a rarity upon China's bar-lifting policy to international banks in domestic markets since December 11, 2006, subsequent to a five-year buffer of China's WTO entrance at the end of the year of 2001.

In regard to the selected Chinese enterprises for an in-depth investigation, the scope of the present research is primarily confined to the banking industry due to the reasonable considerations as follows. First, although there are only eight Chinese banks among 128 Chinese corporations listed in Fortune 500 global corporations, China's banks are the largest profit-makers of all industries within Chinese Fortune 500 companies. According to the latest Global 500 statistics of 2013,[4] the "Big Four" state-owned banks, namely the Bank of China, the Agriculture Bank of China, the China Construction Bank and the Industrial and Commercial Bank of China performed exceptionally excellent and individually earned annual profits ranging from 22.1 to 37.8 billion USD. ICBC, in particular, has been extensively regarded as the world's most profitable bank. Second, unlike the dominant Chinese industries of petroleum or heavy machinery industries in Global 500, banks are service providers of each individual customer, making the quality of their external corporate communication in the new media era extraordinarily crucial. Third, ever since the 2009 global financial crisis initiated by subprime mortgage loan, there is an increasing awareness of the credibility of banks (Perez and Rodriguez del Bosque 2012), resulting in a question mark of the banks' identities in addressing their stakeholders. More succinctly, public listed banks are worthy of adequate and timely research attentions for the messages they deliver and the modes they select in communicating with the general public.

To summarise, the research objectives are three-folded: to identify the multiple identities of Chinese banks on social media; to illuminate the dialogic interactive mechanism of corporate identity formation on social media between corporation and their followers; to establish a theoretical framework which facilitates corporate identity studies on social media.

1.5 Outline of the Monograph

In sum, the monograph is organised into eight chapters. The current first chapter set a relevant scene for the present study to naturally unfold by sketching the research area being contributed, the research contexts as well as the aims of research. Chapter 2 offered a critical review of the voluminous body of research, by delineating the major strands of research in identity formation, construction of corporate identity, interactional sociolinguistics as well as academic achievements in new media discourse studies. It was at the end of this chapter that both research gaps and significance of study were pinpointed. Chapter 3 briefed the brand-new theoretical framework based on which the four research questions were posed. Research methods, research design and data collection details were described and presented in this chapter. Chapter 4 showcased the multiple corporate identities constructed and presented a comparison between the CMB and the BOC. Chapter 5 examined

[4] http://money.cnn.com/magazines/fortune/fortune500/2013/full_list/.

and summarised the impression management strategies employed by Chinese banks on Sina Weibo in constructing corporate identity. Chapter 6 explored the co-construction of followers of corporate identities. Chapter 7 detailed the cross-bank variations in identity construction. Chapter 8 concluded the monograph with a summary of the main findings, discussions and ended with a report of research limitations and implications for future research.

Chapter 2
Literature Review

2.1 Introduction

This chapter critically reviews the extant relevant literature, both theoretical and empirical, on which the theoretical framework is based and elucidated. The literature review basically consists of two sections. The first section describes identity formation and the construction of corporate identity. The second section examines notions and tenets of interactional sociolinguistics and new media discourse studies. Subsequent to acknowledging the existing and available literature, a discussion of research gaps is presented to indicate how the present study helps to bridge the research gap in literature.

2.2 Identity, Corporate Identity and Language Use

2.2.1 Identity Formation and Language Use

The interlocking relation between identity formation and language use is reviewed from the following three prominent perspectives: (1) psychological and sociological perspective (2) linguistic and communication perspectives (3) pragmatic perspective.

2.2.1.1 Psychological and Sociological Perspectives

In simple terms, when we realise the impression of "me" in the eyes of others, the consciousness of identity immediately comes into play. The psychologist Erikson (1964, 1968) maintained identity as a dynamic conception of oneself as a person, which amounted to a subjective sense of sameness felt by individuals within

W. Feng, *Discursive Constructions of Corporate Identities by Chinese Banks on Sina Weibo*, DOI 10.1007/978-981-10-4469-4_2

themselves. Identity as the perception of personal unity was generally regarded as the conviction to remain unchanged and essentially the same. Social identity theory (Tajfel and Turner 1979) problematised and untangled the identity of individuals vis-a-vis larger social groups, such as nations and religions to tackle intergroup discrimination.

Identity formation or identity construction, also known as individualisation, is an evolving, psychological and formative process of socialisation through which one's distinct personality and mentality are determined and become mature and relatively stable against others in social groups (Schwartz et al. 2011). Social belongings and biological traits have endowed individuals with a number of layers of simultaneous identities, be it ethnic and national identity, cultural identity, religious identity or gender identity, a matter of fact affecting all aspects of human societies and a basic truth that policymakers, educators and product designers can never afford to neglect.

It ought to be duly noted that, as one of the most renowned, yet elusive and sophisticated psychological notions, identity has generated accelerating interest and works in both the scholarly and practitioner realms (e.g. Goffman 1959; Leary 1996; Elliott 2001). Identity and its formation have long been an active research area in psychology and a wide variety of disciplines in social sciences (Elliott 2011). Despite that interpersonal development of identity formation can be individualised, there are developed theories describing and categorising the nature and process of identity formation. The crucial theory of psychological development of Erikson (1964) propounded that the particular stage relevant to identity formation, i.e., "identity versus role confusion", takes place during adolescence (age between 12 and 20). If this stage is accomplished, individuals enter into the next stage of "intimacy versus isolation" where they will form strong friendships and a sense of companionship with others. Likewise, Marcia's (1966) well-cited identity status theory proposed a natural progression of four identity statuses: identity diffusion, identity foreclosure, identity moratorium and identity achievement.

While some schools of thought highlighted the sameness feature of identity, other scholars sensed and acknowledged the fluid, dynamic and negotiated nature of identity and its formation (De Fina et al. 2006; Garzone and Archibald 2010). The pioneering attempt of McCall and Simons (1966) in defining identity deemed identity formation as a bidirectional process and linked the role of the actor in relation to the role of other actors as a result of social interaction. More recently, it was argued that views social identity theorists held towards identity were incomplete and static (e.g., Perverelli 2006). Rather than viewing identity construction as "one-way traffic", Perverelli (2006, p. 2) regarded and conceptualised identity, particularly corporate identity, as "the construction of identity by the holder of the identity, the environment in which the identity is constructed". His richer definition of identity pertains to two directions: (1) it comprises three aspects of identity: the holder of the identity, the environment in which the identity is constructed and the construction process; (2) it allows for a multiple definition of identity: an individual can be perceived as having multiple identities in multiple contexts (ibid.). Noticeably, the co-construction of identity has been increasingly echoed. Some believed that "corporate identity formation is not a univocal process: a number of different corporate functions and people contribute to it" (Allori and Garzone 2010, p. 14).

To further trace the source of identity as co-construction, a great name and his seminal philosophy deserved our attention and elucidation. In his groundbreaking book *The Presentation of Self in Everyday Life* published as early as 1959, sociologist Erving Goffman set the basic frontiers in the realm of identity with reference to face and social interactions. In comparing individuals to performers and their everyday presentation to staged performance in front of audience, Goffman (1959) specified that identity is an ongoing interactive construction rather than something given (cf. Irwin 2011). This entails that self is an ongoing social construct, rather than merely an array of visual and invisible attributes wholly controlled and decided by its owner. The efforts individuals attempt to make in the public is front-stage behaviors or, in Goffman's words, impression management. Otherwise in the private domains where they take off masks, individuals act back-stage behaviors. Goffman (1967) gave sufficient prominence to the role of social interaction in constructing personal identity, during which face and face-work are an integral part. The social experience in constructing personal identity is governed by frame (Goffman 1974). After all, a convincing conclusion was drawn on the construction of identity: "this self is a product of a scene that comes off, and is not a cause of it" (Goffman 1959, p. 252).

The research on identity has flourished for half a century or so, resulting in the recognisation of the accelerated interdisciplinary popularity of identity. In recent years, identity appears to be in the social sciences and humanities as everything from reconstructed and reinvented to displaced and disowned to loveless and liquidised. There is indeed an immense and growing literature on identity and the field of identity studies has become of key significance to the social sciences and humanities the world over" (Elliott 2011). A noticeable challenge is the changing milieu of identity being examined, as observed that in a context of globalisation, e-society, the networked or virtual society, the mobility of labor and citizenship, "identity has now become a more nuanced core topic stretching across a variety of sub-fields" (Pullen and Linstead 2005, p. 1).

In summary, among the academic literature revolving around identity and its formation, two developed perspectives drew noteworthy attention: a dialogic perspective and a dialectic perspective. From the dialogic perspective, social constructionists (e.g. Gergen 1994, 1999) deemed individuals as living in a network of relations with others and proposed the concept of a linguistic, relational self where self is realised in language and dialogue, i.e., self is then constructed and re-constructed in a reflective process through continuous interactions and relationships. However, a dialectic perspective such as Vygotskian socio-cultural approach (Rieber and Carton 1987) assumed that all human mental functioning is socio-culturally, historically, and institutionally situated and maintained that identity formation involves an encounter between cultural resources for identity and individual choices for fidelity, values, ideology and commitment.

2.2.1.2 Sociolinguistic and Communication Perspectives

Another key strand of thought in identity and language use falls into sociolinguistic research which explicitly suggested that: "identity is now considered as a primary focus of investigation" (Dyer 2007, p. 108). Not surprisingly with identity as a common theme and drawing heavily on spoken interaction, social constructionist work has been extended to much wider domains penetrating to areas of "gender, ethnicity, childhood and adolescence, adolescence and gender, adolescence and ethnicity, adolescence and social class, ethnicity, national identity and minority languages, 'othering' in the legal system, ethnicity, natural identity and policing, mediated (political) discourse (Irwin 2011, p. 110). However, the applicability of social constructionist approach of identity studies is somehow limited its scope to synchronous face-to-face and one-to-one spoken interaction, as such allowing more timely research on one-to-many non face-to-face written interaction, preferably on institutionalised basis to further explore language and discursive construction of identity.

The extant volume of research, over the past few decades, touching upon the dualistic relationship between identity and language has been cross-disciplinary and primarily inspired by sociology (Goffman 1959, 1967), variationist sociolinguistics (Labov 1972; Lakoff 1975), ethnography of communication (Hymes 1974), socio-psychology (Tajfel 1981), pragmatics (Leech 1983; Brown and Levinson 1987; Gu 1990; Verschueren 1999), ethnolinguistics (Eckert 2000), critical discourse analysis (Fairclough 1995a) and interactional sociolinguistics (Gumperz 1982b; Tannen 1996; Goffman 1981).

By his classic dramaturgical metaphors such as "back stage, front stage and audience", Goffman's (1959) far-reaching sociological conclusions of personal identity regard the self as a social construction or more specifically an interactive construction. However, the concept of self is by no means grounded in individual psychology with psychological constructs such as goals and motives applied, but is more concerned with social rules in social interaction (Schiffrin 1994, p. 105). Goffman's holistic coneptualisation of the self-concept is summarised into a tripartite scheme: the self is a social construction, impressions of self are "given off" rather than "given" and they are interpreted according to conventionalised or socially agreed-upon "rituals" (Tannen 2009, p. 300). In the same page Tannen continued, by "given off" rather than "given", it is meant that aspects of a speaker's "performance" give others an impression of the speaker's self.

Variationist sociolinguistics is a strand of quantitative approach to the interrelationship studies between variables at different levels of phonetic or grammatical structures and linguistic, social-economic environments in which they occur (Labov 1980). In many cases, social factors such as gender, age and class are used to experiment their constraints in language use. The representative figure Labov (1972) distinguished the economic status of speakers in a New York department store by locating the phonological variations of the English syllabus "r" among randomly selected participants. His seminal study was replicated many times in varied settings in various parts of the world. (Variationist) sociolinguistics enabled reliable methods that, apart from their effectiveness in tracing linguistic diffusion processes, "make it possible to use linguistic indices in survey studies of social identity" (Gumperz 1982a, p. 25). In others words, variationist sociolinguistics bridged the systemic connection between linguistic behaviors with linguistic attitudes and opinions, which reflect and reinforce user identity. Another crucial figure Lakoff (1975) proposed her most cited dichotomous view of gender and the general features of female register, ranging from women's favored usage of weak expletives to the use of question tag. Nonetheless, variationist sociolinguistics has been heavily doubted and challenged for their static interpretations of born and essentialist identities of language users, more precisely the automatic causal correlation between individual aspects of linguistic behavior and certain traits of social identity (cf. Camerson 1990).

From the perspective of the ethnography of communication, Gumperz (1982a) stressed the discourse strategies in interpersonal communication and argued that identities can be constructed and created in verbal communications, regardless of the pre-given identities that speakers may have. Gumperz's conceptualisations on identity constructions were not alone. Ethnolinguists claimed that the identities are constructed in the community of practice, which form members' collective way of doing and way of thinking (e.g. Eckert 2000). Major accomplishments of Tannen (1984, 1990, 1996) reside in her gendered discourse studies in relation to its relationship with identity whose anti-essentialist view of identity in gender studies never stops to inspire people to conceive identity as fixed and stable, but rather fluid and multilayered (cf. Garzone and Catenaccio 2009). Adopting a social perspective, critical discourse analysts (Fairclough 1989; 1995b; van Dijk 1988) deconstructed and proved how identities are created as power and ideology are enacted and manipulated by means of the choice of wording, intertextuality and text arrangements.

In conclusion, the bittersweet relationship between identity and language in sociolinguistics has roughly undergone three stages: "identity as social category, identity as a contact phenomenon and identity as practice" (Dyer 2007, pp. 101–105), a static to dynamic evolutionary view of identity from variables such as age, gender, and class to ultimately a negotiated on-going practice.

2.2.1.3 Pragmatic Perspective

Furthermore, pragmatist Verschueren (1999) noticed the various parameters of social speakers, ranging from culture, ethnicity to educational background. Scholars have been aware of the decisive role of context in the construction of identities of speakers (e.g. Butler 1990). Nevertheless, the agent status per se of the language speakers in forming their identities has not been sufficiently valued by pragmatists (Gu and Li 2007). The pragmatic perspective of identity construction owes to the Chinese scholar of pragmatics Prof. Chen Xinren and his followers. Chen's (2013, p. 27) defined "pragmatic identity" or "identity in use" as "the contextualised identity, the speaker/author attributes to himself/herself or the address, be it conscious or unconscious, in the communication process". The pragmatic identity is the de facto identity speakers take in real-life process of communications, different from any other identities they took prior to the process of communications (Chen 2013). According to Chen (2013, pp. 27–28), as compared to social identity, pragmatic identity is characteristic of the following traits: (1) communication-dependent and temporary (2) dynamic and variable (3) resourceful (4) subjective and purposeful. The choice of one's pragmatic identity is bound by the underlying rules as follows: (1) irregardless of the speaker's willingness/unwillingness and likes/dislikes, the speaker has to make choices of his/her pragmatic identity in a given circumstance (2) the instability of the degree of consciousness is noticeable as speaker makes choices of his/her pragmatic identity (3) the speaker's selection of pragmatic identity is driven by his/her needs of communication (4) the speaker's selection of pragmatic identity is dynamic (5) in a given circumstance, the speakers' selection of pragmatic identity is manifested in his/her choice of language/discourse (6) in a given circumstance, the selection of specific pragmatic identity generates specific communicative value and brings about specific communicative outcomes (7) whether or not the speakers' selection of pragmatic identity is appropriate, reliable, effective and polite depends on the given circumstance of the discourse, inclusive of contextual factors, types of occasions, the presence of third-party, social relations of the two parties in the communication, history of interaction, values and beliefs of the other party (ibid.). Having been applied in the studies of promotional discourse undertaken in the drugstores (Yuan and Chen 2013), law discourse and advertisements (Chen 2013) and online B2C pre-sales consultancy of cosmetic products (He and Chen 2015), the rationality of pragmatic identity was verified and the genres of pragmatic identity apply were identified.

2.2.2 Discursive Constructions of Corporate Identity

One of the most dynamic and prolific sub-areas of identity studies resides in understanding the configurations of corporate identity and how it functions in enhancing the corporate public image. The study of corporate identity has benefited from the rich legacy of identity studies and is particularly indebted to the initial work of organisational culture research in the 1980s and 1990s (Pullen and Linstead 2005). Meanwhile, it merits clarifying that there is no fundamental difference in the ways individuals and organisations construct their identities (Hatch and Schulz 2002), and corporate identities are projected and largely under the control of host organisations (Topalian 1984).

To trace back the origin of corporate identity, as early as in the 1950s, graphic design consultants Lippincott and Margulies coined the notion of "corporate identity" (Lippincott and Margulies 1957), discussions and deductions arising from which since then have been excitingly dynamic, resulting in the voluminous literature of corporate identity. Corporate identity, originally evolved from the realm of marketing in the 1960s, has been primarily based on the business practitioners' sales, advertising and the design activities of logos and mission statements (cf. Melewar and Jenkins 2002). During the preceding business undertakings, professionals are in desperate need of a set of identities to locate and represent the corporations and make clear to stakeholders. The root of corporate identity was observed as a strategic manifestation of corporate-level vision and mission, underpinned by the strategies, which a corporation employs in its operations or production (Melewar and Wooldridge 2001).

The conceptualising and evolving process of corporate identity studies has been undertaken for a journey of over half-century. It was discussed and revealed that there were five stages in the brief history of corporate identity and its academic research: 1950s–1970s, 1970s to early 1980s, late 1980s to late 1990s, late 1990s and 2000 (Blamer 1998). As per Blamer (1998), stage 1 was primarily concerned with corporate image and with graphic design. Stage 2 was characteristic of the ascendancy of corporate identity and corporate personality. Stage 3 witnessed greater academic interest, particularly in Europe where emphases were given to the marketers, strategists as well as behaviorists with special attention to behavioral aspects of identity and in particular to organisational identity. However, in stage 4, corporate identity has seen a burgeoning of cross border and cross-disciplinary contact among both academics and practitioners. This sub-discipline has formulated and has attracted increasingly international and interdisciplinary endeavors and out-of-ivory-tower activities. The last stage 5 saw the advent of corporate marketing, bridging gaps for researchers, managers and consultants.

Even though there is still a lack of consensus as to the characteristics of a corporate identity, some existing misunderstandings or "fogs" may be captured anyway. After all, corporate identity entails at least two sets of denotations: (1) the mix of elements which gives organisations their distinctiveness: the foundation of business identities; (2) the importance of several elements including culture, strategy, history, business activities and market scope (Balmer 2001, p. 254). Prior to this synthesis, Balmer's (1998) research was pioneering and significant in summarising the several salient features of corporate identities.

Furthermore, common features of corporate identity were further acknowledged: (1) corporate identity is a multidisciplinary field; (2) it is a term used to identify the essence of what the firm is and thus incorporates many unique characteristics of the firm such as history, philosophy, culture, communication and the industry the firm operates in; (3) it is inseparable from the corporate personality of the organisation (Melewar and Karaosmanoglu 2005, p. 848). A tripartite layers of corporate identity definitions was further teased out and its characteristics were made explicit: "(1) complexity (they are multi-faceted and multidimensional in nature in that they informed by various spatial/temporal dimensions); (2) variability (they are immutable but evolutionary in character); and (3) heterogeneous (they are informed by multidisciplinary perspectives in terms of comprehension and management)" (Balmer 2001, p. 888).

Corporate identity is "the central, distinct and enduring dimensions of a company" (Albert and Whetten 1985, p. 265). From a psychological view, corporate identity in nature can never be separated from planned self-presentation of an organisation, consisting of cues an organisation gives via "its behavior, communication and symbolism" (van Riel 1995, p. 36). Corporate identities, similar to organisational identities as a symbolic process, establish a common definition in terms of who we are and what we stand for, both in and outside the organisation. In accordance to general industry practice, corporate identities are believed to consist of three aspects: corporate design (e.g. logos and corporate colors), corporate communication (e.g. advertising, public relations) and corporate behavior (e.g. values and norms). The crucial task of building a good image for the corporation all points to the significant work of impression management. Indeed, many scholars have recognised the interchangeability of corporate identity and corporate image, between which a profound link has been strengthened across a wide literature of marketing, corporate communication and public relations (Melewar and Karaosmanoglu 2005).

The communication of corporate identity entails its visual communication and discursive communication, of which the latter form shall be the foci of the present study. A holistic taxonomy of corporate identity listed a few defining determinants, i.e., corporate communication, corporate design, corporate culture, behavior, corporate structure, industry identity and corporate strategy, each being categorised into a lower level to contain more determinants (Melewar 2003). It is evident that corporate communication plays a crucially determining role in the defining model of corporate identity. Melewar (2003) also regarded corporate communication as the first and foremost factor in corporate identity determination, which comprised of controlled communication, uncontrolled communication and indirect communication. By controlled corporate communication, he meant that the management tool by which all consciously used forms of internal and external communication is harmonised effectively and efficiently for creating a favorable basis for a relationship with an organisation's stakeholders (van Riel 1995). Conversely, uncontrolled communication usually involves the communication between the employees of an organisation and the external stakeholders through their interaction (Moingeon and Ramamantsoa 1997). Moingeon and Ramamantsoa (1997) indicated customer-to-customer on-line community is in fact a new form of uncontrolled corporate communication. In this sense, the corporate microblogging platform is a prototype of uncontrolled external corporate communication, on which followers' responses are unedited, instantly generated and beyond the control of the corporation or any agents.

It has been aware that nowadays identities arising from corporate communication have become unprecedentedly complicated. Of prime concerns of the preceding literature is the progressive colonisation of life world, entailing a displacement of communicative practices (Habermas 1984), during which transformations contributing to identity construction are seen more and more common from other forms of communication into corporate communication (e.g., Bhatia 1993, 2004; Erjavec 2004; Fairclough 1995a; Maat 2007).

The art of constructing corporate identity has been examined. In the theoretical model conceptualised by Cornelissen and Elving (2003), media and messages are seen as the two crucial dimensions of managing corporate identity. Likewise, by identifying three types of language style on English-mediated corporate Twitter:

emotional bird, social realist and thinking machine, Pacea (2011) concluded that there exists a strong correlation between the language style and the situational parameter of company profile on Twitter. Nevertheless, despite sheer efforts of organisations, corporate identity construction involved other forces derived from other stakeholders, e.g., the public.

In sum, corporate identity literature owes to three philosophical underpinnings: functionalist, interpretive and post-modern (Gioia 1998). Functionalist scholars (marketing perspective) regard corporate identity from a management perspective, deeming it as an objective phenomenon, and thus can be forged and managed, whereas the interpretive studies (the organisational behaviorist perspective) argue that corporate identity as subjective, socially constructed and stakeholders actively interpret the environment based on their interpretations of corporate identity (Gioia 1998; James and Melewar 2008). Post-modern perceptions of corporate identity, however, orient to "an invention for the (often sinister) purposes of parties in power" (Gioia 1998, p. 28).

In the conceptualisation of the theories regarding corporate identity, three strands of thinking that somehow intertwined among one another are noteworthy: (1) the interpretivist view that a corporate identity as an expression of the corporate personality; (2) the functionalist view that corporate identity as an organisational reality; (3) the rhetorical view that corporate identity as all the expressions of a company (Cornelissen and Harris 2001, pp. 60–61). "In the first two theories, communication and symbols were analytically separated from the thoughts and objects being symbolised" and the third rhetorical view of corporate identity focuses on "how language is used to enact or create social structures and how language and other symbol systems are reproduced, maintained and changed through use" (ibid). In other words, the theorised corporate identity has undergone an evolution of an identity from "sameness" to "essences and properties" and ultimately to identity as "identity as appearance", which lays special emphasis on the company's conscious and consistent impression management of the public over time for a trustworthy image and reputation of their own (ibid). The third rhetorical view of corporate identity as all the expressions of a company may be a concert and contemporary manifestation of Goffman's (1959) seminal perception that the individual identity is a product of social interaction, instead of an inner cause or antecedent reality.

In accordance to the interpretivist, functionalist and a rhetorical approach and strand of constructing the corporate identity, some common myths have to be prudently clarified. According to Theunissen (2014), the first myth is on the role of the public in creating corporate identity, which is only recognised for how identity might be perceived through the image created in the minds of the public, thus assuming that corporate identity is in the control of organisations who can manipulate it. The second myth is that corporate identity can change but once it is constructed, it is fixed and needs only to be adapted, updated or modernised every a few years by the corporation. Myths of corporate identity as such can be categorised as static, one-way and corporation-responsible only. Nonetheless, an increasing body of research has questioned these myths and commenced to recognise corporate identity as something that may be co-created, user-generated and resulted from the negotiation between stakeholders and the company (De Fina et al. 2006; Peverelli 2006; Theunissen 2014). The co-creational thinking of corporate identity emphasises on communication and dialogue with the public, rather than the preplanned monologue and rehearsed solo performance of companies. Although dialogic tenets tend to gain momentum in co-constructing corporate identity, it remains an under-explored and under-developed concept in public relations theory and practice (Pieczka 2011; Theunissen and Wan Noordin 2012).

2.3 Identity Construction in Corporate Communication: How?

2.3.1 The Turn of Social Media in Online Corporate Identity Construction

As per Balmer (1998)'s five-stage divide of corporate identity evolution, the 21st century may be foreseen as the advent of corporate marketing. Albeit he did not suggest possibilities enabled by technological innovations, online corporate identity did play an ever-increasingly key role in corporate marketing. Indeed, an influx of scholars (Abdullah et al. 2013; Topalian 2003; Melewar and Navalekar 2002; Allori 2010) has paid attention to the pros and cons of corporate identity construction in the context of corporate websites. In comparison to mass media advertising propaganda, where information flow is hierarchical, downward and purely commercial, online corporate identity construction excels in the sense that consumers are entitled to individualised user experience in accessing corporate websites with ample semiotic resources (Degano 2009, 2010; Hynes and Janson 2010). Nonetheless, the general performance of corporate identity formation during pre new media digital age is accused of being undynamic, slow in updating and interaction, disappointing and unsatisfactory in user engagement. Topalian (2003, p. 1121) raised his realistic criticism:

> Corporate websites could be very powerful vehicles for such identities, yet many sites demonstrate few advances on promotional literature. Many are little more than static on-screen corporate notice-boards, brochures or magazines. Dynamic elements incorporated tend to be "clever" add-ons without serious value for visitors: they miss the opportunity to captivate audiences, raise profiles and build mutually beneficial interactive relationships.
>
> Topalian (2003, p. 1121)

The apparent passé flavor in the choice of corporate websites in corporate communication cast reasonable doubts in its capability of projecting a shining and trustworthy corporate identity. The investigation of the corporate self-presentation of top 20 Fortune 500 corporations indicated that the websites contents are featured with impressing numbers, providing third-party evidence, presenting claims as facts, removing agents and humanising the organisation (Pollach 2005). Pollach (2005, p. 296) noted that in conveying attitudes, these world best-selling brands focused on their size and scope, agents of change, leadership, corporate citizenship, whereas in terms of relationships building, sample brands were good at using personal pronouns but the interactivity of websites were seen poor enough and "in one-way communication only". Another large-scale study by Abdullah et al. (2013) who examined 300 Malaysian and 214 Singaporean corporations found that both Malaysian and Singaporean companies have weak brand personality dimensions which reflect their less satisfactory projection of corporate identities on their official websites.

In fact, interaction with stakeholders is no longer under organisational control due to the prevalence of social media (Luoma-aho and Vos 2010). The increasingly voluminous body of research in regards to corporate identity construction that was conducted in the 21st century was largely inspired by the rise of social media. The need for such a critical perspective was highlighted ever since the emergence of worldwide recognised SNS brands such as Facebook, Twitter and Weibo that revolutionised the way corporate identity used to be constructed, e.g., by emphasising the followers' contribution and the role of shaping corporate identity in the firm-follower interaction (Rybalko and Seltzer 2010; Lillqvist and Louhiala-Salminen 2014; Waters and Jamal 2011). Illuminating insights of these research noticed the valuable role of social media in managing online corporate reputations and having dialogues and conversations with stakeholders via social media seen conductive to companies to promote good relations in the social media environments (e.g. Briones et al. 2011; Cho and Huh 2010). For instance, how American Red Cross made effective use of social media to maintain relationships with stakeholders was discovered (Briones et al. 2011).

Strategies of impression management were also given dedicated scholarly passion vis-a-vis the company-consumer interaction on social media. It is acknowledged that in coping with corporate crisis communication on corporate Facebook fan page, upholding social acceptability and promoting credibility are two major strategies Finnish corporations used to interactively manage a better identity and impression, which can be subcategorised into "conventional politeness, moral discourse, diversion, entitlement and stake, footing and ridicule" (Lillqvist and Louhiala-Salminen 2014, p. 21). However exciting, the sweeping body of research of corporate identity construction in post-social media era seems to have been conducted in Western business perspective and environment. It is imperative that studies on building corporate identity on social media platform can be explored in contexts other than the Western.

2.3.2 Impression Management

Impression management, sometimes used interchangeably as self-presentation, is defined as "the conscious or unconscious attempt to control images that are projected in real or imagined social interactions" (Schlenker 1980, p. 6). Impression management refers to the behaviors individuals engage in influencing and the impressions others have of them (Rosenfeld et al. 1995). In a narrow sense, impression management may also imply the beliefs and practices of organisations' public relations in managing their public images (DuBrin 2011b). Rosenfeld et al. (2002, p. 29) delineated two overarching tendencies both human beings and organisations encounter in managing their impressions: "to be seen by others in favorable manner and to avoid being viewed negatively", which are accordingly named as the acquisitive impression management and protective impression management (Arkin 1981; Palmer et al. 2001). The most commonly researched acquisitive impression management must be ingratiation, being defined as a set of related impression management tactics that have as their collective goal making the person more liked and attractive to others (Jones 1990). In addition to ingratiation, other acquisitive impression management strategies encompass, for instance, self-promotion, intimidation, exemplification and supplication (Rosenfeld et al. 2002).

The founding father of impression management studies is undoubtedly Erving Goffman. Goffman's (1959) dramaturgical metaphor of self-presentation may equally be well applied to agents and organisations other than individuals (Johansson 2007). Corporations and organisations, bearing similar traits as individuals, are actors engaging in performances in various settings in front of their audiences (Allen and Caillouet 1994). The discursive presentation of corporations specifically links to their external corporate communication. Corporate communication may be defined as "an instrument of management by means of which all consciously used forms of internal and external communication are harmonised as effectively and efficiently as possible, in an attempt to create a favorable basis for relationships with groups upon which the company is dependent" (van Riel 1995, p. 26). This powerful definition of corporation communication and its many similar versions accentuate the desired corporate communication outcome: company's favorable image and public relations among its stakeholders. The ultimate goal of public relations discourse strives for an excellent reputation and a good impression of the corporation in the public (Harlow 1976), which in one way or another helps to improve sales figures in the financial statements in the long run. To this end, a series of preferable communicative practices and strategies to public relations professionals were suggested: "known source, clear intent, reasoned argument, factual accuracy, and positive but limited emotional appeal and it is dialogic, respectful of its audiences, open to challenge, ready to amend and willing to reply" (Wood and Somerville 2008, p. 98).

Impression management is regarded as a notion in closest proximity to and serving as an integral part of the corporate identity construction. Indebted to the early significant work done in sociology and psychology, impression management originally conceptualised self-presentation in interpersonal communication (Goffman 1959; Leary 1996). Erving Goffman (1959, p. 208) creatively utilised a series of dramaturgical metaphors to identify a connection between the kinds of "acts" that individuals put on in their everyday life and theatrical performances in social interactions. According to Goffman (1959), in a theatrical performance there is an onstage area where actors/individuals appear before the audience; this is where positive self-concepts and desired impressions are presented. But there is also a backstage or a hidden, private area where individuals can be the real themselves and drop their societal roles and identities. Impression management strategies have been applied to cope with organisation's crisis (Allen and Caillouet 1994). It is argued that corporate Facebook fan page may be seen mainly as a frontstage with some backstage moments as well for external corporate communication (Lillqvist and Louhiala-Salminen 2014). This is probably the same applicable to corporate microblogging site, the most powerful and influential company-consumer communication channel in today's China.

The notion of impression management has been borrowed wisely to improve corporate management and public relations (DuBrin 2011a; Giacalone and Rosenfeld 1989; Rosenfeld et al. 2002). It has been certain that the presentation of corporate image and identity through corporate communications is influential and has paramount impacts on corporate reputation (Melewar 2008). It has been aware that the interlocking relationship between corporate identity and corporate communication in the sense that "managing corporate identity is about identifying the right image for an organisation, and communicating it effectively" (Wood 2004, p. 95). It is also noted that scholarship on corporate identity did pay ample attention to the "how" questions in daily practice of corporation, vis-a-vis the role of language and communication in shaping corporate image, resulting in fruitful empirical studies of discursive construction of corporate identity (e.g., Zhu and Hildebrandt 2013; Yuan 2011). In probing effectiveness in international business sales letters, Zhu and Hildebrandt (2013) innovatively compared persuasion strategies of Chinese and New Zealand businessmen, which are culturally specific from an emic-etic perspective and uncovered the implication of Qing (positive affect)'s role generated by the Chinese identity.

Corporate identities studies have expanded to and given prominence to a variety of industries, ranging from tourism sectors, healthcare sectors to media sectors and elsewhere, flourishing specially in the Internet context (cf. Garzone and Catenaccio 2009). Strategies of discursive identity formation and construction via Internet pay special attention to corporate websites and social media, pertaining to complex and multi-layered identities such as social, national, cultural and ethnic (Garzone 2009).

In essence, the linguistic realisations in impression management of corporations share roots in interpersonal communication. From a genre-based perspective, Bhatia (2004) elucidated this revolutionarily transforming trend from non-promotional discourse to corporate communication and clarified that a growing number of genres, ranging from academic introductions to philanthropic fundraising letters, have appropriated the promotional tendencies and nature of "classic" promotional genres, in terms of communicative purposes, lexico-grammatical structures, move structures and so on. A common feature shared across all the promotional genres is their similar communicative purposes, either "mainly promotional" or "informational as well as promotional" or "mainly public relational and promotional" (pp. 68–69). Bhatia also pointed out how listed companies took advantage of their annual reports, a presumably press release genre and appropriated textual features of sales letters and other promotional genres to construct their amicable, trustworthy identities and brush up their public image (ibid.).

Fairclough (1995a) shed more light on and gave more substance to this issue in his profound and detailed analysis of the changing and transitioning identity of a higher education from a tertiary education provider to a normalised and commercial service provider, being manifested in the self-promotional genre of university leaflets in the UK. Noticeably, the hybridity of marketization and information has succeeded in penetrating into a wider pool of public discourse genres, generating neologisms of hybridised genres which survive and normalise, for example, informalisation (Wouter 1986) and "conversationalisation of public discourse" (Fairclough 1995a, p. 138). Fairclough (1992, 1996) has drawn upon a noteworthy issue of "technologies of discourse" to refer to highly pervasive and homogenised types of discourses in plenty of institutions, e.g., counseling and interviewing as a new form of identity construction in corporate communication, or in his own words, "enterprise discourse" (Fairclough 1995a, p. 112).

2.3.3 Dialogue Theory: The Dialogic Turn in Corporate Communication

There is a scholarly consensus that the dialogue theory is deeply indebted to the early accomplishments of the philosopher Martin Buber (1970) who believed that human communications is an intersubjective process in which parties came to a relationship with trust, openness and respect. Subsequent to Pearson's (1989) earliest exploration of the concept of dialogue, public relations, both in theory and practice, witnessed the strategic dialogic turn from the organisations' monologic persuasion of the publics. Not surprisingly the present dialogic turn in public relations has been magnified since the advent and prevalence of social media in the last decade, which not only enables but also encourages real-time, user-generated contents. Nevertheless, it is asserted that it is technological innovations such as the Internet and social media that have eventually forced companies to employ the attitudes and approaches of dialogic communication in addressing the public (Mersham et al. 2009). Dialogue is defined as "any negotiated exchange of ideas and opinions in public relations practice" (Kent and Talyor 1998, p. 325). Dialogue may be considered as the key element of in-between, for it "represents efforts by parties in a relationship to engage in an honest, open and ethically based give and take" (Bortree and Seltzer 2009, p. 317).

In this sense, dialogue is

> both quality of relationship that arises, however briefly, between two or more people and a way of thinking about human affairs that highlights their dialogue qualities. Dialogue can identify the attitudes with which participants approach each other, the ways they talk and act, the consequences of their meeting, and the context within which they meet.
>
> Cissna and Anderson (1998, p. 64)

As a product of ongoing communication and relationship (Kent and Talyor 2002), dialogue and dialogic communication are claimed to be two-way symmetrical and more ethical than the preceding asymmetrical systems theory of public relations (Theunissen and Wan Noordin 2012). In order to deal with the long-standing unequal relationship between organisation and the publics, dialogic theory requests that organisations should be willing to interact with publics in honest and ethical ways in order to create effective organisation-public communication channels (Kent et al. 2003). Kent and Talyor (1998, p. 324) maintained that:

> Buber's conception of dialogue focuses implicitly on ethics. That is, for a dialogic relationship to exist, parties must view communicating with each other as the goal of a relationship. Communication should not be a means to an end, but rather, as Kant's Categorical Imperative suggested, communication should be an end itself.
>
> Kent and Talyor (1998, p. 324)

In terms of its overarching tenets, there are a series of principles, which are somehow in a similar vein towards each other, all laying emphasis on the equalitarianism, interactivity, mutual benefit and other similar qualities in organisation-public communication. Kent and Talyor (1998) pinpointed five principles that offer guidelines for the successful integration of dialogic public relations and the World Wide Web: the dialogic loop; the usefulness of information; the generation of return visits (RV); the intuitiveness/ease of the interface; and the rule of conservation of visitors. Four years later, they updated and renamed principles of dialogic public relations theory to be the five overarching tenets of dialogic communication: "mutuality", "propinquity", "empathy", "risk" and "commitment" (Kent and Taylor 2002, pp. 25–30). Accordingly, mutuality refers to an acknowledgment that organisations and the public are inextricably tied together. For organisations, dialogic propinquity means that the public are consulted in matters that influence them, and for the public, it means that they are willing and able to articulate their demands to organisations. Empathy refers to the atmosphere of support and trust that must exist if dialogue is to succeed. Risk means that dialogues have the potential to produce unpredictable and dangerous outcomes. Commitment describes three characteristics of dialogic encounters: genuineness and authenticity, commitment to the conversation and a commitment to interpretation (ibid.).

A highlight of dialogic communication theory resides in its alleged ethical nature. The ethical feature of dialogue in Pearson's (1989) work asserted three procedures: that no topic should be excluded a priori from discussion, that no type of communication be considered a priori as inappropriate or irrational, and that during discourse, communicators have the option of changing levels of reflexivity. In spite of the overwhelming advocacy of dialogue theory, it is equally critical to be aware of the potential risks that might shadow dialogic communication in public relations. Due to the fact that dialogue can expose differences as well as similarities, it may in fact not lead to agreement but rather to disagreement (Theunissen and Noordin 2012). The fact is that this is one of the principles of dialogue as per Kent and Talyor (2002), whose theoretical backbones encompass vulnerability, unanticipated consequences and the recognition of strange otherness. The underlying philosophy of dialogue that communication content and outcome are not controlled in the strictest managerial sense poses risks for the claimed relationship building with the public.

Although a stream of scholars recognises, promotes and applies dialogue theory, dialogue is on the whole an under-explored and under-developed concept in public relations theory and practice (Theunissen 2014). Empirical research hitherto that applied and verified dialogic theory in public relations has been limited to: the test of dialogic principles in organisational websites (Capriotti and Pardo Kuklinski 2012; McCorkindale and Morgoch 2013; Madichie and Hinson 2014), the role of dialogic communication in reviving democracy in society (Kent 2013) to a test of dialogic principles on Twitter (Rybalko and Seltzer 2010; Watkins and Lewis 2014), most of which, however, stress its role in relationship building. By and large, extant research indicated that dialogic communication possesses great potential in developing organisation-public interaction.

To date, little research attempted to illuminate the stakeholders' co-construction of corporate identity through dialogues with organisations (e.g. Theunissen 2014). With skepticism about corporations' sole control over corporate identity, Theunissen (2014) noted the irreplaceable role of dialogue in audience engagement in the co-creating process of corporate identity.

In the conclusion, Theunissen (2014, pp. 613–614) claimed that:

> Scholars should explore the impact of dialogue on corporate identity, image and reputation, and understand that developing a corporate identity that is perceived as authentic can only happen by means of a co-creational process.... Accordingly, to create a truly authentic corporate identity, public relations practitioners need to recognize the co-creational impact and the role of communication, and specially dialogue
>
> (Theunissen 2014, pp. 613–614)

Not only the role of dialogue and dialogic communication in corporate identity construction is gradually acknowledged but also dialogue is being boosted in corporate communication in the age of social media. Capriotti and Pardo Kuklinski (2012) held that Web 2.0 that fosters the dialogic communication is generating significant changes in the manner that organisations engage in dialogue with their publics, opening the way towards interactive communication. The dearth of scholarly attention in regards to the dialogic communication on social media is particularly noticeable, despite a few testing attempts, e.g., Kent (2013). According to Kent (2013, p. 341), the purpose of the use of social media in the corporate communication practice should be "to build relationships, solve problems, and enact socially responsible goals." To realise such an overall purpose, he raised six suggestions: (1) parallel, or alternative, social media spaces should be developed where organisational members actually communicate with individuals and not members of a collective, like customers; (2) dialogic social media spaces should not be enacted through existing social media venues like Twitter or Facebook, filled with advertisements and distractions, and poorly designed for substantiative, interactive discussions; (3) the identity of participants should be public and verifiable; (4) clear rules should exist for participation; (5) experts should be sought out and invited to participate; (6) divergent voices should be nurtured and encouraged to participate. The leading global businesses are equipped with excellent experiences in capitalising social media interface to engage stakeholders, as Fortune 500 corporations have made enormous effort in purveying more dialogic spaces to their users where dialogic communication could potentially develop and mature (Rybalko and Seltzer 2010). Nonetheless, cases in the developing world remains much less examined.

2.3.4 *Emotional Branding*

2.3.4.1 Emotional Branding and the Conversational Human Voice

The role of emotions has emerged as a new and vibrant research focus in recent branding and marketing research, particularly its indispensible function of closing company-consumer distance and triggering consumers' strong emotional attachments and bonds to brands (Gobe 2001; Yoo and MacInnis 2005). Emotional branding is defined as the engagement of consumers in a deep, long-term, intimate emotional connection with the brand, which is beyond the benefit based satisfaction, and which creates a special trust based relationship for the development of a holistic emotional experience (Morrison and Crane 2007). Emotional branding can be a sophisticated means of corporate identity construction (Wu and Feng 2015). As the name suggests, emotional branding focuses on customers' emotional attachments to brands and could lead to "higher levels of firm performance and competitive advantage" (Akgun et al. 2013, p. 504).

Since the new millennium, a recurrent theme in the extensive emotional branding literature lies in the discussion of its overwhelming merits, as opposed to the traditional benefit-driven branding communication (Gobe 2001, 2007, 2009; Rossiter and Bellman 2012; Thompson et al. 2006). For instance, it was verified that how brands apply emotional branding to meet customer requirements through bonding, companionship and love (Rossiter and Bellman 2012). Being regarded as the key to marketing success, emotional branding and its strategic value to brand image have been noticed and valued (Thompson et al. 2006).

The developmental divide of emotional branding may be categorised into tripartite phases: "the pragmatist age (1940–1967)", "the evangelist age (1968–1989)" and "the sensualist age (1990–2009)" (Gobe 2009, p. 128). According to Gobe's (2009) elaborations, emotional branding in pragmatist age emphasises on products or service' function, reliability and other pragmatic functions, as manifested by the omnipresent advertising which dominates corporate communication. Evangelist age represents philosophies of justice, equality and sensitivity to the environment, making people realise that they have power and could positively change the course of politics and the world. By influencing people's lives, emotional branding discourse in the sensualist age is lifestyle-oriented and towards hedonism, glamour, fame and the individual expressions, creating its own language, culture and symbols.

In realising the emotional branding, a conversational human voice should not be neglected (Searls and Weinberger 2001; Kelleher and Miller 2006; Kelleher 2009). Kelleher and Miller (2006, p. 413) proposed 11 defining items of conversational human voice: "invites people to conversation; is open to dialogue; uses conversation-style communication; tries to communicate in a human voice; tries to be interesting in communication; provides links to competitors; uses a sense of humor in communication; provides links to competitors; attempts to make communication enjoyable; would admit a mistake; provides prompt feedback addressing criticism with a dialect but uncritical manner and treats me and others as human".

2.3.4.2 The Communication of Corporate Social Responsibility

The communication of corporate social responsibility is a form of the evangelist emotional branding (Gobe 2009), thus constructing an identity as a socially responsible corporation to gain popularity in public. Corporate social responsibility is also called corporate conscience, corporate citizenship, social performance, or sustainable responsible business (Wood 1991). The term corporate social responsibility (CSR) gained popularity in the 1960s and has remained a term used indiscriminately by many to cover more narrowly construed legal and moral responsibility (DeGeorge 2010). CSR is defined as the "economic, legal, ethical, and discretionary (philanthropic) expectations that society has of organisations at a given point in time" (Buchholtz and Carroll 2008, p. 40). CSR roughly refers to the efforts corporations strive to make for a more positive impact through its activities on the environment, consumers, employees, communities, stakeholders and all other members of the public sphere who may also be considered as stakeholders. However, in spite of the heterogeneous nature of CSR, a common approach is corporate philanthropy through which corporations are seen as donors to communities, neighborhoods or even foreign countries, in an attempt to create an image of a caring corporate citizen.

As a fundamental part of corporate marketing strategies, CSR has served as a verified means to strengthen corporate image (e.g., Maignan and Ferrell 2004). Aside from traditional means to construct and project corporate identity such as logo design symbolism, CSR has been recently employed as a new approach to study corporate identity. The projection of CSR-based corporate identity is more effective than symbolism (Pomering and Johnson 2009). As an example, the roles that CSR played in the Spanish banking industry were examined to construct corporate identity and it was revealed that CSR communication did generate brand value and a good corporate reputation (Perez and Rodriguez del Bosque 2012). It has also been proved that CSR communication is important to inform others about corporate social actions, which helps the value creation. Accordingly, banks investigated believe that "CSR communication should be a bidirectional process, both upward and downward, when rather than just transmitting information, they also have to pay attention to grasp stakeholders' concerns and suggestions" (ibid., pp. 158–159). In this regard, corporate image is a partial outcome of CSR communication.

The four-step pyramid of CSR outlined by Carroll (1991) is perhaps most widely cited, wherein he believed a company's CSR activities comprise four segments: economic, legal, ethical and philanthropic obligations. In an empirical study, it was revealed that economic responsibilities of corporations were given the most emphasis across the globe, followed by philanthropic activities in emerging nations such as Bangladesh (Belal 2008). Legal responsibilities of enterprises are seen in the third place and last are the ethical responsibilities. In addition to the CSR pyramid of priorities, corporate philanthropy was incorporated in Kotler and Lee's (2004) six major marketing communication strategies (cause promotion, cause-related marketing, corporate social marketing, corporate philanthropy, corporate volunteering and socially responsible business practice) to refer to that corporations' general CSR policy as a marketing communication strategy, which may be unrelated to a specific product promotion. Grounded in such models and theories, the communication of CSR in the Indian context was surveyed and analysed, revealing that Indian corporations have primarily pursued a philanthropic platform with a focus on community development projects to communicate CSR with their stakeholders (Planken et al. 2010).

Shifting the focus to the Chinese context, a focus on CSR communication involved the indispensable role of media. Research on China's newspaper discourse of CSR confirmed that the media is a major stakeholder in defining and promoting CSR (Tang 2012). It was also found that Chinese newspapers predominately define CSR as companies' responsibilities towards communities, employees, and customers. Nonetheless, the legacy media in CSR communication is limited as "China's leading newspapers have not yet played an active role in facilitating a social dialogue about CSR" (Tang 2012, p. 285). Moreover, multiple rationales for Chinese businesses' CSR have been investigated by examining China's print media (Liu et al. 2011). By contrast to print media, CSR communication on China's social media has not received due attention up until now.

2.4 Interactional Sociolinguistics

Interactional sociolinguistics is a sub-discipline of linguistics that makes use of discourse analysis to study how language users create meaning via social interaction (Tannen 2006). As one of the six key approaches to discourse analysis, according to Schiffrin (1994), interactional sociolinguistics is elaborated and defined as follows:

> As an approach to discourse, interactional sociolinguistics offers theories and methods that enable researchers to explore not only how language works but also to gain insights into the social processes through which individuals build and maintain relationships, exercise power, project and negotiate identities, and create communities.
>
> Gordon (2011, p. 67)

Prominent figures such as John Gumperz, Erving Goffman, and Debora Tannen represent key thinkers in this discipline. One of the most noted defining features of interactional sociolinguistics is its interdisciplinary nature, as interactional sociolinguistics is known for its "qualitative interpretative approach to the analysis of social interaction that developed at the intersection of linguistics, anthropology and sociology" (Gordon 2011, p. 67). Boxer (2002, p. 14) also noted that: "work in interactional sociolinguistics derives from sociology, linguistics and anthropology". Interactional sociolinguistics usually draws on naturally occurring data for analysis with methods of tape-recording or video recording.

2.4.1 The Anthropological Insights from John Gumperz

As opposed to the variationist sociolinguistics, the anthropologist John Gumperz together with Dell Hymes developed a brand-new perspective of sociolinguistics whose joint contribution created a research paradigm called the ethnography of communication. Gumperz's (1982a) own approach has been latterly named as interactional sociolinguistics. The founding father of interactional sociolinguistics Gumperz roughly referred to his own approach as "an interpretive sociolinguistics approach to the analysis of real time processes in face to face encounters" (Gumperz 1982a, p. vii). Gumperz's (1971) early work and research interests have centered on speech variation and cultural anthropology in different ethnic groups. His fieldwork research, using participant observation and survey methods in northern Indian villages paid special attention to code-mixing variations, speech community, language diversity, social groups and, in summary, how linguistic structures and meanings were realised in social interaction (see Gumperz 1971, 1974). It is interactive conversational behaviors that define the boundaries of interactional sociolinguistics. A considerable amount of the work that Gumperz devoted his time fell into cross-cultural everyday conversational interaction, focusing specially on the speaking and listening, e.g., back channeling by means of taped and transcribed linguistic data.

In his classic Discourse Strategy published in 1982, although Gumperz stated that "we are still far from a general theory of verbal communication which integrates what we know about grammar, culture and interactive conventions into a single overall framework of concepts and analytical procedures" (1982a, p. 4), his own attempts have offered illuminating insights for meaning making and decoding in social interaction, particularly with what Gumperz called contextualization cues and conversational inference. As a less explicit element in everyday face-to-face conversation, contextualization cues continuously and permanently mediate and signal speaker-hear interactions, assisting conversations to undergo a more smooth and desirable process than otherwise. As Gumperz (1982a, p. 131) described and defined,

> A contextualization cue is any feature of linguistic form that contributes to the signaling of contextual presuppositions. Such cues may have a number of such linguistic realisations depending on the historically given linguistic repertoire of the participants. The code, dialect and style switching processes, some of the prosodic phenomena we have discussed as well as choice among lexical and syntactic options, formulaic expressions, conversational openings, closings and sequencing strategies can all have similar contextualising functions. Although such cues carry information, meanings are conveyed as part of the interactive context, the meanings of contextualization cues are implicit.
>
> (Gumperz 1982a, p. 131)

By contrast, conversational inference is defined as "the situated or context-bound process of interpretation, by means of which participants in an exchange assess others' intentions, and on which they base their responses" (Gumperz 1982a, p. 153). In simple terms, conversationalists "make active predictions about what would come next, rested on the line of interpretation suggested by on-going talk as measured against prior interactive experience" (Tannen 1992, p. 10). Contextualization cues and conversational inference are interrelated by means of varied speakers' contextualization cues, listeners' accurate (or inaccurate) inferences are ubiquitously affected in conversations. In many cases, contextualization cues are "the strategies used for implying an illocutionary act of the speaker, whose communicative intentions are highly context-dependent" (Schiffrin 1994, p. 100).

In summary, learners' realisation and appropriate responding acts to a contextualization cue, be it linguistic or paralinguistic, are one of the prerequisites for successful social interactions. Should the listener fail to achieve in doing so, misunderstandings or a failure in communication might occur. The ability of human realisation and responding acts to contextualization cues may be culturally and historically conventionalised, thus leading to a higher risk of interethnic and intercultural miscommunication. Interactional sociolinguistics recognised diversity, be it cultural or linguistic, that shapes the social world.

In essence, a contextualization cue relates to any conventionalised but usually subconscious or unconscious feature of linguistic forms that contribute to the signaling of contextual presuppositions and ultimately the interpretations among conversation participants. Contextualization cues show that features Saussure devalued as "marginal" (e.g., intonation) are inseparable from those Saussure valued as "core" (e.g. syntax and grammatical affixes)—and they are of core importance in communicating meaning (Gumperz 1982a, p. 16). Any linguistic strategies of signaling contextualization cues can be the use of discourse strategies. In Gumperz's view, speakers do not follow conversational rules, but rather are guided by interpretive norms, which are continually reinforced or revised in the light of on-going interpretation (Tannen 1992). In short, Gumperz's major contribution lies in the recognition and indication of the ways interactants make conversational inference about each other in social interaction.

2.4.2 *The Sociological Insights from Erving Goffman*

Although Erving Goffman did not turn his interest towards language until a rather late phase of his career life, his theoretical backbone and work, beginning with *The Presentation of Self in Everyday Life* (1959), has been crucial for discourse analysts and interactional sociolinguists who study language in social life (Tannen 2009, p. 300). Having said that, by setting the earliest foundations of symbolic interactionism, Goffman (1959, 1967) raised three seminal metaphorical and theoretical notions of face, frame and footing in both describing and prescribing how individuals' identities are constructed during social interaction. By virtue of 'face' he meant the "positive social value a person effectively claims for himself by the line others assume he has taken during a particular contact (Goffman 1967, p. 5)". 'Frame', in his opinion, entails the definitions of a situation that are built up in accordance with the principles of organization, which govern events (Goffman 1974). Goffman (1981, p. 128) propounded the notion of "footing" in his most sociolinguistic book *Forms of Talk*, well elucidating the social construction of speaker identity by separating out individuals from the roles they play in conversational interaction. Footing roughly refers to "the participant's alignment, or set, or stance, or posture, or projected self (ibid.)" and further Goffman continued, "a change in footing implies a change in the alignment we take up to ourselves and the others present as expressed in the way we manage the production or reception of an utterance. "A change in our footing is another way of talking about a change in our frame for events" (ibid.).

Notice the nuances in the different participative roles that speakers might adopt —they can act as "an animator, or sounding box, an individual active in the role of utterance production" (Goffman 1981, p. 144), or an author, "someone who has selected the sentiments that are being expressed and the words in which they are encoded" (ibid.) and a principal, "someone whose position is established by the words that are spoken, someone whose beliefs have been told, someone who is committed to what the words they say" (ibid.). As elaborated for fuller comprehension by Irwin (2011, p. 103), there are three voices involved in any utterance: "there is the animator, the person that utters the words; there is the author, the person that originated the beliefs and lastly there is the principal, the person whose viewpoint is currently being expressed". They take on the role of the speaker if they use their own words and they take on the role of principal if they speak sincerely. They form what Goffman defined as the "production format" of an utterance in interactional conversations (Goffman 1981, p. 146).

Albeit complicated, Goffman's footing has generated an increasing wealth of research in its interpretations and applications across varied domains, (e.g. Johansson 2007; Wortham 1996; Su 2009). For instance, Wortham (1996) mapped out the participant deixis used as a technique for discovering a speaker's footing. Su (2009) demonstrated the changing of footing by code-switching in managing face-threatening communicative tasks.

Nevertheless, in addition to continuous recognition and alignments over time, Goffman's theorisation and conceptualisations are not without criticisms. Unfortunately Goffman passed away in 1982, one year subsequent to his publication of *Forms of Talk* where footing was substantively pondered over. As such, however, philosophical and profound, a series of detailed self-applications and instantiations of footing were necessary for a comprehensive picture of understanding.

In spite of the alleged imperfection of Goffman's underpinnings, the inherent intertwinement and confluences between Gumperz and Goffman's conceptualisations remain clear. As a student of Goffman, Schiffrin (1994) noted a number of intersections in between. In her view, one way of describing Gumperz's contextualization cues is a framing device, i.e., interlocutors indicate the frame (e.g., serious, joking, business, chat) in which an utterance should be interpreted.

> In sum, Goffman's focus on social interaction complements Gumperz's focus on situated inference: Goffman describes the form and meaning of the social and interpersonal contexts that provide presuppositions for the decoding of meaning. The understanding of those contexts can allow us to more fully identify the contextual presuppositions that figure in hearers' inferences of speakers' meaning.
>
> (Schiffrin 1994, p. 104)

As Goffman (1981) himself recognised, what indicates shifts in footing and alignment are not just the way we manage the product of an utterance, but also the kinds of devices identified by Gumperz as contextualization cues.

2.4.3 The Linguistic Insights from Deborah Tannen

Deborah Tannen is most known for her work, both academic and non-academic whose achievements are in gendered linguistic studies from a social constructionist perspective, in light of linguistic variations across gender. But being a student of John Gumperz, she contributes to interactional sociolinguistics with inspiring insights into everyday conversation analysis, noticeably in the workplace domains and those among friends. Not surprisingly, she found a confluence among Gumperz, Goffman and her own work in terms of the understanding of situated interpretation in social interaction and even called Gumperz "a contemporary Goffman" (Tannen 2009, p. 302). In the eyes of Tannen (2009), framing can be contextualization cues signaling meaning as well as sociocultural knowledge and face may be the contextualization cues combined in patterned ways to serve the interactive goals of involvement and independence.

Acknowledging and combining the notion of frame and face as well as under the influence of Robin Lakoff's communicative style, Tannen (1984, 2005) raised her theoretical framework of conversational style, which contains a bipartite scheme: involvement and considerateness. Conversational style has provided "a foundation for understanding both human interaction and the workings of language in any context" (Tannen 2005, p. xvi).

Tannen (2009, p. 302) operationalised conversational style as follows:

> In the style I call "high-involvement" you show you're a good person by putting on record your connection to others (for example, by fast rate of speech and short interturn pauses, talking-along to show attention and enthusiasm, and relatively loud and quick displays of listenership. In the style I call "high-considerateness" you show you're a good person by not imposing (for example, by relatively slower rate of speech and longer interturn pauses, avoidance of overlapping talk, and relatively understated displays of listenership.
>
> (Tannen 2009, p. 302)

In face-to-face communications, high involvement features are overtly signaled through the use of the following items: topic (prefer personal topics; shift topics abruptly; introduce topics without hesitation; persist, if a new topic is not immediately picked up, reintroduce it, repeatedly if necessary), pacing (faster rate of speech; faster turn taking; avoiding interturn pauses, salience shows lack of rapport; cooperative overlap; participatory listenership), narrative strategies (tell more stories; tell stories in rounds; prefer internal evaluation, i.e., the point of a story is dramatised rather than lexicalised) and expressive paralinguistics (expressive phonology, marked pitch and amplitude shifts, marked voice quality, strategic within-turn pauses). Tannen (2005) confirmed that a significant amount of bonding is formed through the adoption of high-involvement devices in conversations among friends, the outcome of which is rewarding and is described as "we find talk between us easy and satisfying" (p. 106).

2.4.4 Face and Linguistic Face-Work in Social Interaction

Originated from the Chinese culture, as broadly acknowledged, face, a complex metaphor of self-esteem, honor, respect and dignity, serves as an eternal parameter that governs entire human interactions (e.g., Hu 1944; Brown and Levinson 1987; Goffman 1967; He and Zhang 2011; Scollon and Scollon 1995, 2001). Although face is inherently a Chinese concept in origin (Ho 1976), it is sociologically universal and present in many languages in its idiomatic sense. The notion of face metaphorically refers to an individual's sense of dignity or prestige in social interaction.

Erving Goffman officially pioneered face study in Anglo-Saxon societies, whose tenets and principles well acknowledge the social and instinctive needs of human beings. According to Goffman (1967), the term face may be defined as the positive social value a person effectively claims for himself by the line others assume he has taken during a particular contact. Face is an image of self-delineation in terms of approved social attributes—albeit an image that others may share, as when a person makes a good showing for his profession or religion by making a good showing for himself (Goffman 1967). By face-work, Goffman (1967, p. 12) meant "to designate the actions taken by a person to make whatever he is doing consistent with face. Face-work serves to counter 'incidents'—that is, events whose effective symbolic implications threaten face". Goffman's observations on the interactional order and his sophisticated notions of face and face-work, as Bargiela-Chiappini (2003) argued, should be the starting point for a re-appraisal of politeness and its fundamental role in the social order.

It was claimed that Goffman's face definition entails three aspects (Lee-Wong 2000). First, face defined in the Goffman sense is a socio-psychological construct, the psychological need to be seen in a positive light by an other. Second, face in practice means taking a social stand based on the evaluation of the situation and the participants. Third, in a social encounter, face is implicated: a line is taken by each interactant and/or each interactant is seen to be taking a line (ibid., pp. 23–24). In short, it may be inferred that Goffman's face view is much more sociological oriented than otherwise, e.g. psychologically oriented. From a sociological perspective, face-work is an integral part of social interaction as Goffman maintained that there is no such thing as faceless communication. On the basis of the fact that communication is a typified social process that involves at least more than one person, face-work is therefore nicknamed as "diplomacy and social skills" (Goffman 1967, p. 13), both requesting a high degree of sophistication in social actions. Having given prominence to the maintenance of face as a condition of interaction instead of its objectives, Goffman compared face-work in social interaction to traffic rules by which each member of the society is bound, guided and benefited from.

Subsequent to Goffman's paradigm, another powerful face theory must be attributed to Brown and Levinson (1987), whose underpinnings perfectly recognised the paradoxical fact of human face wants. By definition, face is something that is emotionally invested and that can be lost, maintained, or enhanced and must be constantly attended to in interaction (Brown and Levinson 1987). Brown and Levinson (1987, p. 13) insisted on a dyad concept of face that "a highly abstract notion of face which consists of two specific kinds of desires attributed by interactants to one another: the desire to be unimpeded in one's actions (negative face), and the desire (in some respects) to be approved of (positive face)". According to Brown and Levinson (1987), in association with the universal face wants, there are linguistic face-threatening acts (FTA) to be redressed by politeness strategies. Positive politeness is directed to entertain and satisfy the addressee's positive face. By contrast, speech acts addressed to protect the negative face, or his wants to have his freedom of action unhindered and his attention unimpeded, is called negative politeness. The hub concept of negative face is representative of Brown and Levinson's (1987) expansion and unique contribution, on top of Goffman's framework (Lee-Wong 2000). All in all, Brown and Levinson's (1987) gestation was built on the basis of a psychological or psycholinguistic perspective to explicate individual's emotions and desires towards one another's social action.

From another perspective of sociology, the Chinese writer Lin Yutang (1935, pp. 199–200) offered his sense of face with literary comments,

> Interesting as the Chinese physiological face is, the psychological face makes a still more fascinating study. It is not face that can be washed or shaved, but a face that can be "granted" and "lost" and "presented as a gift". Here we arrive at the most curious point of Chinese social psychology. Abstract and intangible, it is yet the most delicate standard by which Chinese social intercourse is regulated.
>
> (Lin 1935, pp. 199–200)

In a similar vein to Goffman, Lin's (1939) early definition gave prominence to the social functioning trait of face in daily interaction and for the first time highlighted the concept of face as the overarching guideline of Chinese values. Another pioneer Hu (1944, p. 45) dichotomised the face concept into "mianzi" and "lian" to mean social status and moral characters respectively. Gu (1990, p. 241) related face to its politeness function in Chinese social interaction and identified the interrelations between them: "(a) face is the essential element of politeness, to be polite is to be face-caring; (b) face and politeness hold a means-to-end relation between each other". He laid special emphasis on the first principle of face (statement a), which is contrary to Brown and Levinson's (1987) framework.

Having followed Hu's (1944) differentiation of face, Hwang (2004) further illuminated that lian represents the collective respect members of the community hold for persons with high moral standard and mianzi means social reputation that individuals strive to claim in the Chinese society. Grounded in Confucius thinking and the psychological perspective, Hwang (1987, 1997, 2004) recognised the long-standing social stability function of politeness and face, coupled with their cultural and philosophical roots that request a sense of dignity and shame in personal moral behaviors, and which resulted in numerous tenets of Confucianism having to do with face and politeness. By drawing upon face-work as the power game among Chinese, Hwang (1987, p. 953) termed two basic parties of communication as the "petitioner" and "resource allocator" in the game of a series of face-related behaviors (e.g., face-giving, face-loss and face-maintaining) for obtaining and competing for resources, be it economic, social, cultural or symbolic, four kinds of resources defined by Bourdieu (1986) that one looks for in the social arena. Giving prominence to face in relation to the self concept of Chinese people, Hwang (2004) pinpointed that a Chinese concept of self is neither independent self nor interdependent self in the Western sense (Markus and Kitayama 1991), but a "relational self" (p. 317) that is always weighs the self-image and connections in relation to other interactants in the social interactional process.

Though complexity may arise, there is a consensus among Chinese scholars towards face that it is more of a collective conceptualisation in the Chinese mindset to constitute personal face, and the face of one's larger social group, most typically one's family and, for example, one's institution and even nation. As a representation, the concept of Chinese face may thus consist of three layers: individual, relational and group mianzi, catering for face wants both in the individual and group sense (He and Zhang 2011).

Despite the voluminous and far-reaching research that has succeeded in the investigations of the boundaries and implications of face concern and face-work in face-to-face interactions, increasing requests were called for to entertain the delicate nature of virtual face-work. The complexity of face-work in computer-mediated communication is undoubtedly heightened in light of the absence of facial, body and prosodic cues (Baym 1995). To respond to such requests, West and Trester's (2013) ethnographic investigation of face-work on personal Facebook pages, having applied Brown and Levinson's (1987) framework, offered timely insights and a close-up of virtual face-work practices. Based on their analysis of four classic types of socialisation which face is inevitably engaged in: "friending", "self-presentation", "replying and responding" as well as "issuing birthday wishes and event invitations", they explicated how face is threatened, mediated, negotiated and navigated between posters and their Facebook friends (West and Trester 2013, pp. 134–138). Specifically, West and Trester (2013) presented the deference and violations of face and varied kinds of FTA through addressers' maneuvering and addressees' corresponding awareness of and reflections upon face during social media interactions.

From a relational perspective, another key study of face-work on the Chinese SNS Weibo by Wu and Lin (2017 forthcoming) identified and re-defined the diversified speech acts among 4012 items of Weibo celebrities' updates, e.g., congratulating, directives, promising, promoting assets, sharing information, showing concern and stance, daily and festive greetings, in terms of how they contribute to the social self in the virtual interaction. These relational acts performed by Chinese celebrities demonstrated once again Arundale's (2006) argument that the much-used distinction between self-face and other-face is problematic and in fact self and other are dialectically linked for both parties comprise the other to the self, mutually defining one another in their face-work practices.

2.4.5 *Conversation Analysis*

Conversation analysis as a distinctive and recognised approach to the analysis of social interaction is derived from the ethnomethodological tradition in sociology and has been widely used in interactional discourse analysis (see Stivers and Sidnell 2013). The seminal works of conversation analysis began with three people around 1970: Emanuel Schegloff, Harvey Sacks and Gail Jefferson. In fact conversation analysis is one of the six approaches to discourse analysis, parallel to interactional sociolinguistics (Schiffrin 1994), which allows examinations of both casual conversations (e.g. Schegloff 1968, 1988; Tannen 1984) and institutionalised conversations in professional settings (e.g., Sinclair and Coulthard 1975; Yu 2010; Yu and Wu 2015) and in intercultural conversations (e.g., Cheng 2003). As the name of conversation analysis implies, talk-in-interaction has been a recurrent theme. Both strands of conversation analysis and interactional sociolinguistics view conversations from the lens of social interaction focusing on naturally occurring conversation data. Conversation analysis does not see an inherent distinction between the formal and the informal, the everyday and the institutional, rather "they see talk-in-interaction as a social process which is deployed to realise and understand the social situations in which talk is used" (Liddicoat 2011, p. 6).

Conversation analysis operates on a systematic ground that involves analysis of turn-taking machinery (Sacks et al. 1974), adjacency pairs (Schegloff and Sacks 1973), opening and closing conversation (Schegloff 1968) and repairs (Schegloff et al. 1977). Turn-taking machinery refers to speaker change in conversations. According to Sacks et al. (1974), there are two separate but interrelated components in turn-taking: turn constructional units (TCUs) (turns that made up of units) and turn allocation component (current speaker selects next speaker or next speaker self-selects). Schegloff and Sacks (1973) called turns at talk as pairs and paired utterances adjacency pairs, which are the basic unit of social interaction. The initiation turn is called "first pair parts" (FPP) and the flows arising from such initiations are accordingly called "second pair parts" (SPP), as exemplified as question-answer, greeting-greeting and offer-acceptance/refusal (Schegloff and Sacks 1973, p. 74).

Further, the relationship between FPPs and SPPs is constrained by the type of FPP produced (Liddicoat 2011). Schegloff and Sacks (1973) also termed relevance rules: FPP creates a context of dialogue and SPP is supposed to respond to the preceding FPP in a relevant way with either preferred actions or dispreferred actions, which load "different interactional import" (Liddicoat 2011, p. 144). Viewed from a social perspective, actions display alignments with speakers of FPP such as greeting, acceptance, gratitude and agreement are preferred actions with more interactional import and otherwise (e.g. declines and disagreements) are dispreferred actions in SPP (see Sacks 1987).

As a discipline with a history of approximately merely half a century, conversation analysis not only allows but also requests increasingly intercultural and interdisciplinary endeavors. To date, the conversation analysis of Mandarin owes to a series of seminal work accomplished by the team led by Prof. Guodong Yu and Prof. Yaxin Wu in the Shanxi University of China, whose contributions are focused on but not necessarily confined to professional settings as to medical communication and a number of speech acts in the everyday spoken Mandarin (see Yu 2010; Yu and Wu 2015; Yu and Wu 2017).

2.5 New Media Discourse

2.5.1 An Overview

New media discourse, also known by other names of similar connotations such as the most widespread terminology computer-mediated discourse (CMD) (Herring 1996, 2004), digital discourse (Thurlow and Mroczek 2011), digital networked writing (Androutsopoulos 2011) or discourse 2.0 (Tannen and Trester 2013), entails highly situated communication practice and outcome via modes of newly emerging computer science technologies, for example Web 2.0. The fact that new media differs from "traditional" media lies in a number of aspects, made available by everlasting technological advances: content source, quality, frequency, performance, immediacy and usability. Social media platforms of Web 2.0 enable, as

Cormode and Krishnamurthy (2008) stated, the co-mingling of commentators and creators where every visitor has the opportunity to click, comment and create. Against the backdrop of the present-day universal production and consumption of Web 2.0 platform technology, new media discourse has been revolutionised to evolve rapidly from the “older” one-to-many online communication, for example website, to many-to-many real-time communication on a single social media platform, with the most representative being the microblogging brand Twitter and social networking site Facebook (cf. Androutsopoulos 2010).

Herring (2007) developed the concept of facets to mean the individually describable attributes of a complex (multifaceted) entity before a further distinguishing between medium (technological) and situation (social) facets of computer-mediated discourse. Major technological/medium facets, as Herring (2007) denoted are: synchronicity (whether communication is synchronous or asynchronous, i.e., whether or not the participants are online at the same time); message transmission (one- or two-way); persistence of transcript (how long messages stay on the system); size of message buffer (number of characters per message); channels of communication (potential for multimedia content); technological affordances of systems (e.g., whether they permit anonymous messaging, private messaging, filtering and quoting); and message format.

According to Herring (2007), the social or situational facets are specifically inclusive of: participant structure (one-to-one, one-to-many, many-to-many; public/private, degree of anonymity; group size, number of active participants…); participant characteristics (demographic: gender, age, occupation; language proficiency, computer skills, role and status in real life; attitudes, beliefs, ideologies…); purposes (of group, and goal of interaction); topic or theme (of group or exchanges); tone (serious/playful, formal/casual, cooperative/sarcastic); activity (debate, game, collaborative writing, information exchange, virtual sex); norms (of social organisation, of appropriateness, of language) and code (language variety, writing system, font…).

The discourse of social media in Web 2.0 era is very reasonably coined as discourse 2.0 (cf. Tannen and Trester 2013). Herring (2013) reconceptualised the tripartite aspects of Web 2.0 discourse as: familiar aspects (with CMC discourse), reconfigured aspects (topical coherence, turn-taking, threading and intertextuality) as well as emergent aspects (collaborative text product and multimodal analysis approach). Herring (2013, p. 11) located a few reconfigurations such as status updates being structurally and functionally reconfigured in comparison to “action descriptions” and “emotes”. It was also indicated that retweetings, “a prime new example of a discourse phenomenon”, are constitutive of interaction management (ibid., p. 12). Given the new technological functions made unprecedentedly possible by social media platforms, what struck ‘traditional’ media most is the interaction mechanism that social media are devised to feature, which gives substance to the lavish and interesting use of face and politeness strategies at the linguistic level. From the perspectives of four major social media interaction activities, namely, friending, self-presentation, replying and responding as well as issuing birthday wishes and event invitations, West and Trester’s (2013) ethnographic study unveiled how face-threatening acts (FTAs) are avoided and how massive face-work is accomplished on Facebook, e.g. through intertextual links.

In addition to the technical, pragmatic and sociocultural features exerted by new media, the extant findings concertedly suggested that one salient linguistic feature of new media discourse is its overt informality and orality in the form of literacy (Crystal 1987, 2001; Soffer 2012; Cameron and Panovic 2014), which is premised to wield long-term impact. The underlying interactional, vernacular, playful and occasionally interpersonal essence of new media discourse allows and orients its users to employ multiple linguistic, semiotic and multimodal resources, including emoticons, photos and video clips, all of which are believed to ascribe to the attracting feature of social media (e.g. Thurlow and Mroczek 2011). The challenges and arts of engaging user participation and their user-generated contents on social networking sites call for and bring together linguistic awareness of heteroglossia (Ivanov 2001), which is defined as "the simultaneous use of different kinds of speech or other signs, the tension between them, and their conflicting relationship within one text" (ibid., p. 5). In this regard, new media discourse is born as hybrid and dynamic, ready to encompass an endless list of emerging characteristics, as technologies usually upgrade from time to time. Wu et al. (2016) summarised the primary two sociolinguistic approaches for intercultural new media studies: variationist and interactional sociolinguistic paradigms, taking into consideration both the linguistic variations as well as issues like face, identity and rapport. A good manifestation of the interactional sociolinguistic paradigm is Li and Wu (2016) which examined the multinationals relational speech acts that aim at maintaining and strengthening rapport with their social media followers.

New media discourse, which to a great extent inherits the nature of what Crystal (2001, p. 24) named "netspeak" or "webslang", may be viewed as a social dialect from a sociolinguistic viewpoint Feng and Wang (2017). The excellent work of documenting such a variation of the English language was initiated in the 1980s by Crystal (1987, 1988), followed by scholarship on other languages such as French (Anis 1998), German (Beißwenger 2001), Chinese (Wang and Chen 2006; Gao 2006, 2012) and English used by second language learners (Lee 2013), shortly throughout the first decade of the 21st century (Androutsopoulos 2006a).

Nonetheless, increasing attention should be devoted to the new media discourse in the Chinese language, the target language of the present research. The Internet usage of modern Mandarin has been well-noted for its neologisms and impact on non-virtual Chinese usage in the globalisation age (Liu and Tao 2012; Yu et al. 2001; Wang and Chen 2006; Gao 2004, 2006, 2012). The edited book by Liu and Tao (2012) noticed and acknowledged the emerging trends that the Chinese language has undertaken in the era of globalisation. Gao (2012), for instance, well documented the varied features of the Chinese Internet language at the lexical, syntactic and discourse level. At the lexical level, Gao (2012) identified borrowing, compounding, analogy, calquing, metaphor and personification, phonological fusion, explanation, morpheme repetition, near homophonization, semantic shift and word decomposition. Whilst at the sentential level, Chinese Internet language undergoes novel usages, such as a change in sentence word order; the use of sentence-final redundant words; a change in word category; the use of an unusual sense of a word and the use of bound morphemes as free morphemes. The most prominent feature of Chinese Internet language, however, is its Englishlization (Gao 2006). Equally important, at the discourse level Gao (2012) precisely pointed out that Chinese Internet language is characterised with a bilingual code, i.e., a written spoken linguistic style as well as a jesting style. Furthermore, as to the underlying motivations of such language use, it was revealed that using Chinese Internet language helps to construct eight identities of the young and educated Chinese netizens: as entertaining and interesting, technologically well-informed and being able to keep up with social development, modern, fashionable and cool, internationally orientated or transnational, unconventional and even rebellious, young, fresh, innocent, deterritorialised or unconfined by geographical and/or sophisticated and not easily seen through (Gao 2004).

2.5.2 Microblogging Discourse

Etymologically, one of the entries of the word 'log' is known as a record of performance, events, or day-to-day activities, according to the Merriam-Webster dictionary. Jorn Barger named this so-called online journal 'weblog' in 1997[1] and Merholz said in 1999 that people would treat it as 'we blog', giving birth to the term blog we use ever since then.[2] Blogs are defined as "web sites or parts of web sites that are associated with specific individuals and comprise regular entries describing those individuals, their experiences, feelings and actions" (Mckinlay and Mcvittie 2011, p. 182). On this basis, the English word "microblogging" was coined to shorten the length of a "blog". Microblogging is an online broadcast medium that exists in the form of a mini weblog. A microblog differs from a traditional blog in that its contents are typically shorter, usually within 140 words and characters in length, in both actual and aggregated file size. Microblogging service providers allow their users "to send a message to another individual or to an indefinite number of others, to report on daily activities, forward messages or information from others, share links and so on" (Page 2012, p. 93). Microblogging communications are known for their fast-paced and ephemeral nature (ibid.). To mitigate this, a number of useful signs are invented to keep track of the communication threads, for instance, the @ symbol is used to indicate a piece of message addressed to particular users (Honeycutt and Herring 2009), and the # symbol is used to trace topic threads (Boyd et al. 2010). These small messages are sometimes called microposts or tweets, all of which are arranged in reverse chronology.

---

[1]"After 10 Years of Blogs, the Future's Brighter Than Ever". Wired. Published on 17 December 2007.

[2]"It's the links, stupid". The Economist. Published on 20 April 2006.

As a burgeoning genre in the everyday life of modern societies, language in the blogosphere has drawn increasing research attention. At the textual level, the saliency of hybridity of all genres' characteristics existing on microblogging sites called for increasing attentions. For example, Myers (2010) summarised a number of salient stylistic markers of language in the blogs:

> In the part that blog imitating a letter, there are some traces of the sort of interactive language often found in computer-mediated texts: it starts with a question, (You know how you used to have something going on in the kitchen…?) and ends with "xo" (hugs and kisses, I'm told). Further down, in the comments, we have conversational particles ("oh my"), typographical imitation of paralinguistic features (I'm sooo making this), the ubiquitous exclamation marks ("Look delicious!!") and non-standard use of lower case ("this is sweet!").
>
> (Myers 2010, p. 19)

Perspectives other than linguistic features in microblogging communication are also worthy of attention. Given the highly communicative nature of microblogging networks, multimodality is one of the most attractive features that allows for real-time sharing of emoticons, pictures and videos for interesting enhancement of content and users' deeper social engagements. In terms of motivations, it was verified that Twitter gratified its users' psychological need to connect with others in the virtual world (Chen 2011). As Androutsopoulos (2010) stated, users of new media have become intertextual operators, indeed, the multimodality and intertextuality of microblogging are demonstrated via the process of referring to images in texts, and referring back and forth among the original poster and his/her followers, e.g., in comments and counter-comments.

In comparison to alternative "older" text messaging systems such as short message texting (SMT) or instant messaging (IM), microblogging discourse has garnered much less research output, and the research on microblogging has unsurprisingly focused on the English-written Twitter (Lee 2011), leaving other languages and other microblogging aspects somewhat unattended.

In addition to the research on the linguistic forms of microblogging, its linguistic functions are regarded as even more significant. The communicative functions of social media's text-making practices have been identified, namely, "what you are doing right now", "everyday life", "opinion and judgment", "reporting mood", "reporting away messages", "initiating discussion", "addressing target audience", "simply posting quotation", "simply playful silence" and "interjection and using humor" (Lee 2011, p. 112). Furthermore, microblogging's role and application as a new literary genre in politics (Larsson and Moe 2012) and education (Lomicka and Lord 2012; Guth and Helm 2012) have been drawn upon more frequently. In most of the cases, its interactive nature in communication has raised much research interest (e.g. Page 2012).

Corporate social media networking sites (e.g., microblogging) has unsurprisingly replaced corporate websites in drawing research attention and generating increasingly favorable stakeholder relationships, in the studies of the corporate interactive communication practices on social networking sites (e.g., Fischer and Reuber 2011; Rybalko and Seltzer 2010) and the crisis communication of multinationals on the microblogging of the local host countries (e.g. Yin et al. 2015). The findings suggested that the dialogic communication on Fortune 500 companies' corporate Twitter accounts help to engage their stakeholders (Rybalko and Seltzer 2010). It has also been revealed that the Twitter updates of nonprofit organisations primarily existed as one-way communication only, despite the potential for dialogue and community building on the social networking site. In their own words, "rather than capitalising on the interactive nature and dialogic capabilities of the social media service, nonprofit organisations are primarily using Twitter as a means of sharing information instead of relationship building" (Waters and Jamal 2011, p. 323). The use of microblogging in enhancing corporate reputation has attracted research attention. Li et al. (2014) examined the dynamics of communication through a corporate Twitter channel and their contribution to corporate reputation. They also discovered that deeper relationship among users of firm-specific Twitter led to higher user engagement practices.

On the whole, the research into new media discourse has substantially favored a register approach, giving substance to the variations of linguistic forms in the new mode of communicative environment. Nonetheless, it needs to be noted that current research of new media discourse somehow neglects to dig deep for a more profound understanding of the underpinnings for the variations caused, such as identity construction and face-work in spite of only a few attempts (e.g. Gao 2006), and equipped with a more solid and cross-disciplinary method of analysis, e.g., the interactional sociolinguistic and ethnographic approach for a bottom-up dynamic depiction of what is really taking place in the Web 2.0 era. As such, the present study of microblogging discourse from the interactional sociolinguistics point to a gap in the literature examining the corporate-follower interactive process of communication on organisational microblogging.

2.6 Research Gaps and Significance of the Present Study

Due to the very recent advent of social media, the majority of previous scholarly endeavors failed to fully explore the dynamic construction of corporate identity in the milieu of new media, and focused instead on the external corporate communication means such as websites and press conferences. Albeit that increasing claims have been made towards the co-construction of corporate identity by means of dialogic communication (Theunissen 2014), the concepts lack verification and remain under-researched in terms of linguistic empirical evidence, particularly in the social media and non-Anglo-Saxon context.

From an interactional sociolinguistic stance, the desirable dialogic communication mechanism in public relations may be realised through the interactional discourse strategies and conversational style employed by both the corporation and its followers. As such, the present research contributes to the existing body of research by offering a dynamic, two-way interactive perspective of corporate identity construction, with a special focus on interactional discourse strategies and conversational style. Toward this end, a new framework of corporate identity co-construction in new media is proposed.

The second innovation lies in the target genre to be researched. The majority of interactional sociolinguistic research has so far been devoted to interpreting cross-cultural, face-to-face conversation in the past three decades or so, thus calling for an updated and expanded application in contexts enabled with technological advances, such as the current study of non face-to-face speech-like written conversations on new media. This study examines not only the suggested merits of dialogic communication in public relations, but also attempts to illuminate the mechanism of follower participation and its role in contributing to dialogues and the construction of corporate identity.

In view of the overall discourse milieu, what makes the present study even more significant is its aim to demystify the changing Chinese context, as a typical emerging economic giant. As a dark horse in the world economic arena, China's best-performing industry on the Fortune 500 falls squarely on the banking industry. It is more than timely and crucial to investigate how China's banking industry, as an epitome of developing countries, copes with new media communication challenges and interactively delivering "who they are" in a two-way mode of communication to rebuild investor confidence among stakeholders and downplay the aftermath of the global financial crisis in 2009.

Over the past five decades, corporate identity has maintained its long-standing status as a productive research realm. However, it has been largely confined to the field of management and marketing scholarship, thus allowing many interdisciplinary and updated endeavors from linguists, discourse analysts and ethnographic researchers to work one step further. The literature reviewed has undoubtedly suggested that although companies across the globe are either aware of the significance of social media or are in fact using social media platforms as public relations and marketing devices, the role of social media on corporate identity construction, specifically from discursive perspectives, remain opaque. This call for research is especially urgent and pressing given the sheer fact that social media is widely acknowledged for its intensified interaction mechanism in the communication field. It must be fully acknowledged that prior studies did lend their valuable supports in illuminating the interaction management of computer-mediated discourse in social media environment. Nonetheless only a paucity of academic work has been devoted to corporate identity construction among which research scope is generally focused on either the technological availabilities of interaction and their linguistic variations (Herring 2013) or the linguistic strategies used in peer-to-peer interpersonal communication (West and Trester 2013).

Although corporate social responsibility's role in corporate identity has been previously addressed, its presentation on social media is not yet fully understood and the present research will pay attention to the CSR projection via social media. Lastly, interactional sociolinguistic analysis bears its credibility and acknowledged expertise in analysing face-to-face interpersonal communication. By analysing new media corporate communication, the present study expands upon and diversifies the genres, domains and research scope of interactional sociolinguistic analysis for its broader application in the social sciences. More importantly, in terms of methodology, an interactional approach offsets, if not maximally, the accused subjective interpretation in the traditional public relations by taking into account the neglected audience responses. In this way, a larger and more comprehensive picture of Public Relations communication can be distilled. The findings will be further devoted to a more thorough understanding of the multifaceted nature of corporate identity studies.

In summary, by bridging the noticeable research gaps left unfilled by the extant literature, the significance of this study comprises the following aspects: specifying the identities Chinese banks constructed and projected on social media platforms; offering authentic linguistic insights into the content and modes of interactive communications between enterprises and their followers, in a necessary attempt to facilitate the pedagogical and scholarly studies of new media, business discourse and corporate communication; deconstructing up-to-date social media patterns with characteristics in the external corporate communications in Chinese and exploring the role of interaction in the discursive construction of banks' identities on social media, as a methodological innovation, aside from the traditional one-way corporate transmission of corporate identity.

Chapter 3
Theoretical Framework and Research Methods

3.1 Introduction

This chapter is composed of four main components. The first section establishes a dialogic theoretical framework of corporate identity construction on social media. The second section introduces the research questions of the present study. The third and fourth sections detail the research design and data collection procedures respectively.

3.2 Towards a Dialogic Theoretical Framework

First and foremost, the corporate identity in the present study is defined as the overall image(s) that an enterprise presents to its stakeholders and the general public through certain mode of communication. To reiterate, the sole control over corporate identity being in the hands of the organisation has been questioned and so far simplistically understood. The working framework proposed hereby is initiated with a revisit of dialogue and dialogic communication in the discipline of public relations (Kent and Taylor 1998, 2002; Theunissen 2014). Dialogue is deemed as a quality of relationships in public relations (Cissna and Anderson 1998). It is regarded as more ethical than a corporation's sheer persuasion that clearly favors one party's interests (Theunissen and Wan Noordin 2012). A dialogic communication between company and its followers on social media is most desirable, as it emphases "equality, agreement and mutual benefit" (Stoker and Tusinski 2006, p. 160).

W. Feng, *Discursive Constructions of Corporate Identities by Chinese Banks on Sina Weibo*, DOI 10.1007/978-981-10-4469-4_3

Fig. 3.1 A two-way dialogic corporate identity construction framework on social media

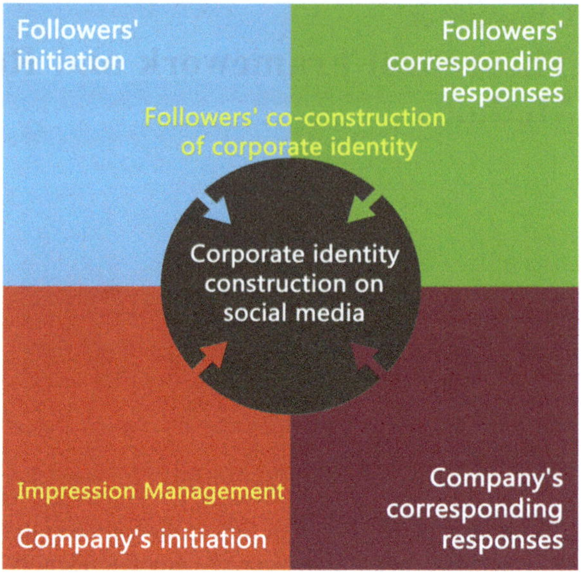

The proposed dialogic theoretical framework, drawing upon a social constructionist perspective, is rooted in interactional sociolinguistics (see Fig. 3.1), particularly the seminal work on identity and interaction accomplished by Goffman (1959, 1967). Social constructionist sociolinguistics indeed made considerable contributions in identity and language studies. Yet as new modes of communication emerge, new modes of interaction vis-a-vis identity come into being and there thus exists a call for new theoretical frameworks to be created, interpreted and applied.

In response to the notion of footing, which Goffman (1981) depicted as a speaker's identity in social interaction, i.e., the animator, author and principal in his production format, I hereby propound four roles enacted by the hearers (i.e. the banks' microblogging followers), namely the active contributors, interlocutors, listeners and lurkers on social media. By active contributors, I mean the followers who either speak specifically and exclusively to banks by putting @ in their self-initiated microblogging posts or those who made comments on corporations' microblogging contents and such comments being reposted by corporations with their responses/feedbacks. By interlocutors, I refer to those who make comments and voice their views but whose comments have not been reposted by corporations and so do not appear on the corporate microblogging contents. The listeners, however, are involved in reposting and liking, making only minimal interactive effort. Lastly, the lurkers do not usually signify their existence but are constitutive of the mainstream followers of corporations. The deconstructions of the hearers as a collective group on social media are commensurate with and illustrated by the performance and/or efforts made in interacting with the speaker.

3.3 Research Questions

The research questions that guide the aims of this research are as follows:

RQ1: By means of corporate Weibo updates, what identities have the two Chinese banks constructed?

RQ2: What impression management strategies have the two Chinese banks employed in the management of their identities and images?

RQ3: What are the dialogic patterns/types in the firm-follower interaction? In what ways did the followers play a role in the co-construction of corporate identities on corporate Weibo?

RQ4: Are there any variations between the state-owned bank and the non-state-owned bank in their corporate identity construction? If yes, how differently do they present themselves on the Weibo interface?

3.4 Graphic Depiction of the Theoretical Framework

As the two-way dialogic corporate identity construction framework on social media (Fig. 3.1) shows, the two-way corporate identity construction on social media consists of two pairs of initiation and responses, driven by both corporation and its followers. In the first pair of initiation-response, company posts and updates contents on corporate social media account, which generate responses of the followers. In the second pair of initiation-response, followers initiate interaction and company responds. While the company's self-initiated updates are considered as the impression management of its corporate identity, followers' initiation and responses make up the co-construction of the corporate identity.

During the dialogic communication between company and the followers, company's initiation may be interpreted as its impression management contributing to corporate identity construction, which helps to set the tone of the two-party dialogic communication afterwards. Both the followers' initiation and responses to company's initiation are included in the co-construction of corporate identity. The first pair of initiation-response (company's initiation and followers' responses) is postulated as the most frequent forms of dialogic communication, as the second pair of initiation-response (followers' initiation and company's responses) takes place less frequently. Despite its scarcity, the value of the second pair of initiation-response (followers' initiation and company's responses), characterised by followers' authentic participation, should be given sufficient attention and is a highly sensitive indicator in the corporation's impression management process. The capability of generating followers' initiation and responses allows companies a distinct advantage and competitive edge in gaining trust over the publics and adapting to the demands of the stakeholders.

3.5 Methods of Analysis

To ensure the maximum reliability of any possible conclusions, the present study integrated a tripartite of methods of analysis: thematic analysis, interactional analysis and in-depth qualitative interviews. While thematic analysis was employed to discover the Chinese banks' corporate identities in the social media self-presentation, interactional analysis is used to analyse the corporations' impression management strategies as well as the firm-follower dialogic patterns in the followers' co-construction of corporate identities. In-depth interviews with key informant media creators illuminate stories behind the curtain and help to contextualise communicative intensions and rationale.

Thematic analysis is the most common form of encoding qualitative data (Guest 2012), spinning across a wide range of disciplines like sociology, literature, psychology, cultural anthropology, economics and many other fields. Thematic analysis "enables scholars, observers, or practitioners to use a wide variety of types of information in a systematic manner that increases their accuracy or sensitivity in understanding and interpreting observations about people, events, situations, and organizations" (Boyatzis 1998, p. 5). Coding is the primary process for developing themes and patterns within the raw data by recognising important moments in the data and encoding it prior to further analysis and interpretation (Boyatzis 1998). The interpretation of these codes, on the basis of a codebook, can include comparing theme frequencies, identifying theme co-occurrence, and graphically displaying relationships between different themes (Guest 2012). In so doing, thematic analysis is useful in examining large amounts of data, perhaps seemingly unrelated to each other, and converting qualitative data into quantitative information in a systematic way, which allows further conceptualisations and arguments on the handful identities of banks constructed on the Sina Weibo.

Interactional analysis, as a method of analysis in the present study, involves a combination of conversation analysis and interactional sociolinguistics analysis. As reviewed in the literature, the concepts such as "face", "face-work" (Goffman 1967, p. 1), "footing" (Goffman 1981, p. 128), "conversational style" (Tannen 1984, p. 7), as well as power and solidarity in interactional sociolinguistics and notions like turn-taking (Sacks et al. 1974) and adjacency pairs (Schegloff and Sacks 1973) in conversation analysis lend support to the present study. As face is a relational phenomenon, it may only be analysed during interactions (Spencer-Oatey 2007) and face-work is almost universal in social interaction. Conversation analysis is used as a powerful tool for analysis talk-in-interaction and one of its good examples is the initiation-response-feedback pattern identified in classroom discourse (Sinclair and Coulthard 1975). The examination of the realisation forms of these terms helps to locate the banks' impression management strategies and their interaction/dialogic patterns with followers in social media communication.

In-depth key informant qualitative interviews of media creators in both banks were designed for more thorough and deeper understandings of the backstage communication intentions and process, responsive to the call for discourse-centered online ethnography (Androutsopoulos 2008), combing systematic analysis of the discourse produced online with direct interaction between the researcher and the discourse producers. Interviews were carefully transcribed according to the procedures of Boyatzis (1998) for data analysis. Qualitative interviews are useful in diagnosing the current state and rationale for communicative events (Packer 2011). The significance of in-depth key informant interviews lies in the exploration of 'what is behind the curtain' and reasonable interpretations of textual evidence for corporate communicative intensions. In-depth interview investigations with media creators are inseparable in the providence of contemporary socio-cultural and socio-political milieu based on which Weibo updates are created day by day. Through interviews, the researcher "gains some understanding of the psychological and social factors, which may affect language use in the speech community" (Lee-Wong 2000, p. 55).

In summary, my research on the discursive constructions of corporate identity was designed and operationalised in a multi-dimensional way and mainly in three components. First, thematic analysis was conducted for identifying identities of each bank on Weibo. Second, both corporation-initiated Weibo updates were examined for the extraction of their impression management strategies using interactional sociolinguistic approach. The point of probing banks' impression management strategies resides in the intension to track down their own tactics and efforts in projecting identities and images on social media. The third dimension of research design was concerned with the other side of the coin, by drawing on the co-construction of corporate identity to examine the followers' interaction with banks' posts, i.e., likes, reposts and comments and their key roles in shaping the corporate identity construction of the banks. Lastly, a comparison was conducted for locating interbank variations in identity construction, impression management and the interaction with followers. The endeavors were devoted to investigate how corporate identities were being constructed, co-constructed and negotiated in firm-follower interaction.

3.6 Data Collection

To facilitate the research objectives of the present research, the selection and retrieval of microblogging texts concern two premium Chinese banks for a thorough in-depth investigation, namely, the Bank of China and the China Merchants Bank, a wholly state-owned bank versus a non wholly state-owned or, a joint-equity bank, both of which fall into the Fortune 500 categories. The rationale for the selection and pairing as such was based on their unique industry status. On the one hand, with a century-old history and the widest global network, the BOC takes pride in acting as a reputable brand name and the icon of China's banking industry throughout the world. On the other, founded in 1987, the CMB is the first non-wholly state-owned bank in China. It is also one of the very few banks which is headquartered in Shenzhen, Guangdong province—a border-crossing city of Hong Kong—rather than in Beijing, the majority choice of headquarters for others banks. The presumable contrast between the BOC and the CMB might lead to varied corporate identities and relevant impression management strategies.

Entire textual updates initiated by the CMB, including followers' initiated updates that have been reposted by banks, during 1 September, 2013 to 30 September, 2016, amounting to a totality of 1382 items, were collected for analysis. As of the BOC, due to its abundance of corporate tweets, a randomly sampled data consisting of 1423 items of tweets were extracted during the same time span, i.e., ranging from 1 September, 2013 to 30 September, 2016. While the banks' textual posts being collected, a few key numbers indicative of followers' interactive responses, i.e., numbers of likes, reposts and comments, and the exact time spots were also documented. All the dialogues with active contributors for a conversation analysis of interaction patterns/dialogic types were extracted too.

3.7 Data Collection Methods

The selection of textual data was decided upon the reputation of social media networks and the representativeness of the banking corporations. In view of the complexity of research design, data for the analysis was extracted from two reliable sources, textual and ethnographic. Firstly, the microblogging updates of the BOC and the CMB are downloaded from www.weibo.com and saved in separate Word files. Meanwhile, in-depth interviews with bank managers were arranged for an ethnographic study in order to shed crucial light on the rationale for their corporate microblogging practices.

The rationale for a selection of Sina Weibo as the data source is primarily derived from its outstanding industry status and its imperative role in shaping public sentiments. A hybrid of Twitter and Facebook, NASDAQ-listed Sina Weibo (Weibo is the Chinese phonetic system pinyin for microblogging) definitely takes a leading position among the most popular social media sites in the Cultural China region (including Chinese mainland, Hong Kong, Taiwan, Macau and Singapore) with its 69.7% market share in the Chinese microblogging industry as per the 36th report of the China Internet Network Information Center in 2015. With an alleged similar market penetration of Twitter in USA, Sina Weibo was launched by the Beijing-based SINA Corporation on 14 August 2009, and have 297 million active users (active at least once per month) as of 302016, an increase of 34% as compared to the same period of 2015.

According to the Sina database, by the second quarter of 2016, Sina Weibo has 282 million subscribers and 126 million daily users, an increase of 33 and 36% respectively as compared to the same period in 2014. In addition to active individual users, Sina also confirmed that more than 5000 companies and 2700 media organisations in China use Sina Weibo. The users of Sina Weibo include Asian celebrities, movie stars, singers, famous business and media figures, athletes, scholars, artists, organisations, religious figures, government departments, and officials from Hong Kong, Mainland China, Malaysia, Singapore, Taiwan, and Macau, as well as well-known international individuals and organisations, including Leonardo DiCaprio, Stephen William Hawking, Bill Gates, David Cameron, David Beckham, Christine Lagarde, Coca Cola, MacDonalds, Toshiba and many non-government organisations.

In terms of demographics, the gender ratio of Weibo users saw a balance of 55.5% for male users versus 44.5% for female users, despite a majority of well-educated users with university diplomas (77.8%). Users of Weibo over 30 years old reached more than 80% of entire users, indicating a long-lasting user habit into the coming decades.

Accompanied by numerous celebrity users and with the blended features of Twitter and Facebook, Sina Weibo is home to at least 100 million updates daily. According to Sina Weibo datacenter statistics, by 30 September 2016, the younger generation of China or future mainstream customers is their major players. The post-1990s generation accounts for half of the total user pool, at 53% and the post-1980s generation covers a little more than one third with 37%. Only 8% of users belong to the post-1970s generation. Sina corporate microblogging is also home to almost 30% of the Global Fortune 500 companies, a mix of corporations from 35 nations. Even though other brands of social media in China have appeared, such as Renren.com and WeChat, the recognised power of the earliest microblogging icon Sina Weibo, particularly in shaping non-interpersonal communication and public sentiment, is unparalleled.

3.8 Graphic Description of Textual Data

See Table 3.1.

Table 3.1 Description of textual data

Sina corporate microblogging platform	Bank of China (wholly state-owned)	China Merchants Bank (non wholly-state owned)
Time span	1 September 2013 to 30 September 2016	1 September 2013 to 30 September 2016
Number of followers	3,510,731	6,561,879
Number of updates in total	1429	1387

Chapter 4
Heterogeneous Corporate Identities of Banks on Sina Weibo

4.1 Introduction

This chapter uncovers respectively the multi-faceted identities projected by the CMB and the BOC on the Sina Weibo. The coding schemes and the results for multiple identities were introduced, followed by instances of each corporate identity. What was presented afterwards was the discussion of the prominence of heterogeneous identities of both banks on social media with reference to the extant research.

4.2 Heterogeneous Identities of the CMB on the Sina Weibo

In an attempt to uncover and discern corporate identities the CMB projected on the Sina Weibo, a thematic analysis of the selected 1393 tweets between 1 September 2013 and 30 September 2016 was conducted. As illustrated in Table 4.1, the evidence indicated the multifacetedness of the CMB's corporate identities projected on the Sina Weibo, containing five prominent identities: the companion identity, the journalist identity, the authentic identity, the CSR identity and the specialist identity.

The most prominent companion identity of the CMB, realised as an intimate, witty and caring friend of its followers in the 825 items on social media, accounting for 59.5% of the entire microblogging updates. This is an identity which best epitomises the involved 'playing cuteness' conversation style, demonstrating solidarity and politeness strategies in addressing and engaging the followers of the CMB. The witty element of this friend identity was reflected in its health tips, jokes, book extracts, philosophical remarks and chicken-soup-for-the-soul style of microblogging updates. Secondly, by means of 290 items of tweets, or 20.9% of the total CMB corpus, the CMB skillfully projected itself as a well-informed (financial)

W. Feng, *Discursive Constructions of Corporate Identities by Chinese Banks on Sina Weibo*, DOI 10.1007/978-981-10-4469-4_4

Table 4.1 Coding schemes and results for the multiple identities of the CMB projected on the Sina Weibo

No.	Corporate identities of the CMB	Descripitive statements	Operational definitions of coding	No. of updates	% in total updates
1.	Companion identity	An intimate, witty and caring friend	Updates caring about followers' interests and demonstrating friendliness towards followers, including useful life and health tips and those bearing philosophical implicature	825	59.50
2.	Specialist identity	An authoritative financial specialist and industry expert	Updates discussing and commenting on financial prospects	16	1.20
3.	Authentic identity	A financial products seller or financial institution	Updates advertising and promoting its banking service and financial products	214	15.40
4.	Journalist identity	A well-informed (financial) newsman	Updates of informative news reports, especially relating to the financial and economic domains	290	20.90
5.	CSR identity	A socially responsible corporation	Updates manifesting banks' corporate social responsibilities, e.g., environment-friendly posts.	30	2.20
6.	Other identities	Others	None of the foregoing applies	12	0.80
Total				1387	100

newsman, actualised through informative news reports, especially relating to financial and economic domains, though some of which were reposted or quoted ones. Thirdly, approximately 15% of the entire microblogging updates projected the CMB's authentic identity as a financial product seller or a financial institution, who advertised and promoted its banking service and financial products, coupled with official announcements relating to a variety of the CMB's banking services. Fourthly, as a trendy component of present-day corporate communication, information that presented the CMB as a socially responsible corporation was rather limited, accounting for merely 2.2% of total posts on its Sina Weibo account. Lastly, the weakest specialist identity of the CMB may be found in 16 tweets, a slight share of 1.2% amongst the total microblogging updates.

As is seen clearly, to a great extent, the companion identity as an intimate, witty and caring friend of followers dominates the CMB's microblogging sphere. It may be further elaborated that such an identity is the most desirable one for the CMB's social media self-presentation. Displayed below are sample individual microblogging updates exemplifying each identities of the CMB, where companion identity, journalist identity, authentic identity, the identity as a socially responsible bank and specialist identity are manifested in Extracts 1, 2, 3, 4 and 5 accordingly.

Extract 1: 意外和明天不知道哪一个先到，真的，珍惜当下。

贊(65)|轉發(47)|收藏|評論(12) CMB 15082015 22:57 來自 iPhone 6

Extract 1: It is hard to say whether the unexpectedness or tomorrow occurs first, really. Cherish the present moment.

Like (65)|Repost (47)|Collect|Comment (12) CMB 15082015 22:57 from iPhone 6.

Extract 2: 【塑料货币你支持吗?】 英国央行18日发布公告，2016年和2017年将发行两款币值为5英镑和10英镑的聚合塑料币，头像将采用英国前首相丘吉尔和著名作家简•奥斯丁的形象。与纸币相比，塑料货币更安全更环保成本更低。目前世界上大约已有20多个国家和地区发行了塑料货币。央视报道: http://t.cn/8kNiI4G

贊(32)|轉發(37)|收藏|評論(43) CMB 19122013 21:02 來自 iPhone客户端 | 舉報

Extract 2: 【In support of plastic cash?】 On the 18th, the Bank of England announced that two denominations of £ 5 and £ 10, made of polymer plastic materials, will be issued in 2016 and 2017. The avatar image printed on the bank notes will be the former British Prime Minister Churchill and the well-known writer Jane Austen. Compared with paper-made bank notes, plastic bank notes are safer and more environmentally friendly with lower costs. There have been over 20 countries and regions in the world where plastic bank notes have been issued. Report of CCTV:http://t.cn/8kNiI4G.

Like (32)/Repost (37)/Collect/Comment (43) CMB 19122013 21:02 from iPhone app.

Extract 3: 【重要通知】 小招家的攻城狮又要开始忙活了。我行将于18日20:
00至20日20: 00对北京市，山东省，河南省，辽宁省，黑龙江省所辖机构实
施系统升级。期间业务可能会受到一定影响，详情及升级城市请看大图。

贊 (7)|轉發(23)|收藏|評論(24) CMB 18102013 14:27 來自专业版微博 | 舉報

Extract 3: 【Important notice】 Engineers of the CMB are busy with system upgrading. The CMB is about to upgrade systems in Beijing, Shandong, Henan, Liaoning, Heilongjiang from 20:00 of 18th to 20:00 of 20th, during which business transactions might incur inconveniences. For details please refer to the uploaded big pictures.

Like (7)/Repost (23)/Collect/Comment (24) CMB 18102013 14:27 from Weibo.

Extract 4: 大家还记得雅安的小伙伴们吗?去年4月20日，老天给他们开了一个大大的玩笑，现在怎么样了?小招的同事们带着祝福探访了重建中的雅安，儿童服务站，避灾篮球场，农房重建，金葵花温暖包等项目，满满的正能量哦，请看大图! 希望小招的爱心捐款能够为雅安的重建贡献一点点力量

@壹基金

贊(28)|轉發(39)|收藏|評論(13) CMB 10012014 21:25 來自新浪微博 | 舉報

Extract 4: Do you remember the buddies in the earthquake-stricken Ya'an. On 20th April last year, God has made a practical joke against Ya'an, but how about the situations now? Staff of the CMB has visited projects such as the Children's Service Station, escapable basketball courts, rural housing reconstruction and Golden sunflower package. Lots of warmth and positive energy are presented. See pictures please! Hope the donation of the CMB contributes to the reconstruction of Ya'an.

Like (28)/Repost (39)/Collect/Comment (13) CMB 10012014 21:25 from Sina Weibo.

Extract 5: 小招在智联招聘和北京大学相关机构联合举办的2013中国年度最佳雇主评选中荣获第一， 同时入选最具社会责任十强雇主。在这里我要感谢小伙伴们一路上的支持和努力, 2014期待更多小伙伴加入我们!

贊(73)|轉發(250)|收藏|評論(102) CMB 17122013 16:34 來自新浪微博 | 舉報

Extract 5: The CMB won the champion in the competition of Best Employer of the Year in 2013, organised jointly by zhaopin.com and the Peking University. Meanwhile it was awarded as the one of the top 10 socially responsible employers. I hereby would like to be grateful for your support all the way. Look forward to more pals to join the CMB in 2014!

Like (73)/Repost (250)/Collect/Comment (102) CMB 17122013 16:37 from Sina Weibo.

4.3 Heterogeneous Identities of the BOC on the Sina Weibo

Similar to the multiple nature of the CMB's corporate identities on social media, a thematic analysis of 1429 items from the BOC Sina Weibo updates throughout a time span of three-year indicated a multifaceted identity package, containing five corporate identities: the companion identity, the specialist identity, the authentic identity, the journalist identity and the identity as a socially responsible corporation. Nonetheless, the proportion of the BOC's corporate identities showed dramatic variations as compared to those of the CMB.

The more balanced spectrum of identity package of the BOC is composed of the same five identities as found in the CMB microblogging: specialist identity, companion identity, authentic identity, journalist identity and CSR identity, as shown in the Table 4.2. Firstly, the centrality of the BOC's corporate identities was reflected in its specialist identity, as either an authoritative financial specialist and industry expert or a long-standing, worldwide, best-performing bank. While the authoritative financial specialist may be found in the 434 items or 30.40% of total updates, the very unique and exclusive identity of the BOC as a long-standing, worldwide, best-performing bank was manifested in 139 items, or 9.7% of the microblogging contents, thus making the specialist identity the most prominent throughout as many as 573 items or 40.1% of the BOC corpus. In the second place, companion identity of the BOC as an intimate, witty and caring friend of the followers was projected through 368 items, taking up 25.8% of the BOC tweets. Thirdly, the most unsurprising authentic identity of the BOC was related to 270 items or 18.9% of the total contents. The fourth journalist identity, informing the CMB's followers of informative news reports, especially relating to financial and economic domains, accounted for 8.60% in proportion. The weakest CSR identity was reflected through merely 83 tweets, a slightest coverage of 5.8% amongst the BOC's Weibo contents.

Similarly, below manifested individual microblogging updates exemplifying each identities of the BOC respectively. That is, the companion identity (Extract 6), the specialist identity (Extract 7), the authentic identity (Extract 8), the identity as a

Table 4.2 Coding schemes and results for the multiple identities of the BOC projected on the Sina Weibo

No. of identities	Corporate identities of the BOC	Descriptive statements	Operational definitions of coding	No. of updates	% in total updates
1.	Companion identity	An intimate, witty and caring friend	Updates caring about followers' interests and demonstrating friendliness towards followers, including useful life and health tips and those bearing philosophical implicature	368	25.80
2.	Specialist identity	An authoritative financial specialist and industry expert	Updates discussing and commenting on financial prospects	434	30.40
		A long-standing, worldwide, best-performing bank	Updates highlighting its glorious century-old history, its global operation networks and its awards	139	9.7
3.	Authentic identity	A financial products seller or financial institution	Updates advertising and promoting its banking service and financial products	270	18.90
4.	Journalist identity	A well-informed (financial) newsman	Updates of informative news reports, especially relating to the financial and economic domains	123	8.60
5.	CSR identity	A socially responsible corporation	Updates manifesting banks' corporate social responsibilities, e.g., environment-friendly posts	83	5.80
6.	Other identities	Others	None of the foregoing applies	12	0.8
Total				1429	100

Note Identity No. 2 and No. 4 were calculated together for the specialist identity of BOC in Table 4.2

long-standing worldwide bank (Extract 9), as a well-informed newsman (Extract 10) and as a socially responsible corporation (Extract 11).

Extract 6: 工作一周积累了不少脏衣服吧?如何清洗才能让自己心爱的衣物保持如新?童鞋们戳大图, 赶快学习起来!(Via窍门百科)

贊(6)|轉發(69)|收藏|評論(8) BOC 09112013 16:16 來自专业版微博 | 舉報

Extract 6: Bothered about the accumulated, plenty of unwashed dirty clothes at the end of a busy week? What kinds of wash can result in clean clothes, as brand-new? Classmates can be informed of by clicking the pictures.

Like (6)/Repost (69)/Collect/Comment (8) BOC 09112013 16:16 from Weibo.

Extract 7: #中银视界# 周四美联储宣布基准利率不变，强调关注全球局势。利率决议公布后金价短线冲高至1128美元/盎司，之后逐步回吐涨幅。今日关注美国第四季度GDP数据等。请关注《每日市场点评》之“国际金价冲高回落 关注美国经济数据”

贊(6)|轉發(115)|收藏|評論(3) BOC 28012016 15:02 來自专业版微博 | 舉報

Extract 7: # BOC horizon # the Federal Reserve Bank announced Thursday that benchmark interest rate remained unchanged, stressing a concern over the global situation. Subsequent to its announcement of interest rate decision, short-term gold price shot up to $1128/ounce. Nevertheless afterwards, the gold price gradually decreases its gains. The fourth quarter GDP statistics of the US economy will be focused today in detail. Please pay attention to our column “the soaring and falling of international gold price and the US economy statistics” in “Daily Market Review”.

Like (6)|Repost (115)|Collect|Review (3) BOC 28012016 15:02 from Weibo.

Extract 8: 【快乐经济行 惠享9.1折】新加坡，曼谷，吉隆坡……独具特色的东南亚风光让人流连忘返。即日起至2014年3月31日，凡持长城环球通信用卡金普卡，中银南航明珠信用卡金普卡用户，购买南航特定路线机票，可享9.1折优惠哦!这个“十一”还不行动起来! http://t.cn/z8D4e2B

贊|轉發(2)|收藏|評論 BOC 30092013 13:39 來自专业版微博 | 舉報

Extract 8: Singapore, Bangkok, Kuala Lumpur, and Southeast Asia…… unique Southeast Asian scenery is unforgettable. From now until March 31, 2014, holders of the BOC Great Wall credit card (Gold and normal), the BOC China Southern Airlines credit card (Gold and normal) will benefit from 9% off discount for purchasing certain routs of the China Southern Airlines. Be quick to seize the opportunity during the National holiday this year! http://t.cn/z8D4e2B

Like (0)/Repost (2)/Collect/Comment BOC 30092013 13:39 from Web.

Extract 9: #中银足迹# 从1912年成立至今，中国银行已走过了102年的路程。足迹遍布中国内地，香港，澳门，台湾及全球37个国家。在许多陌生而新鲜的城市，我们期待着与你的温暖邂逅。从今天开始，就请和@中国银行一起踏上微博环球旅程。最近恰逢匈牙利总理到访中行，我们的第一站就去匈牙利吧。

贊(13)|轉發(29)|收藏|評論(7) BOC 18022014 16:00 來自新浪微博 | 舉報

Extract 9: Since its inception in 1912, the BOC has gone through 102 years of journey, whose footprints are all over Chinese mainland, Hong Kong, Macau, Taiwan and 37 nations worldwide. In many unknown and fresh cities, we look forward to a warm encounter with you. From today on, please embark on a microblogging global journey with @Bank of China. As Hungarian prime minister happens to visit the local BOC branch, let's head for the first stop of our journey in Hungary.

Like (13)/Repost (29)/Collect/Comment (7) BOC 18022014 16:00 from Sina Weibo.

Extract 10: 【2013年十大新闻图片】美国《时代周刊》近日评选出2013年度十大新闻图片，向我们展示了2013年最震撼人心，最令人难忘的瞬间。痛苦和灾难终将过去，愿新年的阳光充满更多爱与希望。(来自腾讯网)

贊(5)|轉發(19)|收藏|評論(3) 05122013 BOC 17:26 來自专业版微博 | 舉報

Extract 10: [2013 Ten News Picture] Time magazine of the US has selected top 10 news pictures to show us the most stirring, most unforgettable moments of 2013. As grief and disaster have past, wish that there will be more love and hope in the new year (from Tencent).

Like (5)/Repost (19)/Collect/Comment (3) BOC 05122013 17:26 from Weibo.

Extract 11: 【中行获颁“母亲健康快车十年推动奖”】近日，中国银行获颁中国妇女发展基金会“母亲健康快车十年推动奖”。2013年，中行支持大型公益项目“母亲健康快

车"，为山东，安徽，湖北等地贫困地区捐赠了48辆流动医疗车，为贫困妇女送去健康。http://t.cn/8kuGvbp

贊(6)|轉發(2)|收藏|評論(3) 27122013 BOC 17:56 來自新浪微博 | 舉報

Extract 11: 【Bank of China was awarded the "The Decade Promotion Award of the Mother Heath Express"】 China Women's Development Foundation has recently awarded the Bank of China the decade award of promoting Mother's Health Express. In 2013, the Bank of China supported the large-scale public project "other Health Express", donating 48 mobile medical vehicles to poverty-stricken women in provinces like Shandong, Anhui, and Hubei. http://t.cn/8kuGvbp.

Like (6)/Repost (2)/Collect/Comment (3) BOC 27122013 17:56 from Weibo.

4.4 Corporate Identities Realised on Corporate Social Media

The findings have verified Blamer's (1998) five-stage classifications of corporate identity in which the fifth stage (2000 onwards) is orientated to corporate marketing, as evidenced that not only real identities of both banks emerge on and off through Weibo marketing activities, other located identities, whether the amicable, agreeable companion or the reliable specialist, pave the way for instant online or future offline marketing transactions. In addition, the findings lend their supports to characteristics of corporate identities, ranging from complexity, variability to heterogeneous (Balmer 2001).

Apart from this, there are also new insights of corporate identity construction that are derived from corporate social networking sites. Corporate communication on social media has revolutionised the way enterprises used to address customers in the "bureaucratically accepted modes of communication" (Gumperz 1982b, p. 7), e.g., in the 'old' mass media. This has pointed to the fact that while identity categories, as manifested in ethnicity, gender and class, have still remained as special interest to sociolinguistics, corporate identity has been diluted and emerged to be opaque on social media, the corporate identity in the era of social media has been overwhelmingly oriented to relationship building, a call for an idealised objective of public relations (Briones et al. 2011). The surged motivation of building relationships with followers in the social media sphere has witnessed a mobilisation of all possible linguistic symbols and resources in the firm-follower communication.

4.5 Summary

Although grounded in the beliefs that talk itself is constructive of social reality, we are still looking at how meanings and actions are realised in practices (Gumperz 1982b, p. 3). Hence the study has adopted a dialogic perspective of identity construction, relying on the reflective process where relations with others are constructed through linguistic resources and dialogues. It was found that the corporate identities of both banks are multifarious and inter-related. While the CMB and the BOC have presented their identities as a companion, a well-known (financial) newsman, a financial product seller or a financial institution, a socially responsible corporation and an authoritative financial specialist and industry expert, the constitution of the identity package may vary substantially between the two banks. Specifically, while the CMB has primarily emphasised its companion identity, the BOC both wishes to be a companion and aspires to look professional, best-performing and long-standing, with a global impact, a unique identity of the BOC on its corporate social media.

Goffman's (1959) construct of identity is essentially an orientation of 'my your me', stressing the rituals that govern social interaction. The presentation of corporate self on social media centers on the on-staged self, comforting to rules and regulations of the "front and the setting" (Goffman 1959, p. 22). The findings inevitably suggested that social media does have been discovered a new front and setting, where rituals of social interaction have been drastically updated, in stark contrast to the traditionally prestigious-looking identity that banks used to favor and present in the traditional modes of media.

Chapter 5
Framing Who We Are: Impression Management Strategies of Corporate Identity Construction on the Sina Weibo

> A performer who is disciplined, dramaturgically speaking, is someone who remembers his part and does not commit unmeant gestures or faux pas in performing it.
>
> Erving Goffman (1959, p. 216).

5.1 Introduction

The current chapter will extract and examine the impression management strategies artfully and skillfully used to construct corporate identities on Sina Weibo. The research revealed two principal impression management strategies used by the CMB and the BOC which emerged from the data sources described in the Chap. 3, namely, humanising and popularising the corporate self and persuading followers into trusting (and eventually trading with) the corporate self, each of which is constituted by three sub discursive strategies for the framing of a huamnised and trustworthy corporate identity.

5.2 Humanising and Popularising the Corporate Self

In realising corporate identity construction on the social media, three types of discursive strategies Chinese banks utilised were identified: (1) 'playing cuteness' as a conversational style; (2) positive politeness strategies and face-work; (3) material benefits to followers, e.g., interactive lucky draws and downloadable apps.

W. Feng, *Discursive Constructions of Corporate Identities by Chinese Banks on Sina Weibo*, DOI 10.1007/978-981-10-4469-4_5

5.2.1 'Playing Cuteness' as a Distinctive Conversational Style in Corporate Weibo

The literary translation of the neologism "卖萌" (*mai meng)* is "selling cuteness". Based on 萌's (*méng*) literary meaning of sprouting and the symbolic meaning of spring, the denotation of "萌 (*méng*)" has been extended to the metaphorical description of infants, pets and girls, or anyone who is characterised as adorable, innocent and lovely. Originating from the Japanese animation industry, this character "萌 (*méng*)" is considerably popular among the younger generations of China. Members other than younger people in the Chinese community appear to take a tolerant view on the widespread usage of the character 萌. Its phrasal verb is "卖萌 (*màiméng*)" or 'playing cuteness' as is pragmatically translated in English, referring to the behaviors of pretending to be cute or acting in a cute way in an attempt to attract the audience attention or gratify the authors' specific psychological and/or communicative needs. The Chinese phrase "卖萌" (playing cuteness) has received both public and scholarly attention since 2011, when it was voted and indexed as one of the top annual buzzwords, as documented in the Report of the Annual Language Situation in China (2011).

From the theoretical perspective, the tendency of playing cuteness in the discourse practices of the corporate Weibo conforms to what Tannen (1984, 2005) termed high involvement conversational style, a style that is fully dedicated to the engagement of addressees. In her influential framework, Tannen (2005) explicated four aspects that characterise the features of high involvement: topic, pacing, narrative strategies and expressive paralinguistics. Despite pacing not being intrinsically fit for the analysis of written microblogging contents, the deliberate selection of interpersonal topics and a high degree of diversity in the topic range, the eagerness in storytelling and sharing, the intentional use of emoticons, new words and marked language forms are evidence of the highly involved playing cuteness conversational style found in both banks' Weibo updates. According to the recognised study of English and many other languages including Chinese by Biber (1988, 1995), information and involvement were acknowledged as the two major communicative parameters in analysing the linguistic style of any given genre. As Biber (1988) revealed, face-to-face conversation was ranked as the second most involved genre with a huge amount of involvement features, just next to the most involved genre of telephone conversations in a pool of 23 registers and genres. Despite the social media as virtual rather than face-to-face communication, its defining feature of user engagement and high involvement may never be overlooked, a perception that scholars keep stressing in discussing the genre of computer-mediated discourse (Herring 2007; Crystal 2001). Involvement is characteristic of the "fragmented, generalised packing of content with affective and interpersonal focus" (Biber 1995, p. 145), a comprehensive portrayal of the corporate Weibo updates.

The findings suggested that on the corporate Weibo, the involvement features of playing cuteness as a distinctive conversational style were embodied in the address forms, in the employment of neologisms and new expressions, and the humoristic expressions exclusive to the post-1980s and -1990s generations in China (the Generation X and Y in the United States). By and large, the very conversational style of playing cuteness is suggestive of a sociable and perhaps even spoiled girlish identity in the corporate self-presentation on social media, invoking an equal, relaxed camaraderie in firm-follower communication. The detailed analysis below will focus on the involvement features and the distinctive traits of playing cuteness as a conversational style in corporate social media communication.

An effective means to evoke an involved style, address forms are perceived as a recurring realm of research in politeness, interactional sociolinguistic studies as well as in the practitioner communication practices (Brown and Levinson 1987; Gu 1990; Tracy and Robles 2013; He and Ren 2016). Although it is common sense to all that address forms function as the opening session of human communications, the awareness of the pragmatic function of address form that defines and denotes differentiated relationships between and among communicating parties fell well short of satisfaction (e.g. Tracy 2002). In the discussion of identity implications of address forms, Tracy and Robles (2013) advocated a couple of facets to be of prime concern to impression management and identity construction: the degree of closeness or distance and the degree of equality between the two parties.

> By the forms people select to address others and refer to self, they present how they view themselves in relation to actions and others. Uses of different pronouns, for instance, (I, you, he/she, they, we, etc.) can indicate closeness and moral judgment.
>
> (Tracy and Robles 2013, p. 65).

It was observed that the avant-garde playing cuteness conversational style on both enterprise' social media tended to be featured with the use of playful, light-heartedly amusing and melodramatic address forms and phrases prevalent on the Internet, many of which showed the trait of the deviant, non-standard orthography exclusive to the post-1980s and -1990s generations in China.

A handful of representative self-address forms were located in the analysis of the BOC data: 中国银行 (Bank of China in full); 中行, 中银 (abbreviations of the Bank of China, i.e., zhonghang or zhong yin); 小编 (junior editor); 我们 (we/us); 全体中行人 (the entire BOC staff). In the meanwhile, there is a multitude of address forms to call the BOC's followers: 小伙伴们 (little buddies), you, (你); 宅男宅女们 (homebodies/shut-in); 大家 (everyone); 您 (honorific second-person pronoun); 亲们 (dear); 童鞋 (classmates); 亲爱的粉丝们, 客户们 (dear fans and clients); 网友 (cyber friend) and 客户 (client).

It was discovered in the Weibo updates of the China Merchant Bank (pinyin: Zhao Shang yin hang) that little + the first character of the CMB in pinyin was most commonly used as the self-address form. Other preferable self-address forms of the CMB included: 小招 (pinyin: Xiao Zhao, translated as little Zhao), 招行 (Zhao Hang), 我们家 (our family), 小招家 (little Zhao's family) and我家 (my family). The recurring and most frequent self-address form is the humanised and involved小招 (pinyin: Xiao Zhao, translated as little Zhao). In addressing followers, the CMB employed a wide variety of individualised address forms and funny nicknames, such as小伙伴们 (my little buddies), 你 (you), 朋友 (friends), 童鞋 (classmates),

北鼻 (baby), 宝宝 (baby/darling child), 大家 (everyone), 各位亲 (my dears), 剁手族 (shopaholic), 客户 (clients) and粉儿 (followers or fans).

Over two decades ago, Gu (1990) justified the appropriate address forms as one of his four overarching maxims of politeness in the Chinese context, illustrating that the self-denigration maxim fundamentally ruled how to appropriately address others in China. According to Gu (1990, p. 246), the addressing practices of "my worthless name is Zhang" and "what is your honorable surname" are not only culturally acceptable but also practically advocated. Similarly, in the examination of the historical transition of address forms to their contemporary uses in China, Pan and Kadar (2011) interpreted and exemplified some currently prevalent address forms in China, e.g., the unisex address forms of today's China 同志 (comrade) and a long list of its embedded flexible usages, e.g., surname + job titles (e.g., Director Li, Teacher Wang and Doctor Zhang).

Nevertheless, the advent of the social media may be interpreted as a driving force for the termination of the high-water mark of the "polite" address forms in China as one of the defining features of politeness argued by Gu (1990) and Pan and Kadar (2011). The underlying rules of addressing they discovered do not work the same well in the context of Chinese corporate social media. The findings explicitly indicated that in the corporate Weibo context, almost all denigrated address forms, the unisex address "comrade" and job title address forms that Chinese people used to favor and depend on in face-to-face communication have long become passé. In other words, despite the cultural and historical preference, the self-denigrated, other-elevated address forms, together with their honorific forms, are not any longer the prerequisites for appropriate address forms and the deficiency of these "polite" address forms signals an extinctive trend in the corporate social media communication.

On the contrary, address forms in fashion in the corporate Weibo context demonstrated distinct characteristics of creativity and the playing cuteness style. The playing cuteness style was best manifested in the banks' babyish, informal and creative way of addressing their followers. One likely motivation of the enterprise's intentional adoption of such address forms in fashion is to keep pace with the pop culture and to disguise itself for the most possible acceptance by and mingling with their social media followers. It was observed that address forms guided by such audience design (Bell 1984) fell into at least two categories: those that "play young" and those that mock followers. It should be emphasised that the address forms that play young attempted to imitate the tone of infants and children whose pronunciation of vocabulary was either somehow inclined to be close to the standardised form but in fact inaccurate, i.e., near homophonization (Gao 2012) or where the word choice was typified as childish. Illustrations of playing cuteness address forms may be 童鞋 (classmates) and 妹紙 (younger sister), rather than the standard Chinese 同學 (classmates) and 妹子 (younger sister). Notice the usage of 童鞋, which is deviant in orthography and where a near homophone strategy is applied, represents the awkward attempt of a language-learning infant in striving for pronouncing the accurate phrase of 同學 (classmate). In the sub-consciousness of users, the use of near homophones addresses the flavor of cuteness that might be best and vividly demonstrated. Whether or not correct in orthography, fashionable and Internet address forms such as 各位亲 (my dears), 小伙伴们 (little buddies), 萌妹子 (cute girls), 女神 (goddess), 童鞋 (classmates), 妹紙 (younger sister), 孩紙 (child), 北鼻 (baby) are instances of the "play young" forms of address, all relevant to the projection of the banks with a childish and innocent identity. Secondly, the address forms that play cuteness by mocking followers are humoristic, as exemplified in the creative, hyperbolic and intimate usage of the Internet slang, e.g., 剁手族 (shopaholic), 宅男宅女们 (homebodies/shut-tin) and 女汉子 (tough girl/girls as independent and capable as men), most frequently used among pals and in domains of informality for the sense of humor. The pervasive use of the symbolic Internet address forms 亲 (dear) was borrowed from online customer service jargon, namely the Taobao (the largest Chinese online shopping brand) linguistic style, where customer service staff invented and applied this unisex and jesting address form to address any customer and potential customer involved in the online shopping.

Given the socio-pragmatic function of the address forms as a proven approach in the enterprises' strategic self-positioning and their efforts in the alignment of the followers, the predominance of the play cuteness address forms is ultimately aimed for the corporate impression management and identity construction in social interactions. A brilliant manifestation of the globalised kidult culture, the 'playing cuteness' style of addressing followers that the banks employ, which they would never practise elsewhere in reality, is tailor-made and audience designed on corporate social media to cater for the youthful followers. The consistency of the playing cuteness style of address throughout the corporate social media enabled banks to have no difficulty in establishing considerable amount of involvement and solidarity, identifying and labeling themselves not only as non-virtual individuals but also as carefree, intimate friends of their followers. In self-reference for instance, the China Merchants Bank (Zhao Shang Yin Hang in Chinese pinyin) constantly referred itself to 小招 (Xiao Zhao/little Zhao), an effective means to humanise the CMB as if it is a real human being surnamed Zhao rather than a lifeless profit-driven banking corporation. Another excellent example of humanisation was the self-address form 小编 (junior editor), by which the corporation covered its authentic identity and took a fairly objective journalistic and editorial stance. "Bianji" (the Chinese pinyin for editor) is merely a job title, instead of an individual's name and the address form of "little + first character of job title" is nothing but conventional and sounds similar to the way a person is addressed by little + the first character of his/her name in the daily life in China. Likewise, capitalising on the core value of family in the Chinese culture, the self-address forms of the China Merchants Bank: 我们家 (our family), 小招家 (little Zhao's family), 我家 (my family) perfectly illustrated the decorative and humanising effects these address forms created, as if banks were not profit-making corporations but rather intimate friend's families, people whom followers were familiarised with and welcomed to drop in on from time to time.

The playing cuteness conversational style, realised by the creative, in fashion address forms on corporate social media, subconsciously and effectively helps to humanise and animate banks into real and amicable persons in the flesh. The prevalence of the tactful address forms applied to play cuteness, characteristic of zero power distance and maximum solidarity, attaches great significance to the followers' cognitive and affective needs, thus leading to a well-received impression of the corporate self.

In addition to address forms, the playing cuteness conversational style was strikingly manifested by a variety of attention-demanding netspeak (Crystal 2001), such as neologism, buzzwords, unconventional set phrases and marked sentence structures, both at the lexical and sentential level. Below are several good examples. The buzzword expression 重磅福利 (heavyweight welfare), by no means an unmarked phrase in Chinese, has gone viral on social media and is an exaggeration of the benefits to followers that they can take from the following Weibo updates. 来自星星的银行 (the bank who came from the star), is smartly nicknamed after *You Who Came from the Star*, a huge hit Korean romantic soap opera in late 2013 that achieved the greatest vogue especially among the post-1980's generation across Asia. The expressions of 记得牵着她来领银子 (remember to leash her for collecting your silver) stood in contrast to the normal verb-object agreement in Chinese but indeed demonstrated a drop of amusement and persiflage. The humorous expression 比月光族更凶残: 月欠族, translated as "those who are monthly overdrawn clan are more deadly than those who live from paycheck to paycheck", made a jest of the contemporary social tendency that youngsters are increasingly affected by consumerism and becoming shopaholics. Tailor-made for catering to the need of the younger generations to be treated with egalitarianism and through having fun in the non face-to-face communication, these creative expressions in modern Chinese language demonstrated a light sense of humor, dramatically underplaying the traditionally hierarchical linguistic practice in the face-to-face communication.

Presented below are a number of notable netspeak expressions in the Weibo context:

Extract 12: 【熊猫遇上树】 当熊猫宝宝遇到树, 各种可爱的姿势就来了, 有木有萌到你啊～

贊 (22)|轉發 (41)|收藏|評論(12) BOC 23022014 日 10:00 來自新浪微博 | 舉報

Extract 12: 【When pandas meet trees】 When the baby pandas meet trees, all of the cute gestures are coming, have you been sold the cuteness～

Like (22)/Repost (41)/Collect/Comments (12) BOC 23022014 10:00 from Sina Weibo.

Notice that Extract 12 is titled as 【熊猫遇上树】 (When pandas meet trees). The sentence structure "A meets B" is adopted when they are comparable to each other, such as when East meets West. The title "When pandas meet trees" itself manifests a marked and funny expression in modern Chinese. What adds to the playing cuteness conversational style is the netspeak word choice of "有木有", a deliberate typo of 有没有 (have you ever) as if of a child having difficulty in the accurate spelling, and the new word of "萌" (cuteness) in its verb usage. The playing cuteness conversational style is reinforced with the non-standardised punctuation "～" rather than a question mark, a paralinguistic symbol, signaling an easygoing, cute and fun key of speaking, if not spoiled. As far as the contents, it is a sheer fun-sharing update, highly personal and mostly likely to be present in a personal social media update. Hence, a humanised image and impression of the BOC is managed, eliciting dialogic responses and catering for followers' needs of entertainment and information.

Extract 13: 今天是正月初八, 春节后第一个工作日, 此刻状态是 "不想上班" 的童鞋请举个爪!

贊 (189)|轉發 (134)|收藏|評論 (70) CMB 07022014 08:08 來自 iPhone 客户端 | 舉報

Extract 13: Today is the 8th day of the Chinese Lunar New Year, the first working day after the spring festival break. Those classmates whose mode is "no mood for working", claws up!

Like (189)/Repost (134)/Collect/Comment (70) CMB 07022014 08:08 from iPhone app.

The involved Extract 13 played its cuteness to elicit consensus and interaction as if an indulging child, reluctant to go to school upon the completion of a festival's celebration. Indeed, the topic of 不想上班 (no mood for working) can be quite personal and sensational for open discussion during the early office hours (8:08 am) of a workday. The playing cuteness conversational style was highlighted with contextualization cues (Gumperz 1982a) of the marked jokes of 童鞋 (classmates) and 举个爪 (claws up), with an interactional discourse strategy such as instances of an Internet "recognizable in-group code" (Tannen 2005, p. 36), which signal a humanised, personal and intimate relationship with the followers. The neologism 举个爪 (claws up) was completely intelligible and dialogic in nature and the corporate update clearly attempted to evoke as much solidarity and dialogue in addressing followers as friends.

Extract 14: 中国人民银行定于2月28日发行第二届夏季青年奥林匹克运动会金银纪念币一套。该套纪念币共4枚, 其中金币1枚, 银币3枚, 均为中华人民共和国法定货币。等等, 这么萌, 真的是央行发行的吗

贊 (18)|轉發 (90)|收藏|評論 (43) 2 月 19 日 CMB 19022014 21:06 來自新浪微博 | 舉報

Extract 14: The People's Bank of China is scheduled for the issuance of the second session of the Summer Youth Olympic Games set of commemorative coins, one gold and one silver. The total of four sets of commemorative coins includes one gold and three silver, all are legal currency in the People's Republic of China. Hold on, so cute as it is, is it really issued by the People's Bank of China

Like (8)/Repost (90)/Collect/Comment (43) CMB 19022014 21:06 from Sina Weibo.

As Extract 14 instantiates, the playing cuteness conversational style was found pervasive across corporate Weibo and was represented in its hybridisation with classic news releases. At the end of the news update Extract 14, the fashionable sentential structure 等等, 这么萌, 真的是......嗎 (hold on, so cute as it is, is it really issued by the People's Bank of China) was marked with certain amounts of liveliness and affability. In so doing, the serious journalistic reportage of financial news is immediately diluted with a playing cuteness ending of the CMB. It is found that the perfect combination of the objective news contents and the corporations' own playing cuteness style comments is rather representative of the news release style on corporate social media.

The findings also revealed that the flourishing of playing cuteness as a conventionalised conversational style on corporate Weibo dissolves the performance individuals take on the social front or the front stage in real society's interaction. A recurrent theme in Goffman's (1959) constructs revolved around the degree to which an individual's activity is bound by social interaction. Goffman (1959) regarded impression management as performance and individuals as performers who act on both the front stage and the backstage. In the front stage, usually during social interaction, a performer conforms to dramaturgical disciplines by keeping in mind his own appearance, manner and having his all activities mobilised to live up to officially accredited values and expectations, whereas in the backstage, where he is away from his audience and social interaction, the performer is substantially less constrained by his screenplay.

Nevertheless, the findings implied that in social media interaction, the case seems to be vice verse. Corporate Weibo has framed the Internet as a front stage where carefree playing cuteness is not only possible but also feasible and necessary. Notice also that in face-to-face interaction, playing cuteness as a conversational style is still subject to many visible and invisible cultural and situated restraints in reality. China at large is claimed to be a country with excessively high power distance and in-group interests are significantly valued over strangers' interests (Hofstede 1983). The emergence of playing cuteness on the Internet has revolutionised the way Chinese people used to address strangers and friends. A fundamental alteration of the stage focuses on the fact that in real life playing cuteness is confined within intimate relationships, but Chinese corporate social media has successfully expanded its audience construction to consist of anyone making his/her virtual presence, most being strangers and not necessarily customers. It was also observed that the new media literacy characteristic of playing cuteness style, realised through either address forms, netspeak expressions or emoticons, has even gradually emerged as expected, unmarked and formulaic way of expressions on the Internet, rather than creative and avant-garde literary practice on the corporate Weibo context. The credibility of this observation was elaborated further by the insider interviews in the Chap. 7. In essence, the conversational style of playing cuteness as an effective and powerful means of impression management, represented by the linguistic intimacy and various discourse strategies, contributed to a brilliant corporate self-presentation and initiation in the firm-follower dialogic communication. The conversational style of playing cuteness per se, a kind of enthusiasm unconstraint as termed by Tannen (2005), has become a contextualization cue to be indicative of the solidarity and camaraderie enterprises seek to establish in plesasing and engaging their followers.

5.2.2 *Politeness and Face-Work Strategies*

Denoting the projection of self-image and actualising impression management, face-work is by nature a specific front-stage behavior that is deliberately performed in charge of other people within the mixed social connections (Hwang 1987). A key determinant in interpersonal relationships, the proliferant face-work practice remains at the core of human social interactions. It was discovered that banks were tactfully in control of politeness and face-work on their corporate Weibo, by anointing the positive faces of their followers, in accordance to their consistent efforts of humanising and popularising themselves. Having said that face is a relational phenomenon, it can only be analysed during social interactions (Spencer-Oatey 2007). The politeness and face-work strategies of corporate social media updates were elaborated and illustrated through the speech acts of (1) regular greetings to followers; (2) expression of gratitude towards followers; and (3) the persiflage of followers and self-ridicule, all of which are consistent with Leech's (1983) remarks of politeness: being polite entails making others feel comfortable and maximising the benefits to hearers. Two distinctive strands of face-work in the three aforementioned categories of speech acts performed by the two banks were observed: as summarised and defined in the present study: (1) the "playing safe" face-work that focuses on the conventional, unmarked and normative efforts of either establishing or maintaining social relationships, e.g., the acknowledgement of power distance; and (2) the over-done face-work that entails the creative, marked efforts of anointing others' faces, e.g., the linguistic intimacy designed for building the maximum solidarity in the communication with unfamiliar parties.

5.2.2.1 Regular Greetings to Followers

As expected, considerable amounts of politeness-related speech acts on corporate Weibo were identified, among which regular daily greetings such as good morning and good night dominated, dotted with festival wishes and New Year related wishes during both the Western and Chinese festivals. Corpus statistics revealed that there were as many as 151 instances of greeting good morning and 157 instances of good night in the CMB updates, whereas no single similar expressions were found in the BOC corpus. Furthermore, a stark contrast of performance did make its presence in terms of formality in the insurance of New Year wishes between the CMB and the BOC.

The BOC made no hesitation to offer positive faces and timely New Year greetings to followers in a formal but sincere tone, as Extract 1 illustrates.

Extract 15: 新年的钟声已敲响, 在这 "1314" 的难忘时刻, 心中满溢的是感谢与期盼—感谢这一年每位客户对我们的支持与鼓励, 更期盼新一年继续为您奉上全体中行人的热忱与真心。中行祝您2014新年快乐, 万事如意!

贊 (45)|轉發 (123)|收藏|評論 (36) BOC 01012014 00:00

Extract 15: As the bell of New Year tolling, at the turning point of 2013–2014, fully filled in my heart is the gratitude and expectations. I am grateful to supports and encouragement given by every client during the past year. What I look forward to is that in the New Year the BOC staff presents our warmth and sincerity to your excellency. The BOC wishes you a happy New Year and all the best!

Like (45)/Repost (123)/Collect/Comment (36) BOC 01012014 00:00.

The Extract 15 empolyed both the positive and negative politeness strategies. In the last line of Extract 15, the BOC addresses its clients with sincere New Year wish with expressions such as 中行祝您 2014 新年快乐, 万事如意! (The BOC wishes you a happy 2014 and all the best!) The positive politeness of this greeting showed the BOC's awareness to satisfy its followers positive face wants/needs at a critical moment of the year and to let followers feel being "ratified, understood, approved of, liked or admired" (Brown and Levinson 1987, p. 62). The positive face and politeness strategy echoed Goffman's presentational rituals that maintain face-work as a condition for interaction (1967, p. 12).

Giving massive followers a general face, the BOC modestly self-bragged, a padded and indirect face threatening act, by saying 心中满溢的是感谢与期盼—感谢这一年每位客户对我们的支持与鼓励 (fully filled in my heart is the gratitude and expectations. I am grateful to supports and encouragement given by every client during the past year) to refer to their followers' acknowledgement and encouragement towards the bank during the past year of 2013. 心中满溢 (fully filled in my heart), 期盼 (look forward to) and 为您奉上 (presented … to your Excellency) cued a great extent of "self-effacement" (Brown and Levinson 1987, p. 70), a full range of respectful attitude and gratitude in a traditional or unmarked politeness manner, positioning the BOC in a lower social status and showing respect for followers, by adopting a negative politeness strategy. It has been discovered that the power distance and status-oriented mindset of politeness continued to function well in the Chinese culture and Weibo practice, despite the apparent playing cuteness style. In this crucial Spring Festival moment, "other-elevation" address form of politeness such as the honorifics 您 in Chinese (Gu 1990), if not self-denigration, continued to perform as a lubricant in social media interactions. During the two-sided polish of face-work, both the BOC and followers' lovely faces were saved and maintained. I name the unmarked and normative face-work employed herein in Extract 1 as the "playing safe" face-work.

Rather than the BOC's greeting of formality being actualised in four-character formulaic set clichés like 新年快乐, 万事如意 (Happy New Year and All the Best), the CMB's greetings were enlivened with involving linguistic features, e.g., interpersonal questions and discourse markers of colloquialism. Its lively style set the basic tune of affability with a distinctive persona and humor, manifested in the caring, involving questions that resonates among real friends interactions. It was specially realised through its linguistic orality such as in the non-professional address form 各位 (everybody) (instead of professional address form 客户 (client) by the BOC), in the word choice of 话儿 (words), 快快查收 (be quick to receive) and in the use of modal particle such as 啦 (la). An alternative strategy of conversationalised greeting as such was every-day, cool and easy to digest. Despite the same positive face strategy, the CMB downgraded positive face and politeness use by means of linguistic orality. It is consistent with Wu and Hui's (1997) identification of orality in the use of loose and short clauses, frequent modal particles and non-literary word choice.

Extract 16: 大年初一, 小招给各位拜年啦! 祝福的话儿都在图里, 快快查收

贊 (72)|轉發 (105)|收藏|評論 (49) CMB 31012014 09:10 來自 360 浏览器超速版 | 舉報

Extract 16: First day of the Chinese New Year, Xiao Zhao is greeting you the best year! All greeting words are in the photos below. Be quick to check out.

Like (72)/Repost (105)/Collect/Comment (49) CMB 31012014 09:10.

Extract 17: 回家的票订好了吗?

贊 (35)|轉發 (103)|收藏|評論 (32) CMB 11012014 23:03

Extract 17: Have you successfully bought the tickets to go back to hometown (during Spring Festival)?

Like (35)/Repost (103)/Collect/Comment (32) CMB 11012014 23:03.

In the everyday conversation amongst Chinese, a single concrete inquiry concerning addressees' interest (e.g., current problems and worries) could be perfectly viewed as a form of greeting. In a similar vein to the last update, in contrast to the BOC, the utterances of the CMB are framed in a "conversational human voice" (Kelleher and Miller 2006, p. 395), as evidenced in the interpersonal eliciting question "have you bought the tickets to go back to hometown (during the Spring Festival)?" Note that added in this conversational human voice was a sense of humor to provoke amusement with reference to the common sense of the transportation rush during the Chinese Spring Festival and widespread complaints about such a plight.

5.2.2.2 Expressing Gratitude

Similar to greetings, the corporations' speech act of appreciation was found to be a routine positive politeness strategy and face giving to followers, regardless of cultural variations. The long-standing practice of corporations' speech act of appreciation corroborated Dabrowska (2013, p. 201) who discovered that gratitude expression was recorded as the second popular politeness strategy of Facebook, just next to birthday wishes.

Extract 18: 新年快到了, 灰常感谢大伙儿在13年滴支持, 既然这样, 怎么好意思没点表示呢! 所以, 小招准备了一些小礼品, 快快转发或评论此微博, 马上领红包! http://t.cn/8F5z8BI

贊 (233)|轉發 (2413)|收藏|評論 (16371) CMB 22012014 10:55

Extract 18: The New Year is approaching. Big thanks to you guys for supporting us for 13 years. How come there are linguistic thanks only! So, Xiao Zhao has prepared some presents to those who repost and comment! Be quick and ready to receive the gift money! http://t.cn/8F5z8BI

Like (233)|Repost (2413)|Collect|Comment (16371) CMB 22012014 10:55.

Extract 19: #周年感恩#企业问卷调查结果显示: 在48%的童鞋心目中我们是专业严谨风, 有62%的小伙伴希望看到更多财经金融类内容……感谢大家提出的建议, 我们定

会更加用心将这条 “围脖” 越织越长。最后，感谢大家积极的参与，恭喜中奖的童鞋们! PS.小编可会不承认自己是女汉纸哟!

贊 (7)|轉發 (5)|收藏|評論 (25) BOC 12102013 19:16 來自专业版微博 | 舉報

Extract 19: #Anniversary thanksgiving# our questionnaire findings revealed that: in the mind of 48% classmates (referring to followers), Our Weibo has a professional and rigorous style. There are 62% little buddies (referring to followers) who expect more financial and business microblogging contents…… Thanks very much for your suggestions and we shall definitely continue to make efforts in the BOC Weibo. At last, thanks for your participation and congratulations to those classmates who have won our presents! PS: As the editor of the BOC Weibo, I would not be admitting that I am a tough girl!

Like (7)/Repost (5)/Collect/Comment (25) BOC 12102013 19:16.

The CMB expressed its gratitude to followers in the Extract 18 where both the positive and negative politeness strategies were empolyed. While the playing cuteness style reflected through the use of netspeak 灰常感谢 (thanks very much) and 滴 (of or ’s) demonstrated the CMB’s in-group identity and contributed to the giving of a positive face to the followers, the request to call for the followers’ action to comment and repost may be interpreted as an evident negative face strategy, impeding the freedom of the CMB’s followers. However, the FTA was immediately padded with the corporations’ generosity of gifts offering, the second round of positive politeness strategy.

Notice in the Extract 19 that there was a hashtagged topic or column named #周年感恩# (the anniversary of thanksgiving), an indication of a series of speech acts of appreciation by the BOC. In Extract 19 by 感谢大家提出的建议…感谢大家积极的参与 (Thanks very much for your suggestions…thanks for your participation) dual appreciations in cliché entailed a heartfelt sincerity with unmarked positive face-work, or playing safe face-work.

Like the CMB, the BOC’s sense of humor and in-group identities were manifested in the positive face strategy to show approval and likeness for followers, entailed by playing cuteness address forms “童鞋” (classmates), “小伙伴” (little buddies), “围脖” (Weibo), “女汉纸” (tough girl), “小编” (junior editor) in Extract 19. “小编可会不承认自己是女汉纸哟” (I would not be admitting that I am a tough girl!) might be regarded as an overdone face-work, uttered in a cute and spoiled tone to indicate the BOC’s intimate relationships with followers. Meanwhile, having vividly cued the kidding and lovely style, “怎么好意思没点表示呢” (How come there are linguistic thanks only) also hints an over-intimacy between the CMB and its followers, meaning we are so close and how can I not be generous enough, thus signaling an overdone face-work.

5.2.2.3 The Raillery of Followers and Self-ridicule

Politeness can be culturally bound, being one of the commonest reasons why Brown and Levinson (1987) never lacked criticism of their claimed universality in politeness and face theory (e.g., Chen 2001; Kasper 1990; Locher and Watts 2005). The banks’ ridicule of followers in a humorous and unmalicious way highlights and features their context-bound impression management strategies, which they rarely practise on other contexts of written external corporate communication, be it a website or leaflets. Mocking one's friends in a just-kidding manner is likely to be maneuvered to make both parties feel relaxed and comfortable, a strategy far from being impolite and one that contributes to friendship strengthening. It is perfectly understandable that jokes of specific types can only be strictly produced and consumed within peer group, or even in a tiny circle of best friends, otherwise communicative failure resulting from embarrassment and astonishment might occur. On both banks' postings it was located some culturally specific jocose posts ridiculing followers' personal weight and their modest financial situations, namely jokes which drastically threaten addressees' positive faces for the intention of intimacy improvement.

Extract 20: 大过节的, 谁提 "减肥" 跟谁急

贊 (48)|轉發 (135)|收藏|評論 (51) CMB 03022014 22:15

Extract 20: It is spring festival time and the diet issue is of course dismissed, whoever brings it up to me.

Like (48)/Repost (135)/Collect/Comment (51) CMB 03022014 22:15.

Extract 21: 我就想知道, 春节除了吃, 大家还干了些什么——看书的敢不敢留下书名? 花钱的敢不敢报上位数?长膘的别说人艰不拆, 人类都懂, 直接说几斤吧。

贊 (29)|轉發 (72)|收藏|評論 (111) CMB 04022014 23:15

Extract 21: I just want to know, what have you been doing expect indulging in cuisine? Those who were reading and those who were spending money, do they dare to report book names and the sum of money? Those who put on weight do not be shy, as everyone is cognitively informed of it. Let me put it in a more straightforward way, just tell me the how many kilogrammes you gained.

Like (29)/Repost (72)/Collect/Comment (111) CMB 04022014 23:15.

Extract 22: 记得我在2013年的目标是减掉10斤肉, 现在快到年底了, 离目标就差20斤了……(图片源自网络)

贊 (9)|轉發 (62)|收藏|評論 (18) BOC 15112013 12:16

Extract 22: I still remember that my objective was to lose 5 kilogrammes, as the New Year's Eve is approaching; I am close to my objective with only 20 lb in between…… (Photo from Internet)

Like (9)/Repost (62)/Collect/Comment (18)/BOC 15112013 12:16

Extract 23: 作为2013年最会败家的水瓶男和天蝎女, 请发表一下你们的获奖感言

贊 (18)|轉發 (630)|收藏|評論 (226) CMB 14012014 11:09.

Extract 23: As the shopaholic of the year 2013, Aquarii males and Scorpionis girls, please comment on your award-winning.

Like (18)/Repost (630)/Collect/Comment (226) CMB 14012014 11:09.

Extract 24: 今天非常气愤, 扇了我钱包一耳光……其实也没什么, 就是希望它能肿起来, 最近它瘦得我都看不下去了! (图片源自网络)

贊 (23)|轉發 (149)|收藏|評論 (39) BOC 16112013 22:16

Extract 24: I was so pissed off today and slapped my wallet…nothing serious; I just wish it gets swollen for recently it has been losing enough weight! (Photo from Internet)

Like (23)/Repost (149)/Collect/Comments (39) BOC 16112013 22:16.

Jokes and humor might be heavily culture-bound, as they allow shared common knowledge and cognitive experience to provoke laughter and a relaxing atmosphere among given speech communities. By reference to shared common knowledge, solidarity of computer-mediated groups can be enhanced (Baym 1995). Research shown that face-work was accomplished by creating common ground through jokes and self-deprecating style of humor (Bury 2005). Consistent with Bury (2005), the findings suggested that common ground and face-work are claimed on the topic selection of weight gain and loss, overconsumption through either self-deprecation (self-ridicule) or other-deprecating comments (the raillery of followers). The evidence showed that on the Chinese corporate Weibo, jokes and humor, as means of face tribute, are tied to younger generations' everyday concerns and worries extending from weight loss, lack of money, reluctance to go to work and go to sleep, oversleep, procrastination to the shopping addiction, all relating to the lack of self-discipline and the materialism orientation spread among the younger generations of China.

While Extracts 20, 22 and 24 were instances of self-deprecating jokes on weight loss, Extract 21 and 23 illustrated other-deprecating jokes, anticipating a humorous effect by the tease of followers' lack of self-control in consumption. The subject "I" in Extract 22 and 24 adopted a humanised narrative tone, as though complaining although oneself in his/her personal account. In the same conversational human voice, the CMB's self-ridicule 谁提减肥跟谁急; 离目标就差20斤 (The diet issue is of course dismissed. I might be pissed off against whoever brings it up to me; I am achieving my objective of weight loss with only 10 kilograms) and the persiflage of the CMB's followers on the issue of weight loss 长膘的别说人艰不拆, 人类都懂, 直接说几斤吧 (Those who put on weight do not be shy and reluctant to talk about it, as everyone is cognitively informed of it. Let me put it in a more straightforward way, just tell me how many kilogrammes you gained.) masked the real trading relations and are manifestations of the over-done face-work, characteristic of linguistic and stylistic informality. Another example of the CMB's self-ridicule 它瘦得我都看不下去了 (Recently it has been losing enough weight) on its embarrassing financial challenges was the evidence of the corporation's efforts of rapport management (Spencer-Oatey 2002). Thanks to the portrayal of the CMB as a small potato, both topics of weight loss and financial shortage are dialogic and able to trigger resonance among female followers and followers of young employees who might also be similarly stuck in their real lives. The self-denigration style of sharing personal but prevalent problems and the attempt to seek consensus in Extracts 20, 22 and 24 were negative politeness strategies and positive face-giving acts to followers. Extracts 21 and 24 are apparent persiflage of followers by threatening their positive face in eliciting 直接说几斤吧 (Let me put it in a more straightforward way, just tell me the how many kilogrammes you gained) and identifying 水瓶男和天蝎女最会败家 (Aquarii males and Scorpionis girls as the shopaholic of the year). As evidenced by the hundreds of reposts and comments in number, Extract 23 in fact triggered a super topic and rounds of exciting and debatable discussions on which match of horoscope and gender tends to be shopaholic and profligate among the CMB followers. Nonetheless, the CMB's good-willed bold-on-record FTA in Extract 23 were dramatically padded with a light-hearted buffer of the award-winning speech invitation 请发表一下你们的获奖感言 (please comment on your award-winning).

On the whole, the display of topics in Weibo updates that caters for followers' interests and concern may be a useful positive face and politeness strategy (Brown and Levinson 1987). However, in the aforementioned cases, face-work on corporate social media has been seemingly 'overdone', in a desperate exchange for attention, involvement, solidarity and linguistic intimacy, as shown in greeting, thanking and climaxing in the raillery of followers and self-ridicule. The overdone face-work is hereby defined as the impression management that is not in accordance with the actual relationship but grounded in imaginary or desirable relationships, such as between celebrity in TV commercials and the audience, a boy and the beloved girl he still desperately pursues. In Hwang's (1987) words, face-work is effected in strict view of guanxi between petitioner and resource allocators in the Cultural China. Nevertheless, evidence interestingly suggested that corporation's overdone face-work or fabricated face of excessive linguistic intimacy on social media is by no means marked and intensely favored by their followers. In theory, the over-done face-work clashes with the sincerity principle of politeness, argued by Gu (1990) and in practice it might be related to the practice of flattery, hypocrisy and even ass-kissing. In accordance with Hwang (1987), it is inferred that the discourse practice of corporations' face-work is instrumental and to seek recourses as a petitioner from their potential resources allocator of followers.

5.2.3 *Offer of Free Material Benefits to Followers*

The last impression management strategy being observed is the corporations' generous offering of free material benefits to their followers, as evidenced, for instance, by its irregular practice of lucky draws. On the BOC updates, it was observed that there were 23 instances of lucky draws, boldly encouraging followers with advertising language to engage in reposting the referred microblogging contents, @ the credit card microblogging account of the BOC, answering riddles and quizzes, voting or spending a certain sum by debit/credit cards and so forth, for a free iPad, iPad Mini, museum and concert tickets, or prepaid mobile bill coupons of 20–1000 RMB. Similarly, the CMB organised and sponsored 13 lucky draws among its followers in attempt to stir repost numbers, mobile banking applications and so forth. Several days subsequent to an advertising calling for participation, banks would follow-up and @ specific lucky followers to collect their presents.

The extraordinary popularity of the lucky draws on corporate social media was manifested in the huge numbers of reposts, comments and likes, indicating followers' super active interaction. Characteristic with wits and perfect timing, the successes of lucky draws are attributed to strategically planned online public relations events or marketing devices, aiming at the enhancement of brand recognition and reputation. Having saved millions in advertising expenses, both banks wasted no chance to build up their humanised, caring and generous images in the heart of their millions of followers.

A recent study by Men and Tsai (2013) identified the motivations of Chinese Sina Weibo users in corporate SNS communications, with the first motivation being information-seeking, followed by entertainment and social integration purposes, or in summary information and entertainment, in contrast to that of American social media users who are strongly motivated to seek remuneration (e.g., awards, discounts and sweepstakes) (Tsai and Men 2012). The present findings however have located the overwhelmingly exceptional enthusiasm of interaction or interactivity of followers, in reposting and commenting shown below, as compared to the average degree of interaction of regular updates.

Extract 25: 【转微博, 赢门票】 中国银行支持的 "地中海文明—法国卢浮宫博物馆藏文物精品展" 现已亮相中国国家博物馆。10月29日至2014年2月10日, 280件卢浮宫珍品带您感受地中海流域不同文明间的碰撞, 交流与融汇。11月6日前关注并转发此微博, 有机会获得展览门票两张哟!(共10个名额) http://t.cn/zRKHNvj.

贊 (8)|轉發 (406)|評論 (82) BOC 31102013 17:26 來自专业版微博

Extract 25: [Repost microblogging and win museum tickets] The Mediterranean civilisation- the exhibition of selected exhibits of Le Louvre sponsored by the BOC has just made its début at the National Museum of China. From 29th Oct to 10th Feb., 280 pieces of treasures of Le Louvre will enable you to experience the cross-cultural communication and civilisations along the Mediterranean regions. Repost this microblogging post before the 6th of November and you might win 2 tickets for free (10 tickets in total). http://t.cn/zRKHNvj.

Like (8)/Repost (406)/Comment (82) BOC 31102013 17:26

Extract 26: #中行医达通#小编向您推荐医院挂号就诊攻略, 让看病挂号不再难, 缴费更简单, 不必反复排队, 告别长长等待。10月21日—10月25日, 关注@中国银行 转发此微博, 即有机会获取iPad mini, 活动结束后由新浪平台抽取5名幸运小伙伴。奔走相告啦! http://t.cn/zRMpQC4 http://t.cn/zRM0gDa

贊 (26)|轉發 (1061319)|評論 (399022) BOC 21102013 18:01 來自微活动-#中行医达…

Extract 26: #BOC hospital-easy card# Junior editor is recommending a short-cut for hospital registration, saving your time of lining-up to register, to wait and to pay. From 21st Oct to 25th Oct, follow the CMB microblogging and repost this item of microblogging and you might win an iPad Mini. There will be 5 lucky buddies at the end of this event. Why not tell everyone this piece of news! http://t.cn/zRMpQC4 http://t.cn/zRM0gDa

Like (26)/Repost (1061319)/Comment (399022) BOC 21102013 18:01.

Extract 27: 又送福利喽, 伙伴们在肥家的路上看到我们家的广告, 请马上拿出手机拍下来, 蓝后分享到微博或朋友圈, 只要有10个好友转发或点赞, 凭截图发微博@招商银行 就有机会获得一份神秘礼品, 共50份! 活动持续至2月28日, btw, 马上第一波抽奖了哦^_^

贊 (41)|轉發 (177)|評論 (48) CMB 27012014 22:07 來自 iPhone 客户端

Extract 27: More free gifts. Buddies, on your way back home if you see the CMB advertisements, please take photos at once and share it on your social media sites. @CMB with a snapshot of 10 likes or reposts and you might win a gift and there are up to 50 gifts in total. The event is on until 28th of Feb, btw, this first time of drawing lots is right on the corner^_^

Like (41)/Repost (177)/Comment (48) CMB 27012014 22:07.

Extract 28: 小伙伴们, 2014年的热刷188活动又来啦! 只要你在6月30日前持我行62银联一卡通单笔消费满188元, 就可抽取WMF QUALITY ONE系列锅具两件套, 乐扣乐扣玻璃4件套! 3月起普惠礼还会重磅回归! 1月27日前, 转发本条微博并@ 三位好友, 小招将随机抽取两名送出WMF BRILLIANT系列锅具三件套!

贊 (88)|轉發 (8550)|評論 (4014) CMB 21012014 21:07 來自 iPhone 客户端

Extract 28: Little buddies, spend RMB 188 by CMB bankcards and win! Only if you spend RMB 188 with the CMB bankcards, and with the card number starting with 62, you are eligible to win WMF QUALITY ONE cookware, Lock & Lock 4-piece set glassware! A drawing lot gift offering will be on again from the beginning of March! Repost this post and @ at least three followers on or before the 27th of January and you might win WMF BRILLIANT 3-piece cookware!

Like (88)|Repost (8550)|Comment (4014) CMB 21012014 21:07.

Material benefits such as free gifts in Extracts 25 to 28 prove to be a promotion megahit in enhancing banks' popularity, as shown by the excessively considerable number of likes and reposts, such as the surprising 8550 times of repost and 88 times of like clicking in Extract 28. As represented by the free tickets in Extract 25, iPad mini in the extract 26, mysterious gift in Extract 27 and WMF Brilliant 3-piece cookware in the Extract 28, the free-of-charge gifts, in turn treat, reciprocity and thoughtful small favors, the lucky draws PR events enabled the network of social relations between the corporations and their followers to be established and cemented.

5.3 Persuading Followers into Trusting (and Eventually Trading with) the Corporate Self

To convince followers that they are trustworthy financial institutions, the banks of China primarily employed the following sub-strategies: (1) the change of footing along posts: establishing power or solidarity; (2) devoting themselves to follow-up and interaction; and (3) detailing company awards and the benefits of promotions or launches.

5.3.1 The Change of Footing Along Posts: Establishing Power or Solidarity

The pair of terms "power" and "solidarity" was initially raised to describe and prescribe indices resulting from choices of pronouns (see Brown and Gilman 1960). Later on, they were noted as two social cognitive factors to underline broad sociocultural contexts where interpersonal interactions occur (Hwang 1995, 2004). Power and solidarity have been recurrently investigated in disciplines such as pragmatics, sociolinguistics and intercultural communication to examine conflicts, constraints, style and successes arising from real-life interpersonal interaction (e.g. Scollon and Scollon 1995). Power emphasises the hierarchical relationship, while solidarity stresses the horizontal relationship by means of involvement and independence in verbal communication (Yu 2010). Power emanates from the text producer's ability to impose his or her plans at the expense of the text receiver's plans. In contrast, solidarity is the willingness of the text producer to relinquish power and work with his or her interlocutors as members of a team (Hatim and Mason 1990). The delicacy of maneuvering between power and solidarity in communication has been well noted (ibid).

As noted earlier, as one of the profoundly essential notions of Goffman (1981, p. 128) footing refers to "the participant's alignment, or set, or stance, or posture, or projected self". "A change in our footing is another way of talking about a change in our frame for events" (ibid). As Goodwin (1996) held, shifting frame is not undertaken capriciously, rupturing the ongoing discourse, but occurs in orderly ways as a practical solution to interactional dilemmas, reshaping the speech event, or constructing the distance from the tone of the activity in progress. In simple words, the change of footing keys speakers' identity and role shifting. As an instance, Nao (2011) identified how the change of footing marked switched roles and identities taken up by native-English speaking teachers when teaching Japanese students. Despite a few endeavors (e.g. Nao 2011), increasing attention should be given to the pragmatic and sociolinguistic functions derived from the diplomatic and strategic exploitation of the change of footing in an attempt to establish a dynamic, duly and desired social distance towards the audience.

The findings revealed that the radical and continual change of footing might occur from time to time among the companion identity, the journalistic identity and the CSR identity as in the case of the CMB and among the specialist identity, the companion identity, the journalistic identity and the CSR identity as in the case of the BOC. By taking up a specialist footing, the BOC wields its power as a century-old industry giant, issuing authoritatively concise in-depth financial briefs. The companion footing is marked with a playful and considerate frame, in both banks' corporate Weibo, as the purveyor of life jokes, lighthearted remarks and/or funny scenarios or chicken-soup-for-the-soul sentiments. Journalistic footing, pervasive in both the BOC and the CMB updates, is characteristic of its informational nature and demonstrates tabloid-like soft news in the midst of general economic and social updates. As is self-evident, the footing of the specialist delivers power, while the other three footings–peer, journalistic and CSR–are primarily solidarity-orientated, seeking consensus and camaraderie. In fact, the BOC Weibo features a number of hashtagged columns to regularly offer exclusive insider expertise, such as 中银动态 (News of BOC), 中银视界 (Vision of BOC), 黄金市场 (Gold market) and 每日汇评 (Comments on daily foreign exchange), for constructing a high-end and authoritative stance. Nonetheless, the commonality of the three footings resides in the shared intent to create a hybridised, trustworthy and reliable image in their impression management process on their corporate Weibo show.

Extract 29: #中银视界#昨日汇市缺乏焦点数据，各非美货币延续震荡走势，晚间公布的美国房地产及制造业数据均差于市场预期。今日重点关注美国零售销售数据，周四凌晨美联储将公布利率决议，偏向鸽派的结果或继续打压美元。请关注《每日市场点评》之"美国数据继续趋弱，美联储议息或延续鸽派" http://t.cn/zRSlgJw

贊 (1)|轉發 (320)|收藏|評論 (2) BOC 29102013 13:51 來自专业版微博 | 舉報

Extract 29: #BOC Vision# The exchange market of yesterday was in lack of data currency. Non-US currencies continue concussion and the U.S. housing and manufacturing data released yesterday evening were worse than market expectations. Today's focus is on the U.S. retail sales data. On Thursday morning the Fed will announce its interest rate decision. It is expected that this decision of dove-like bias might continue weighing on the US dollar. Please pay attention to the "Daily Market Review" to see how "U.S. data weakening and continuation of dove-like FOMC" http://t.cn/zRSlgJw.

Like (1)|Repost (320)|Collect|Comment (2) BOC 29102013 13:51.

Extract 30: #每日汇率# 2013年10月29日。此汇率表仅供参考，以中国银行各分行实际交易汇率为准，汇率不断更新中。最新外汇牌价 http://t.cn/hCwmp，更多金融数据 http://t.cn/SqMKM5

贊 (2)|轉發 (38)|收藏|評論 (5) BOC 29102013 09:27 來自微博桌面 | 舉報

Extract 30: #Daily Rates# 29th Oct., 2013. This table of exchange rate is for reference only, as the actual exchange rate is subject to the BOC branch's listing on the spot as the interest rate is always changing. For the latest foreign currency rates refer to http://t.cn/hCwmp, for more financial data http://t.cn/SqMKM5.

Like (2)/Repost (38)/Collect/Comment (5) BOC 29102013 09:27.

The formality and rigorousness in the Extract 29 and 30 were evidently shown both grammatically and lexically, such as in their prolonged clauses and sentences, formal word choice, prudent, four-word set phrases and jargon, in the absence of modal particles, and in the absence of first and second person pronouns and lexicalisation. Jargon like 市场预期 (Market expectations), 打压美元 (continue weighing on the US dollar), 货币延续震荡走势 (currencies continue concessions), 外汇牌价 (Table of exchange rate) and 实际交易汇率 (actual exchange rate) help to shape a footing of the Bank of China as a financial specialist. Prudence adds to the reliability, which tactfully allows hedging expressions, e.g., 仅供参考 (for reference only). The specialist identity of the BOC is successfully constructed in the authoritative financial forecasts and the issuance of exchange rates.

Extract 31: 【马年很神奇】①2014年和2015年的立春都在农历马年内。②神奇的星期五：2014年4月4日，星期五；6月6日，星期五；8月8日，星期五；10月10日，星期五；12月12日，星期五。③中国元宵节和西方情人节在同一天。④马年有点长，共384天，有"闰九月"，农历9月生日能过两次。

贊 (19)|轉發 (242)|收藏|評論 (44) CMB 03022014 11:15 來自 iPhone 客户端 | 舉報

Extract 31: The Year of the Horse is magic. ① The beginning of Spring of both 2014 and 2015 are all in the lunar year of the Horse. ② Magic Friday: 4th of April, 2014 is Friday; 6th of June of 2014 is Friday; 8th of August is Friday; 10th of October is Friday; 12th of December is Friday. ③ Chinese lunar Lantern festival of 2014 coincides with the Valentine's Day. ④ The Year of the Horse is longer than usual to have 384 days in total for there is an leap month of September in 2014. Those who were born in lunar September might celebrate their birthdays twice this year.

Like (19)/Repost (242)/Collect/Comment (44) CMB 03022014 11:15.

Extract 32: 【多家5A景区开售淡季门票，九寨沟降价超50%】 旺季出游，人多路堵价格高，常常变成了花钱找罪受。淡季出游倒是很可以考虑一下哦！11月起，许多著名景区开始执行淡季门票价格，优惠幅度多在25%到45%之间，九寨沟，布达拉宫等降价超50%。来把出行计划提上日程吧！(来自央视新闻)

贊 (4)|轉發 (29)|收藏|評論 (8) BOC 01112013 18:16 來自专业版微博 | 舉報

Extract 32: [Many 5A-grade scenic spots to sell off-season ticket prices and Jiuzhaigou's price reduction over 50%] Travelling during peak seasons may incur jam-packed tourists, higher ticket prices and traffic jams, resulting in a suffering experience instead. Why not consider vacationing during off-seasons! As of November, many 5A-grade scenic spots will begin their off-season ticketing, discounting 25–45% of the normal ticket prices. Jiuzhaigou and Potala Palace even offer a 50% discount. Don't hesitate to plan for your travelling! (Source: CCTV)

Like (4)/Repost (29)/Collect/Comment (8) BOC 01112013 18:16 from Weibo.

A forceful reinforcement of the BOC's footing of Mr. encyclopedia, Extract 31 provided four fascinating and coincidental calendar facts to followers: 2014年和2015年的立春都在农历马年内。神奇的星期五: 2014年4月4日，星期五; …… 农历9月生日能过两次 (the beginning of Spring of both 2014 and 2015 are all in the lunar year of the Horse; Magic Friday; Chinese lunar Lantern festival of 2014 coincides with Valentine's Day. …… Those who were born in lunar September might celebrate their birthdays twice this year.) As illustrated, Extract 32 is a piece of timely and useful travelling news on tickets promotion in many renowned scenic spots of China. Subsequent to the news item from the CCTV, the kind reminder and friendly proposal of来把出行计划提上日程吧! (Don't hesitate to plan for your travelling!) urged the BOC's followers to take advantage of the promotion and plan their vacations in advance. The efficacy of such useful piece of information that targets at followers' interests sheds light on the solidarity-oriented, solicitude-driven journalist footing of the corporate Weibo.

Extract 33: "明天你是否会想起，昨天你写的日记；明天你是否还惦记，曾经最爱哭的你……" 一首 "同桌的你" 勾起我们学生时代的美好回忆，童鞋们戳大图，看到最后，你会想起谁?快@ ta

贊 (6)|轉發 (33)|收藏|評論 (15) BOC 28102013 12:16 來自专业版微博 | 舉報

Extract 33: "Will you remember the diary you wrote in the past; will you think of the past self, the one who used to weep the most in the future"… the pop song "The Deskmate You" takes us back to our memorable schooldays. Classmates, be quick to click and by the end of reading, which of your former classmates would cross your mind? Be quick to @ him/her.

Like (6)/Repost (33)/Collect/Comment (15) BOC 28102013 12:16.

Extract 34: 幸福，不是长生不老，不是大鱼大肉，幸福是每一个微小的生活愿望达成，想被爱的时候有人来爱你，想吃月饼的时候会有小招给您定做，内什么，永远爱你们，早安!

贊 (16)|轉發 (45)|收藏|評論 (29) CMB 19092013 09:05 來自专业版微博 | 舉報

Extract 34: Happiness is not immortal, not a feast with ample meat and fish, but having each tiny wish comes true, being loved when you need it. Xiao Zhao will offer you an individualised box of mooncakes to cater for your wish of eating mooncakes. Well, love you forever, good morning!

Like (16)/Repost (45)/Collect/Comment (29) CMB 19092013 09:05 from Weibo.

Note the amount of solidarity the BOC conveyed with a nostalgic household song of the 1990s 同桌的你 (The Deskmate You) to trigger the old sweet memories of their followers. The advice "be quick to @ him/her" promoted followers to look for their most impressionist desk mates of secondary schools. In Extract 33, the deliberate mentioning of a few lines of the lyrics 明天你是否会想起, 昨天你写的日记; 明天你是否还惦记, 曾经最爱哭的你…… (Will you remember the diary you wrote in the past; will you think of the past self, the one who used to weep the most in the future) resorted to a remembrance of one's innocent past days gone through with their former classmates and a call for a resonance among the BOC's followers. Such a strategy of sentimentality aroused by the felicitous lyrics of the good old times is an indication of the BOC's attempts to strive for a companion identity, encompassing as much as solidarity, warmth and emotional supports. According to the observation of Extracts such as 34, a prevalent strategy of corporations to attach solidarity with their followers is the provision of the chicken-soup-for-the-soul Weibo updates, where no inspirational and philosophical remarks on life, love, truth and career are discussed and summarised. While the sentimental chicken-soup-for-the-soul contents in the form of a sincere, thought-provoking definition of happiness 幸福, 不是长生不老, 不是大鱼大肉, 幸福是每一个微小的生活愿望达成, 想被爱的时候有人来爱你 (Happiness is not immortal, not a feast with ample meat and fish, but having each tiny wish comes true, being loved when you need it) focused on the spiritual attachment to followers, the ending joke about offering customerised mooncakes to followers 想吃月饼的时候会有小招给您定做 and the explicit netspeak expression 内什么, 永远爱你们, 早安! (well, love you forever, good morning!) involved the CMB in the storytelling and further engaged the followers with joy, love and warmth in a specific companion identity at the critical moment of the mid-autumn festival.

Extract 35: "今天天气很冷, 看到你们我心里很温暖。" 面对前来看望的人们, 赵森琴老人动容地说。20日那天, 中行北京方庄地区员工与地区办事处, 北青报工作人员一道, 为社区困难家庭送去了慰问品。多日里的温暖礼物和问候虽微不足道, 却折射出我们践行企业社会责任的真诚。 http://t.cn/8FcDQ0O

贊 (6)|轉發 (14)|收藏|評論 (6) BOC 24012014 16:33 來自新浪微博 | 舉報

Extract 35: "It's rather chilly today, but I feel warm deep in my heart". Mrs. Zhao Senqin sincerely expressed her gratitude to everyone. On the 20th, staff of the Fangzhuang branch, BOC Beijing, together with local officials and staff of the Beijing Youth Daily paid their visits to financially challenged families in the local community with free gifts. The greetings and material gifts, though trivial, do manifest our sincere wishes to take social responsibility.

Like (6)/Repost (14)/Collect/Comment (6) BOC 24012014 16:33.

Extract 36: 今天, 我行携手@壹基金 发布#招商银行企业公益平台#, 此公益平台已在一网通主站和手机银行同步上线。只要你是一卡通用户, 就可通过PC或手机银行签约壹基金月捐计划。不需太多, 每人每月小额捐助就能支持社会公益。你我一点力量, 一点点改变世界。

贊 (17)|轉發 (59)|收藏|評論 (18) CMB 22092013 15:34 來自专业版微博 | 舉報

Extract 36: As of today, the CMB, hand in hand with @ One foundation, jointly released #Merchants Bank corporate philanthropy platform#, which has been synchronised on-line in the CMB website and mobile banking. As long as you are a CMB card user, you can sign up for one fund monthly donation program through a PC or mobile banking. With a regular small donation per month, each individual will be able to support social welfare. A little daily effort from you and me, a daily little change in the world.

Like (17)/Repost (59)/Collect/Comment (18) CMB 22092013 15:34 from Weibo.

Being one of the modern Western values of business management, a footing of corporate social responsibility intends to capture the attention and hearts of the followers for alliance and solidarity, creating a self-image of a giving corporate citizen, rather than a selfish profit generator. The BOC's footing as a socially responsible bank was manifested through a true narrative story. The persuasive effect has been enhanced with direct quotation of the helpless old lady 今天天气很冷, 看到你们我心里很温暖 (It's rather chilly today, but I feel warm deep in my heart) in Extract 35. The CMB's "One foundation" CSR programme seemed to be systematic and regular, preaching to followers for their own engagement. The ending of the parallel structure 你我一点力量,一点点改变世界 (a little effort from you and me, a daily little change in the world) in Extract 36 somehow served as its slogan for recognition, consensus and solidarity, instead of deference, between the CMB and its followers.

The findings of the banks' constant shifting among footings remind us of Goffman's words "a change of tone is involved" (Goffman 1974, p. 126). Goffman maintained that footing change is a persistent feature of natural talk. In Goffman's (1974, p. 128) words, Gumperz's study on the behavior of cross-cultural code shifting that "present in almost every corner of conversational life" claimed that their different stances are the actualisation of the change of footing. It is worth noting that both Goffman and Gumperz conducted research on interpersonal face-to-face conversations, during which speech parameters function as contextualization cues for signaling the change of footing and the speech parameters are far more manifest in the prosodic features than the syntactic ones (Goffman 1974). Despite this, what is at issue is the non face-to-face corporate written 'monologue', i.e., the enterprises' social media impression management. There is evidence that the change of footing per se on social media, realised through topic selection, word choice, syntactic arrangement and so on, has been ubiquitous, presenting either authoritative or egalitarian identities for followers to give maximum credit to. While an element of power being exerted in the BOC's image, solidarity has been strategically incorporated into both banks' impression management, encompassing information and remarks interpreted as encouragements and dialogues in the small talk amongst real-life friends.

5.3.2 *Devoting Themselves to Follow-up and Firm-Follower Interaction*

A friend "in contact" is a friend indeed as social interactions are of vital importance to the establishment of network and the maintenance of friendship. Conversely, a lost contact friend is likely to lead to a dispensable relationship. The findings discovered that to construct a trustworthy identity and image, both banks are aware of the significance of keeping an everlasting, ongoing dialogic relationship with their followers by engaging themselves in different forms of firm-follower interactions.

Specifically, the banks' interactional efforts are maximally manifested by the fact that followers' initiated Weibo updates were well taken care of. It is worth noting that the dialogues between followers' initiated Weibo updates, which appear on the homepage of the banks' Weibo contents, and the banks' corresponding responses is a golden opportunity for banks' impression management and branding refinement. Technically speaking, unless followers' speak directly to banks by @ them, followers' initiated updates would not appear on the banks' Weibo main content. In other words, the banks use key word search to make followers' initiated posts present on corporate Weibo, according to certain criteria of banks, as the way we see. The evidence indicates that there accumulated in total 13 times of active contributors' initiated posts on the BOC and 12 times on the CMB microblogging posts, of which banks managed duly and timely towards building mutual trustworthy relationships in most cases. In some cases, both parties apply a just-kidding tone with the same sense of humor to make the dialogic interaction even more interpersonal.

Extract 37: 感谢您对我们服务的肯定, 客户的满意就是对全体中行人最大的鼓励!

◆◆@Xuhuirebecca

收拾家里无意整理出那么一大袋不再出版の破损零钱，　拿到中国银行滕州分行去兑换，工作人员冯君健工号：54054连句埋怨话都没有，埋头苦干了两小时整理加黏贴，超有耐心，值得赞美! @滕州日报

@中国银行 我在:|新兴中路

贊 (15)|轉發 (102)|評論 (4) BOC 12022014 17:39 來自 iPhone 客户端

贊 (43)|轉發 (83)|收藏|評論 (32) BOC 12022014 15:15 來自新浪微博 | 舉報

Extract 37: Thanks for recognising our service. Customer satisfaction is BOC staff's largest encouragement!

@ Xuhuirebecca

While cleaning up my house, I have somehow found a large bag of slightly damaged currency, which is no longer being issued. I took this bag to BOC Tengzhou branch for conversion, Mr FENG Junjian, staff no. 54054 buried himself in counting and repairing all the changes without any complaints. His patient service is worthwhile for compliment! @ Tengzhou daily @Bank of China I am at Zhongxing middle road.

Like (15)/Repost (102)/Comment (4) BOC 12022014 17:39

Like (43)/Repost (83)/Collect/Comment (32) BOC 12022014 15:15.

Extract 38: 欢迎珍妮的小伙伴们陪伴主人光临～

◆◆@杨啊楸

@导盲犬珍妮 看到这个很骄傲, 这是南宁古城路中国银行里。。。

贊 (22)|轉發 (173)|評論 (10) BOC 09022014 17:12 來自 Android 客户端

贊 (38)|轉發 (111)|收藏|評論 (34) BOC 10022014 11:43 來自新浪微博 | 舉報

Extract 38: The guide dog Jenny and all guide dogs as well as their masters are welcomed～

@Yangaqiu

@ guide dog Jenny. So proud to see her here, this is the BOC Nanning Branch, Gucheng road……

Like (22)/Repost (173)/Comment (10) BOC 09022014 17:12

Like (38)/Repost (111)/Collect/Comment (34) BOC 10022014 11:43

Extract 39: 亲, 我家什么都可以马上有, 除了对象和节操, 这个小招真帮不了…(´•_•`)

◆◆@吾爱凑凑

一大波毫无节操的广告在深圳T3袭来。@招商银行 你们家是不是什么都马上有哇? 求马上中奖!! 我在这里:|深圳宝安国际机场B航站楼…

贊 (5)|轉發 (137)|評論 (12) CMB 25012014 16:43 來自 iPhone 客户端

贊 (45)|轉發 (116)|收藏|評論 (66) CMB 25012014 日 22:01 來自 iPhone 客户端 | 舉報.

Extract 39: Dear, it is true that any wish is possible at CMB's home, but I can do nothing about your wish of a girlfriend and moral integrity…(´•_•`)

@Wu ai cou cou

A number of TV commercials without any moral integrity are currently on at Terminal 3 of Shenzhen airports. @ CMB bank. Did not you mention that any wish is possible in the Year of horse? I beg to win your presents at once!! I am at:/Terminal tower B of Shenzhen international airport…

Like (5)/Repost (137)/Comment (12) CMB 24012014 16:43

Like (45)/Repost (116)/Collect/Comment (66) CMB 25012014 22:01.

Notice the Extracts 37–39 that substantiate firm-follower interactions on corporate Weibo, aiming at an identity worthy of trustworthiness. During Extracts 37–39, there is evidence for a clear turn-taking pattern of dialogue between banks and followers. It was found that such dialogues are either praise-acknowledgement or with a jocose nature. In Extract 37, a follower called Xuhuirebecca started the conversation by praising the service quality of a Bank of China teller with "…his patient service is worthwhile for compliments!" This compliment was followed-up by the BOC immediately with a thanking speech act. In Extract 38, a follower named Yangaqiu initiated a bank-targeted talk with the @ function "guide dog Jenny So proud to see her here, this is the BOC Nanning Branch, Gucheng road…" followed by the BOC's expression of the gratitude. Nonetheless, the interactive conversation pattern in Extract 39 was summarised as gift-requesting joke and gift-declining joke where the tone of speech was kidding and in fact raillery, for example between the follower Wu ai cou cou's "I beg to win your presents at once!!" and the China Merchant's Bank's "but I can do nothing about your wish of a girlfriend and moral integrity…(´•_•`)".

Secondly and interestingly during the follow-up dialogic process, the labor divisions of the banks in their microblogging firm-follower interaction were found to have become even more refined, with comment responses (followers' comments of questions and their unfavorable comments centering on the banks' businesses) all having been outsourced and selectively responded to. In practice, the responsibility of responding to followers' individualised comments has been allocated solely to a third-party, i.e., another independent corporate microblogging account: the BOC customer service and the CMB to CMB direct banking.

Extract 40:

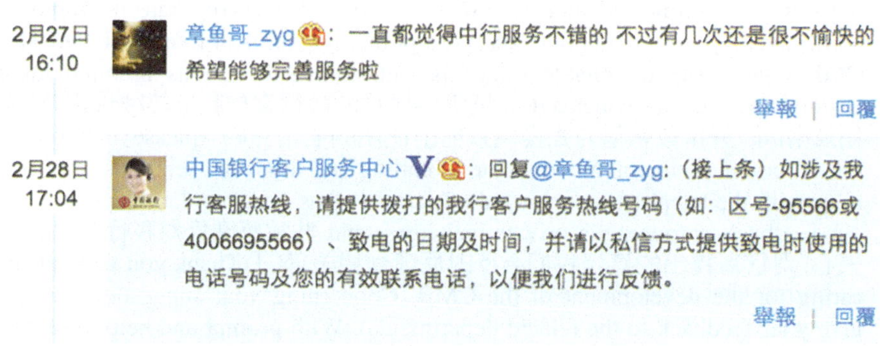
2月27日 16:10 章鱼哥_zyg: 一直都觉得中行服务不错的 不过有几次还是很不愉快的 希望能够完善服务啦

舉報 | 回覆

2月28日 17:04 中国银行客户服务中心: 回复@章鱼哥_zyg:（接上条）如涉及我行客服热线，请提供拨打的我行客户服务热线号码（如：区号-95566或4006695566）、致电的日期及时间，并请以私信方式提供致电时使用的电话号码及您的有效联系电话，以便我们进行反馈。

舉報 | 回覆

Extract 40:

27022014 16:10 Zhangyuge_zyg: I have always felt that service of the BOC is good, however there are also a few unpleasant experiences. Hope service quality of the BOC can be improved.

28022014 17:04 The BOC customer service reply @ Zhangyuge_zyg: If you refer to our customer service hotline, please call our customer service hotline number (area code-95566 or 4006695566), date of calling and time, and send this information to us with the telephone no. you called us as well as your regular telephone no. for our feedback purposes via private messages.

Extract 41:

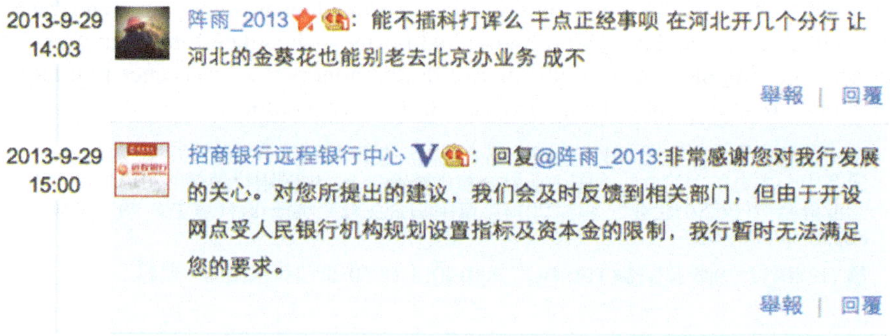
2013-9-29 14:03 阵雨_2013: 能不插科打诨么 干点正经事呗 在河北开几个分行 让河北的金葵花也能别老去北京办业务 成不

舉報 | 回覆

2013-9-29 15:00 招商银行远程银行中心: 回复@阵雨_2013:非常感谢您对我行发展的关心。对您所提出的建议，我们会及时反馈到相关部门，但由于开设网点受人民银行机构规划设置指标及资本金的限制，我行暂时无法满足您的要求。

舉報 | 回覆

Extract 41:

29092013 14:03 Chenyu_2013: Can you stop playing cuteness and joking and get on with serious business? Open more branches in Hebei province to save our trips to Beijing for the CMB sunflower service, can't you?

29092013 15:00 CMB long distance bank center reply @ Chenyu_2013: Thank you very much for caring for the development of the CMB. Concerning your suggestions, we shall give your feedback to the related departments. However we cannot satisfy your needs due to a few policies of the People's Bank of China that restrain the opening of new branches.

In contrast to Extract 37 and 39, Extract 40 and 41 illustrated part of the firm-follower-firm interaction pattern that made their appearance on the comment area of banks' microblogging updates, where one more click needs to be made. In other words, Extract 40 and 41 did not appear on the corporate microblogging homepage. By extremely polite and prompt dialogic turns in Extract 40 and 41, the CMB's professional, reliable image is well-managed with its premium quality customer service, as evidenced in 请提供拨打的我行客户服务热线号码, 致电日期及时间, 并请以私信方式提供致电时使用的电话号码 (please call our customer service hotline number… date of calling and time, and send this information to us with the telephone no. you called us as well as your regular telephone no. for our feedback purposes via private messages) and 非常感谢您对我行发展提出的关心, 对您所提出的建议我们会及时反馈到相关部门 (Thank you very much for caring for the development of the CMB. Concerning your suggestions, we shall give your feedback to the related departments). With prompt and helpful replies to followers' suggestions and complaints, the dialogic channel between the bank and its followers are kept open and transparent, thus helping to persuade customers into trusting the banks and eventually trading with the banks.

5.3.3 *Detailing Company Awards and Benefits of Promotions or Launches*

The publicity of awards and honors, the authoritative recognition to company performance, is a conventional and effective way of self-promotion in public relations practice. In a hierarchical and high power distance culture such as China's (Hofstede 1983), the long-standing practice of official awards and honors guarantee the quality service and product of individual business. It is therefore a certainty that the sensible announcement of official awards and honors is an assistance to improve the banks' overall public image and elevate their reputations.

Extract 42: 【中行获评 "社会责任杰出企业"】 在新华网和中国社科院企业社会责任研究中心主办的 "第六届中国企业社会责任峰会" 上, 中国银行荣获 "2013年度中国企业社会责任•杰出企业" 和 "2013年度中国企业社会责任•最佳雇主" 两个奖项。http://t.cn/8Fqy4ZC

贊 (12)|轉發 (9)|收藏|評論 (14) BOC 20012014 18:50 來自新浪微博 | 舉報

Extract 42: 【The BOC awarded outstanding socially responsible corporation】 In the 6th Chinese corporate social responsibility summit sponsored by Xinhua.net and the Chinese Academy of Social Sciences, the Bank of China took pride in being awarded "The outstanding socially responsible corporation in the year of 2013", and the "Best employer in the year of 2013". http://t.cn/8Fqy4ZC

Like (12)/Repost (9)/Collect/Comment (14) BOC 20012014 18:50.

Extract 43: 【中行荣获"投资者关系百强奖"】 中国银行近日入选英国《投资者关系杂志》(IR Magazine) "2013年大中华区投资者关系百强" 榜单。该榜单由中国内地, 香港和台湾地区370名买方, 卖方分析师和基金经理独立投票选出, 是全球公认最权威, 声望最高的投资者关系奖项之一。 http://t.cn/8krgTH4

贊 (6)|轉發 (9)|收藏|評論 (7) BOC 31122013 16:28 來自新浪微博 | 舉報

Extract 43: 【The BOC awarded as one of the 100 best investor relations corporations】 The Bank of China recently was listed in IR magazine as one of the 100 best investor relations bank in the Chinese Mainland during the year of 2013. The list was generated independently by customers, industry analysts and foundation managers in the Chinese Mainland, Hong Kong and Taiwan, as one of the most accredited and prestigious awards of investor relations in the world. http://t.cn/8krgTH4

Like (6)/Repost (9)/Collect/Comment (7) BOC 31122013 16:28

Extract 44: 小招在智联招聘和北京大学相关机构联合举办的 2013 中国年度最佳雇主评选中荣获第一, 同时入选最具社会责任十强雇主。在这里我要感谢小伙伴们一路上的支持和努力, 2014期待更多小伙伴加入我们!

贊 (73)|轉發 (250)|收藏|評論 (102) CMB 17122013 16:34 來自新浪微博 | 舉報.

Extract 44: China Merchants Bank was named as the champion in the best employer contest sponsored by zhaopin.com and the Peking University. It is also selected as one of the ten most socially responsible employers. We hereby appreciate the support from followers, and look forward to more buddies joining us in 2014!

Like (73)/Repost (250)/Collect/Comment (102) CMB 17122013 16:34.

Extract 45: 下面发布一条高大上的招聘信息, 请各位按捺住内心的小激动。招商银行总行公司金融总部一大批职位正在招募, 比如总行副总经理/总经理助理! 如果你想走向人生巅峰, 那么请速来 2013 中国年度最佳雇主第一名这里报到! 请联系我→http://t.cn/8kNUDEb

贊 (32)|轉發 (270)|收藏|評論 (101) CMB 19122013 11:01 來自新浪微博 | 舉報

Extract 45: Job advertisement time and please hold your breath first. The China Merchants Bank headquarters is launching a great number of posts, such as Vice President and Assistant to the General Manager! If you wish to fulfill yourself, come quickly to join the best employer in China of 2013! Contact me→http://t.cn/8kNUDEb

Like (32)/Repost (270)/Collect/Comment (101) CMB 19122013 11:01.

Extract 46: 【中行医达通—自助就医, 自在通达】 还在为排长队挂号烦恼吗?还在为怀揣大笔现金缴费担心吗?还在为等了几小时却发现专家号已挂完伤心吗?现在再也不是问题啦! 中行推出 "医达通" 服务, 预约挂号在家中, 自助缴费不排队, 让您轻松便捷挂号就诊。详情猛戳大图～http://t.cn/8kTBotx

贊 (11)|轉發 (35)|收藏|評論 (10) BOC 23122013 20:16 來自专业版微博 | 舉報

Extract 46: 【BOC hospital-easy card, self-register so easy】 Frustrated at the line-up for registration in hospital? Worried about having large amounts of money in cash? Disappointed to find the expert registration quotas are all used up after hours of line-up?

Now all problems are gone! The BOC has just issued the hospital-easy card service to enable you make appointments and pay at home. For more details please click the photo～ http://t.cn/8kTBotx

Like (11)/Repost (35)/Collect/Comment (10) BOC 23122013 20:16.

Extract 47: 即日起, 招行 ATM 机全面支持 Apple Pay 取款! 无需插卡, 也无需输入卡号, 只要你的 Apple Pay 绑定了招行一卡通 (或其他银行卡), 即可体验最炫取款姿势! 小招奉上最全攻略↓↓↓

赞 (35)/转发 (68)/收藏/评论 (73) CMB 23032016 12:03

Extract 47: Apple Pay is supported by any AMT of the CMB from today on! No need to insert bank card and neither need to input bank account no… Only if your Apply Pay is bound with your CMB bank card or any bank cards, you may experience the coolest and most fascinating gesture of cash withdrawal from the ATM! Xiao Zhao presents you with details.

Like (35)/Repost (68)/Collect/Comment (73) CMB 23032016 12:03.

The present study indicated that the awards and honors company obtained emerged from the all-embracing contents of corporate Weibo to keep reminding of and reassuring the followers the strengths, merits, breakthroughs and innovations of the BOC and the CMB in regards to their financial services and products as well as the advancement and glory of their brands. Furthermore, the elaboration of product launches and business promotions evinced much concern and a caring attitude towards the interests of followers and persuaded them into taking advantage of these technologically sophisticated benefits. The trustworthy image of the banks, characterised by the powerful persuasive communication and promotional language on the corporate social media, stirs the underlying consumption desires of its followers to become loyal customers of the banks.

In an attempt to enhance the public trust on the Weibo, the BOC highlighted its honorable awards both as the 社会责任杰出企业 (outstanding socially responsible corporation) in Extract 42 and as one of the 100 best investor relations corporations issued by the IR magazine of the UK in Extract 43. In a similar vein, the CMB took pride in Extract 44 and 45 as the 2013 中国年度最佳雇主评选中荣获第一, 同时入选最具社会责任十强雇主 (the champion in the best employer contest sponsored by zhaopin.com and the Peking University and one of the top ten most socially responsible employers). The launch of the BOC's hospital-easy card in Extract 46 is an embodiment of its technology-driven competitive edge.

In pursuit of a higher level of customer satisfaction, the cutting-edge and cool brand image of the CMB may be associated with its strategic cooperation with Apple Pay, the fascinating mobile payment and digital wallet service device launched by Apple Corporation in late 2014, as shown in the extract 47.

5.4 Summary

Language use is “a rich source of information for forming impressions of others and can be used in managing the impressions we convey to others” (Holtgraves 2002, p. 64). In Goffman’s (1959) terms, impressions are front stage image that reflected by language use and are “given off”. There is sufficient evidence that both the BOC and the CMB have employed a couple of impression management strategies: humanising and popularising the corporate self and persuading followers into trusting (and eventually trading with) the corporate self. To undertake “performers’ work of successfully staging the character” (Goffman 1959, p. 208), the CMB and the BOC applied sub-strategies of impression management, such as a playing cuteness conversational style, politeness and face-work strategy, the change of footing, active interaction, material stimulus and branding enhancement.

Chapter 6
Followers' Co-constructing Banks' Corporate Identity on Weibo

6.1 Introduction

This chapter examined how co-constructions of corporate identity take effect, from a dialogic communication perspective. Not only corporate identities projected in firm-follower dialogues were specified for a cross-bank comparison but also the features of dialogic communication were explored.

6.2 Dialogic Communications on Social Media

According to their different interaction modes, followers in firm-follower Weibo interaction may be categorised into four types: active contributors, interlocutors, listeners and lurkers.

6.2.1 Active Contributors

As defined earlier, two types of active contributors were identified. First, there are followers who voluntarily @ banks in their personal Weibo updates. The second type of active followers refers to those who made comments and whose comments being reposted by corporations, thus automatically creating firm-follower dialogues at the corporate Weibo interface. In the second case, it was found that it is corporations who decide the "dialogic value" of followers' comments to be reposted. Active contributors are real and the most significant followers who make the greatest efforts in conversing with corporations (amongst all the four types of followers), wielding their unique and irreplaceable influence on co-shaping

W. Feng, *Discursive Constructions of Corporate Identities by Chinese Banks on Sina Weibo*, DOI 10.1007/978-981-10-4469-4_6

corporate identity. After all, as instances below display, either kind of active contributors has managed to present their words and thoughts on the main page of corporate Weibo, based on which they deserve the most loyal, enthusiastic and major followers with whom targeted enterprises have de facto dialogues on social media in the presence of millions of followers. To analyse the followers' co-construction of corporate identities, a thematic analysis of the firm-follower dialogues was conducted and the results were shown in Tables 6.1 and 6.2.

As Table 6.1 indicated, as the most common corporate identity co-constructed by the CMB's followers (52.2%), a hybridisation of companion and authentic identities has been co-constructed for 60 times during firm-follower dialogues, followed by a pure companion identity co-construction of 40 instances or the second commonest corporate identity in proportion (34.8%). These two types of corporate identities conspicuously account for the majority (87%) of total four identities co-constructed through the firm-follower dialogues on the CMB's corporate Weibo. Authentic identity however, without a companion coat, seems to be downplayed in the firm-followers dialogues in view of its low proportion of 6.9% out of the four corporate identities. The findings also suggested the presence of the CMB's CSR identity as the least key identity co-constructed in the firm-follower dialogues, accounting for only 6.1% out of the 115 instances of the firm-follower interaction in the corporate CMB. That is, the CMB and its followers are exchanging ideas about third-party or social interest, completely irrelevant of the corporate profits. Consequently, the co-construction of the CSR identity contributes to a trustworthier, more favorable image of the CMB, as compared to the sole self-presentation of the CMB as a socially responsible corporation.

Table 6.1 Followers' (Active contributors) co-construction of CI through dialogues (CMB)

Identities constructed via dialogues with active contributors (CMB)	No.	%
Companion + authentic identity	60	52.2
Companion identity	40	34.8
Authentic identity	8	6.9
CSR identity	7	6.1
Total	115	100

Note Coding schemes are based on the definitions of Table 4.2

Table 6.2 Followers' (Active contributors) co-construction of CI through dialogues (BOC)

Identities constructed via dialogues with active contributors (BOC)	No.	%
Authentic identity	4	44.5
Companion identity	2	22.2
Authentic + specialist identity	1	11.1
Specialist identity	1	11.1
CSR identity	1	11.1
Total	9	100

Note coding schemes are based on the definitions of Table 4.2

Nonetheless in the Table 6.2, in comparison with the CMB, the BOC's followers' co-construction of the corporate identity saw a much lower degree of activity. A close examination of the limited interaction indicated that the authentic identity of the BOC as a financial institution was highlighted with four items in the firm-follower dialogues, accounting for 44.5% of all identities co-shaped, whilst two instances of the firm-follower dialogues projected and reinforced the BOC's companion identity, covering a lower percentage of 22.2. Amongst the total nine instances of the firm-follower dialogues, corporate identities co-shaped in the last three dialogues were evenly distributed to a CSR identity, a specialist identity and a combination of authentic and specialist identity, each taking up a weak percentage of 11.1 of the identity co-construction pool.

Dialogues between corporations and their followers are on-staged in Goffman's (1959) words, as they are completely showcased at the interface of the corporate Weibo as part of the main contents of corporate Weibo, without further clicks or retrieval. The findings revealed not only the significance of such dialogues in reinforcing corporate identities but also the binding mechanism of identity co-construction that the co-construction on social media is partially controlled in the hands of the corporations. Specifically, the banks are entitled to repost their followers' comments and initiated a firm-follower dialogue, on the basis of the value of the followers' comments, e.g., entertainment, engagement or information, as in the second interaction mode of active contributors. A more detailed rationale of the corporations in their followers' comments repost and dialogue initiation was revealed with the in-depth interviews in the next chapter.

By means of thematic analysis, a number of specific adjacency pairs (Schegloff and Sacks 1973) were identified respectively in the firm-follower dialogues on the CMB and the BOC's corporate Weibo, as Table 6.3 suggested. Conversation analysts (Schegloff and Sacks 1973; Schegloff 1968) termed an adjacency pair as composed of two utterances by two speakers, one after the other. The speaking of the first utterance (the first-pair part, or the first turn) provokes a responding utterance (the second-pair part, or the second turn). Hence, questions and answers are perhaps the most ritualised adjacency pairs and the most effective way of interaction invitation. Given the varieties of the firm-follower dialogues on Weibo, I extend the broad terms of "statements and replies" (Goffman 1976, p. 263) for analysis.

In Table 6.3, it may be observed that the most noticeable cross-bank variation of followers' co-construction of corporate identity lies in both the frequency and the varieties of firm-follower dialogues. In terms of frequency, the firm-follower dialogues accounted for 7.7% in the CMB corpus but only 0.71% in the BOC corpus. In regards to the variety of interaction, there are as many as five kinds of adjacency pairs in the firm-follower dialogues in the case of the CMB, but only two kinds of adjacency pairs in the case of the BOC.

For a better and comprehensive understanding of the mechanism of firm-follower dialogues on social media, definitions of the varieties of adjacency pairs are provided. To begin with, question has its ritualised meaning, through which followers or corporations raise a question (by @) to initiate a round of

Table 6.3 Adjacency pairs of the BOC and the CMB with active contributors

Bank	Bank of China		China Merchants Bank				
Adjacency Pairs	Question-raillery	Storytelling/praise-acknowledgement	Question-raillery	Storytelling/praise-acknowledgement	Question-answer	Raillery-counterraillery	Storytelling-raillery
No.	1	8	32	26	12	26	19
%	11.1	88.9	27.9	22.6	10.4	22.6	16.5
Total	9		115				
% of total updates							

Note Only the first two turns of the dialogues are examined (usually there are two or three turns in a dialogue)

interaction. Answer is the desired response to a question. An initiation of a question and its follow-up of an answer are composed of the simplest form of firm-follower dialogue. In the present research raillery is meant to refer to the intended human interaction of the playfulness and friendliness of tease and humorous effect. Likewise, the speech act of counter-raillery is herein defined as the goodwilled, playful and friendly reactive nature of the interlocutors. Furthermore, storytelling refers to followers' sharing of narratives, either about their pleasant user experience of bank's customers or about their general life experience somehow but relating to the banking corporation. Praise, as a common speech act, is the expression of followers' approval or admiration, usually of the bank's service. Acknowledgements are banks' positive and unmarked responses to the followers' praise and storytelling, such as the banks' self-modesty towards followers' recognition and compliments on their service quality. By followers' genuine willingness to converse with corporations, the adjacency pair of storytelling/praise-acknowledgement where positive politeness strategy and face-work dominates, intensifies and enhances followers' user satisfaction. This is also the majority type of interaction mechanism of firm-follower dialogue on the BOC Weibo.

As displayed in the Table 6.3, it was found that there are five kinds of adjacency pairs in the firm-follower dialogues on the CMB's Weibo, namely, question-raillery, storytelling/praise-acknowledgement, question-answer, raillery-counter-raillery and storytelling-raillery. The most common form of firm-follower interaction on the CMB corporate social media is the adjacency pair of question-raillery, occurring 32 instances (27.8%) amongst the total 115 times of firm-follower dialogue. The second most frequent forms of firm-follower interaction are found to be storytelling/praise-acknowledgement and raillery-counter-raillery, eaching consisting of 26 items of dialogues or 22.6% in percentage. Next, the adjacency pair of storytelling-raillery counted as 16.5% with 19 times of firm-follower dialogues. The least frequent form of firm-follower interaction in the case of the CMB was found to be the most ritualised interaction pair: question-answer, taking up 10.4% out of the 115 times of firm-follower interaction with 12 instances.

In stark contrast to the official or quasi-official essence of the firm-follower dialogue on the BOC Weibo as represented in the sweeping adjacency pair of storytelling/praise-acknowledgment, the speech act of raillery plays a significant role in the firm-follower dialogues on the CMB's corporate social media, although realised in many different sub-types: as in followers' jesting response to the CMB's question, the initiation of raillery and counter-raillery in-between as well as followers' storytelling in response to the CMB's tease. Accounting for 78% amongst the five kinds of dialogic types, it is certain that raillery strengthened and co-constructed an identity of an intimate companion in the minds of the CMB's followers. Mutual raillery and ridicule of each other signified not only a healthy and relaxed friendship, but more importantly indicated the close psychological gap between the CMB and its followers. That is to say, the CMB is definitely not a companion who can not take a joke.

Extract 48: 喂, 快醒醒, 今天过节呢～ 我真的伤你们这么深吗

@Arnold-Young

平时的心跳: __/_______/_______ 看电影时的心跳: __/___/_/__/_/_/_ 她来电时的心跳: _/_/_/_/_/_ 看到信用卡还款账单的心跳______________: @招商银行

赞 (6) 转发 (160) 评论 (32) CMB 21122013 来自 iPhone 客户端

赞 (37) 转发 (136) 评论 (96) CMB 25122013 11:08 来自微博 Weibo.com

Extract 48: Hey, wake up quickly, today is Christmas Day～ Did I really hurt you that deep

@Arnold-Young

Normal heart beat: __/_______/_______ the heartbeat of watching movies: __/___/_/ __/_/_/_ the heartbeat of receiving her call: _/_/_/_/_/_ the heartbeat at the sight of credit card statement______________: @CMB

Like (6) Repost (160) Comment (32) 2013-12-21 from iPhone app

Like (37) Repost (136) Comment (96) 2013-12-25 11:08 from Weibo.com

Extract 49: 回复 @肥雞燒酒owo吃土ing: 你们这帮磨人的小妖精… //@肥雞燒酒owo吃土ing: 什么时候出银魂的什么时候出银魂的什么时候出银魂的什么时候出银魂的!!!!!!!!! //@招商银行: 我们家出火影了! 出火影了! 出火影了! 出火影了四遍!

@招商银行信用卡-北京

羁绊, 有你, 无所畏!!! 招商银行火影忍者信用卡! 喜欢吗? 点击链接立即申请!!!

赞 (4) 评论 (15) 转发 (53) CMB 26102015 18:18 from Weibo.com

赞 (4) 评论 (37) 转发 (13) CMB 26102015 16:46 from Weibo.com

Extract 49: Reply @肥雞燒酒owo吃土ing: you guys are clinging little fairies…//@肥雞燒酒 owo 吃土ing: When to launch Gintama (credit card) When to launch Gintama When to launch Gintama When to launch Gintama!!!!!!!!! //@CMB: We are launching Naruto (credit card)! Naruto! Naruto! Naruto four times!

@CMB credit card-Beijing

Fetters, you have no fears against!!! CMB Naruto-themed credit card! Like it? Click links to apply immediately!!!

Like (4) Comment (15) Repost (53) CMB 26102015 18:18 from Weibo.com

Like (4) Comment (37) Repost (13) CMB 27102015 16:46 from Weibo.com

Extract 50: 电话那头的帅哥，我们做朋友吧

◆◆@妞小乔的微笑是红色

KITTY 信用卡还款卡被吞，打电话冻结卡。 接线员男同学声音那个好听啊，不小心开了扩音，旁边的女同事听到了凑过来说：太好听了，再打一遍！BTW：卡已拿回!开心！@招商银行

贊|轉發 (17)|評論 (13) CMB 11092013 19:58 來自 iPhone 客户端

贊 (15)|轉發(15)|收藏|評論 (41) CMB 11092013 11:35 來自专业版微博|舉報

Extract 50: The handsome boy over the telephone let us make friends.

@ Niu xiao qiao's smile is red

ATM has swallowed my CMB KITTY credit card, and I called customer hotline to freeze my bankcard. The voice of the call center boy over the telephone was so magnetic. A female colleague of mine was even lured to approach by his charming voice, as I had switched my cell phone to the loudspeaker mode. She urged me to call him once again, "such a good voice, why not call him again?" BTW, credit card has been returned! So delighted! @ CMB

Like/Repost (17)/Comment (13) CMB 11092013 19:58

Like (15)/Repost (15)/Collect/Comment (41) CMB 12092013 11:35

Extract 51: 其实，今天是一次将爱情升华为亲情的绝佳机会，好好把握。 //@抗芒贝笔：#双节要和谐#最完美的计划就是先和男友过好情人节 然后晚上带男友回家吃汤圆～，@中国银行

◆◆@中国银行

#双节要和谐# 就在明天，2014 年的情人节和元宵节即将"狭路相逢"。 是选择浪漫的"二人世界"，还是温馨的"合家团圆"？你是否正在为这个 2014 年的"最大难题"而苦恼呢？快快分享一下你的节日计划吧，@中国银行 还有机会获得精美小礼品呦。

贊 (10)|轉發 (1121)|評論 (141) BOC 13022014 16:00 來自新浪微博

贊|轉發|收藏|評論 (4) BOC 14022014 18:31 來自新浪微博|舉報

Extract 51: In fact, today is a golden opportunity to sublimate your love and cares for family. Do seize the chance. //@ Kang Mang Bei Bi: # perfect match of Valentine's Day and Lantern Festival # The most perfect plan is to spend a Valentine's Day with your boyfriend before coming home to spend the Lantern Festival with your parents in the evening ～, @ Bank of China

@ Bank of China

Perfect match of Valentine's Day and Lantern Festival # Tomorrow of 2014 we see a coincidence of Western Valentine's Day and Chinese Lantern Festival. Would you prefer to spend such a memorable day with the significant other or with your parents and families?

Are you so worried about this "hardest choice" of 2014? Come quick to share your smart plans with us and win free presents by @ Bank of China.

Like (10)/Repost (1121)/Comment (141) BOC 13022014 16:00

Like/Repost/Collect/Comment (4) BOC 14022014 18:31

Extract 52: "公益无处不在, 人人都在参与", 说得太好了! 我们只不过举手之劳, 真的不足道, 但是大家都来参与, 就能凝聚更大的力量!

@贵州青年志愿者

分享一件小事, 昨天去中国银行转账给我们白滩小学免费早餐款, 因是跨行,需交手续费50元, 工作人员看到备注写的是转善款, 当即给我免掉了手续费, 还送了份中国银行的纪念品。 小小的经历, 让我心里暖暖的。 公益无处不在, 人人都在参与。

贊 (25)|轉發 (40)|收藏|評論 (4) BOC 27022014 08:45 來自微博桌面

贊 (28)|轉發 (37)|收藏|評論 (23) BOC 27022014 16:02 來自 weibo.com

Extract 52: Charity is everywhere and everyone may involve. Well spoken! We just made little effort, really insignificant. But if we all come to participate charity, we can gather greater strength!

@ Guizhou younger volunteer

I am to share one true story. Yesterday when we were transferring the charitable breakfast fund to White beach primary school at the Bank of China, we were waived the 50 RMB cross-bank transfer fee by the BOC staff who noticed our written comment of charitable breakfast fund to the school. We were also given a present by the BOC staff for our assistance to the pupils. I felt warmth in my heart although this is a trivial experience. Charity is everywhere and everyone may involve.

Like (25)|Repost (4)|Collect|Comment (4) BOC 27022014 08:45 from Weibo desktop

Like (28)|Repost (37)|Collect|Comment (23) BOC 27022014 16:02 from Weibo.com

Extract 53: 在亚洲、 在欧洲、 在美洲、 在非洲...在您发现精彩世界的路上, 中国银行期待与您的温暖邂逅! 

@陈净在新加坡

今天刚到伦敦, 机场入关处"中国银行"的广告牌甚是醒目, 看着好亲切。 伦敦这个著名的雾都都露出了蓝天, 让北京情何以堪啊

赞 (7) 转发 (4) 评论 (6) BOC 16012014 19:39 from Weibo.iPhone

赞 (8) 转发 (3) 评论 (6) BOC 16012014 13:38 from Weibo.com

Extract 53: In Asia, in Europe, in America, in Africa…wherever on your way to discover the wonderful world, Bank of China looks forward to the warm meeting of you!

@ Chen Jing in Singapore: Just arrived in London today. The Bank of China advertisement at the entrance of the customs office looks so eye-catching, so warm. The famous fog city London clears up, leaving Beijing embarrassing herself

Like (7) Repost (4) Comment (6) BOC 16012014 19:39 from Weibo.iPhone

Like (8) Repost (3) Comment (6) BOC 17012014 13:38 from Weibo.com

Extract 54: 感谢您对我们服务的肯定，客户的满意就是对全体中行人最大的鼓励！

◆◆@Xuhuirebecca

收拾家里无意整理出那么一大袋不再出版の破损零钱，　拿到中国银行滕州分行去兑换，工作人员冯君健工号: 54054 连句埋怨话都没有，埋头苦干了两小时整理加黏贴，超有耐心，值得赞美！@滕州日报

@中国银行 我在:|新兴中路

贊(15)|轉發(102)|評論(4) BOC 12022014 17:39 來自 iPhone 客户端

贊(43)|轉發(83)|收藏|評論(32) BOC 13022014 15:15 來自新浪微博|舉報

Extract 54: Thank you for recognising our service. Customer satisfaction is the biggest encouragement to the BOC staff!

@ Xuhuirebecca

When tidying up my apartment, I found and organised a bag of damaged bank notes, which have stopped publishing. But when I took them to Tengzhou branch of the BOC, the teller Mr. Feng Junjian, staff no. 54054, did not complain at all and it all took him two hours to clean up everything. So patient! @ Tengzhou Daily @ Bank of China I am at:/Xinxing middle road.

Like (15)/Repost (102)/Comment (4) BOC 12022014 17:29

Like (43)/Repost (83)/Collect/Comment (32) BOC 13022014 15:15

As manifested in the extracts 48–54, the co-construction of corporate identity is realised through firm-follower dialogues undertaken on the corporate Weibo. Extract 48 and 49 presented the adjacency pair of raillery-counter-raillery during which the CMB's companion and authentic identity is perfectly shaped. An follower of the CMB named Arnold-Young initiated the firm-follower dialogue by @ the CMB, his graphic account of the heart beat of four occasions, each distinguished by a different driving force: normal period, when his heart beat regular and unmarked; watching movies, when his heartbeat is faster than usual; receiving her calls, when his heartbeat is even faster and fluctuates, humorously indicating the exciting and sweet moments with the significant other; and finally at the sight of his credit card statement issued by the CMB, when his electrocardiograph line is completely straight, exaggerating in a funny way the complicated feelings or suffering of overconsumption by using the CMB credit card. Unsurprisingly, the core component of the follower Arnold-Young's illustrated and creative update lies in its ending part, the vivid portrayal of users' astonishment upon the receipt of their large-sum credit card bank statements. The follower Mr. Young's adoption of self-ridicule and the raillery of the CMB has inspired the CMB, who imitates his the sense of humor and flow of ideas by counter-raillery 喂, 快醒醒, 今天过节呢～ 我真的伤你们这么深吗  (hey, wake up quickly, today is Christmas Day～ Did I really hurt you that deep ) as if Mr. Young's unconsciousness takes place. Feeling wronged, the CMB uses an emoticon to add cuteness to the firm-follower communication, where inevitably the companion and authentic identity of the CMB is actualised.

Likewise, in the first turn of the Extract 49, the CMB announced the new launch of a Japanese comic figure Naruto-themed credit card with the colloquial, childish and playful linguistic style, which is manifested in the repeated linguistic form 我们家出火影了！出火影了！出火影了！出火影了四遍！(We are launching Naruto (credit card)! Naruto! Naruto! Naruto! Four times!). Four times is understood in this context as an expression in jest to indicate the significance of the credit card launch, coined after the present-day Chinese fashionable neologism 重要的事情說三遍 (important matters should be repeated for three times). This creative usage of language sets a relaxing scene to elicit friend-like dialogues. In response, a follower named "肥雞燒酒owo吃土ing" teased back the CMB with his four-times repeated comment 什么时候出银魂的什么时候出银魂的什么时候出银魂的什么时候出银魂的!!!!!!!!! (When to launch Gintama credit card When to launch Gintama

When to launch Gintama When to launch Gintama!!!!!!!!) to express his sincere and strong wish for the CMB's credit card launch of his loved comic figure Gintama. The third turn of just-for-fun dialogue 你们这帮磨人的小妖精… (you guys are clinging little fairies…) is marked with the CMB's counter-raillery attitude, a typical kidding and playing cuteness conversational style through which both its girlish persona and an intimate companion identity are brought into manifestation. The authentic bank identity of the CMB is evidenced through the discussion of credit card launch, a powerful indication of bank-customer relation in the firm-follower interaction.

Different from Extract 49, the dialogue in Extract 50, a storytelling-raillery pair, is initiated by a follower named "Niu xiao qiao's smile is red" to share a recent pleasant user experience of the CMB's customer service to solve her problem of KITTY 信用卡还款卡被吞 (ATM has swallowed my CMB KITTY credit card). Thanks to the help of the 接线员男同学 (call center boy) with a magnetic voice, her credit card was frozen and finally brought back. In the end of the storytelling, the follower expressed her present mood 开心 (so delighted). Instead of taking pride in the quality service of the CMB employee and focusing on authentic, non-interpersonal bank-customer relationships, the CMB's reply to such a storytelling of the follower was found to be a playful, witty and funny raillery, which is uttered in the tone of the girl follower, 电话那头的帅哥，我们做朋友吧 (the handsome boy over the telephone, let us make friends). In the exchange of ideas and emotions, the follower treats the CMB more as a happy-go-lucky companion for sharing and listening than an enterprise with good service. As a result, the CMB skillfully stresses its companion identity with the reply uttered in the follower's tone of persiflage.

In the same vein, the BOC's companion identity is magnified in Extract 51, a question-raillery dialogue with a follower named "Kang Mang Bei Bi". The coincidence of Western Valentine's Day and the Chinese Lantern festival in 2014 is portrayed by the BOC as the 2014 年的"最大难题" (the "hardest choice" of 2014) for a topic eliciting follower's open discussions. Under the hashtaged column #双节要和谐# (#perfect match of Valentine's Day and Lantern Festival#), this question "would you prefer to spend such a memorable day with the significant other or with your parents and families?" has generated as many as 141 answers in comments and one interesting piece of comment is reposted by the BOC. The follower teased the BOC with her personalised countermeasure to the given dilemma 最完美的计划就是先和男友过好情人节 然后晚上带男友回家吃汤圆 (the most perfect plan is to spend a Valentine's Day with your boyfriend before coming home to spend the Lantern Festival with your parents in the evening ~). A smart, jesting answer as such is afterwards replied by the BOC with an encouraging comment其实，今天是一次将爱情升华为亲情的绝佳机会，好好把握 (in fact, today is a golden opportunity to sublimate your love and care for family. Do seize the chance). By the question-raillery dialogue, the BOC's supportive and caring companion persona is portrayed and co-constructed. Nonetheless, in Extract 52 and 53, a couple of storytelling-acknowledgment adjacency pairs, the BOC's CSR identity and specialist identity are primarily promoted upon the BOC's acknowledgement of followers' sincere praise in their storytelling narratives.

Extract 52 presented an adjacency pair of storytelling/praise-acknowledgement. A follower "Guizhou young volunteer" commended the BOC upon its social responsibility contribution after the BOC staff willingly waived the 50 RMB cross-bank transfer fee when he/she noticed the follower's transferring motivation of charity. This face-giving praise was shortly responded by the BOC's modest acknowledgment 我们只不过举手之劳，真的不足道 (we just made little effort, really insignificant) as well as a consensus-bearing and cooperative stance 说得太好了……但是大家都来参与，就能凝聚更大的力量！(well spoken…if we all come to participate charity, we can gather greater strength!). By the exchange of views as regards to social welfare 公益无处不在，人人都在参与 (charity is everywhere and everyone may involve), the BOC smartly projects its identity as a socially responsible bank in a way that is more convincing than self-boasted monologue or advertisements.

In Extract 53, an adjacency pair of storytelling/praise-acknowledgement during the firm-follower dialogue, the ascendancy of a specialist identity over other identities of the BOC was co-constructed through the firm-follower interaction. To follow-up the follower "Chen Jing in Singapore" 's sharing filled with emotions: 今天刚到伦敦，机场入关处"中国银行"的广告牌甚是醒目，看着好亲切 (just arrived in London. The Bank of China advertisement at the entrance of the customs office looks so eye-catching, so warm), the BOC well positioned itself as the prestigious bank of global vision and influence with the second dialogic turn 在亚洲、在欧洲、在美洲、在非洲...在您发现精彩世界的路上，中国银行期待与您的温暖邂逅 (in Asia, in Europe, in America, in Africa…wherever on your way to discover the wonderful world, Bank of China looks forward to the warm meeting of you!). This friendly attitude of acknowledgement and confirmation against a real follower's complimentary remark further intensified the BOC's unique and irreplaceable industry status as a global-scale financial institution with geographic facts.

In another case of Extract 54, one of the BOC teller's professional performance won substantial recognition of the follower "Xuhuirebecca" who initiated the firm-follower interaction by @ the BOC voluntarily. The follower shared with one of her pleasant user experience with the Tengzhou branch of the BOC where a great number of her old, broken banknotes were carefully calculated and patiently handled by a teller named Feng Junjian (staff no. 54054). Her praise was soon acknowledged with the BOC's determination to strive for more excellence in service 感谢您对我们服务的肯定,客户的满意就是对全体中行人最大的鼓励 (thank you for recognising our service). Customer satisfaction is the biggest encouragement to the entire BOC staff!" In Extract 54 what has been apparently co-constructed was the BOC's authentic identity as a banking corporation.

Extracts listed herein (48–54) belong to dialogic communication, defined as the "negotiated exchange of ideas and opinions in public relations practice" by Kent

Table 6.4 Initiating and terminating in firm-follower dialogues

Initiating	Followers (active contributor)	Bank
Responding		Followers (active contributor)
Terminating	Bank	Bank

and Taylor (1998, p. 325). Specific dialogic types identified previously, like the adjacency pair of question-raillery and storytelling/praise-acknowledgement, are inherently two-way symmetrical communication, a consequential feature of dialogic communication. Either the questions initiated by the banks or the storytelling or praise initiated by the followers is dialogic and interactional in nature.

Despite the conformity to the tenets of the dialogic communication, a sketch of firm-follower interaction mechanism is outlined in Table 6.4, in view of Goffman's (1976, p. 264) appeal to "the initiating and terminating" of a conversation to be considered as a total unit of communication.

Note that there are two basic interactions mechanism in the firm-follower dialogues, as shown in Table 6.4. Firstly, followers take initiatives and self-select themselves to address the bank, usually with storytelling or praise, and received their replies from the enterprise. In the second type of the interaction mechanism, the bank initiates dialogues, usually by asking questions and eliciting responses from the followers. The enterprise is replied to by the followers' comments, which are subject to the bank's own choice of reposting. The firm-follower dialogue is terminated with the banks' artful use of back-channel cues, "a clear signal that understanding and sympathy have followed this far" (Goffman 1976, p. 275). It is concluded that in both types of interaction mechanism, both corporations performed excellently as the terminator throughout all firm-follower dialogues, rather than leave their followers unresponded.

6.2.2 *Listeners*

Listeners present themselves as loyal fans of corporations by demonstrating their overt likeness and/or reposting bank-labeled updates through which positive politeness and face-work strategies are well demonstrated. The magic of listeners' nonverbal and minimal-efforts interaction resides in the prompt, real and 100% favorable feedbacks to the banks and in the confidence and recognition transmitted to the corporations. Nevertheless, listeners seem to be more self-contained and uncommunicative, as compared to other types of followers who have their own views exchanged with corporations. To scrutinise the listeners' co-construction of corporate identities, the most liked and reposted bank-initiated updates of both banks are listed below for analysis.

Extract 55: #小招微感恩#没错，今天是5份 iPad Air! 有一份比较特殊（详见图）它还包括之前所有礼物！规则没变，快转发&关注我！有招行卡的朋友可以说说咱家的服务感受，没有的朋友请快去感受一下好吗?请#为小招点赞#(ง •̀_•́)ง，快转吧！

贊 (9056)|轉發 (73073)|收藏|評論 (26566) 22112013 11:28 來自新浪微博|舉報

Extract 55: #CMB is grateful# Yes, you have not mistaken, 5 iPad Airs for today! This is particularly special (see photo for greater details)! Rules have no changes and please spread the information and become my follower ASAP! Those who have CMB cards may talk about your opinions and those who do not have would you please go and get one for a personal feel? Please #Click Like for the CMB#(ง •̀_•́)ง, repost it now!

Like (9056)/Repost (73073)/Collect/Comment (26566) CMB 22112013 11:28

Extract 56: #小招微感恩#今天的是文艺小清新福利，5 份拍立得相机礼包哦！规则和昨天一样（详见图），转发扩散&快关注我！如果觉得小招的服务不错就点个赞吧～#为小招点赞#

贊 (3270)|轉發 (8275)|評論 (5039) CMB 20112013 10:01來自新浪微博

Extract 56: #CMB is grateful# Today's welfare is for art lovers and life lovers: 5 instant photo camera packages! The rules are similar to yesterdays' (see photos for details). Please spread the information and become my follower ASAP! If you feel that the CMB service is not so bad, like this post～ #Click Like for the CMB#

Like (3270)/Repost (8275)/Comment (5039) CMB 2011201310:01

Extract 57: 作为前辈，给想要进入银行工作的学弟学妹们一些有用建议，必看！

贊 (699)|轉發 (20564)|評論 (4016) 17102013 20:42 來自专业版微博

Extract 57: As an older comer, I have some useful tips for fresh graduates and about to-be-graduated who wish to work in banks. A must-read article!

Like (699)/Repost (20564)/Comment (4016) CMB17102013 20:42

Extract 58: 【除夕,不放假!】 有专家解释，很多单位在除夕约定俗成地放一天假，并不安排工作，也就成了法定假日之外的1天"隐形假日"。 你享受到"隐形假日"了吗?明天上班的童鞋请转个发，明天放假的请点个赞，看下比例吧～

贊 (482)|轉發 (239)|收藏|評論 (91) CMB 29012014 22:20 來自 iPhone 客户端|舉報

Extract 58: 【Chinese New Year's eve, no day-off! 】 Experts explain that plenty of institutions conventionally allow their employees to take a day off, or an "invisible holiday", apart from other official holidays stipulated by statutory law. Have you enjoyed the "invisible holiday"? Repost it if you have to go to work tomorrow and click like if you do not have to. Let us see the ratio～

Like (482)/Repost (239)/Collect/Comment (91) CMB 29012014 22:20

Extract 59: #中银视界#黄金引领贵金属下跌，叙利亚紧张局势缓解削弱了黄金作为避险资产的需求，金价上涨乏力使得投资者减少 ETF 的持仓，而金价连续跌破多个重要技术位置，打开了一轮回调的空间。 下周美联储 FOMC 将召开会议。 请关注《每日市场点评》之"金价跌破重要支撑，或将迎来深度回调" http://t.cn/z8peGJk

贊 (1)|轉發 (374)|收藏|評論 (3) BOC 13092013 14:49 來自专业版微博|舉報

Extract 59: #BOC Vision# Gold has lead the fall in price of precious metals. The ease of tensions in Syria has weakened demand for gold as a safe-haven asset. The retard of gold price increase allows investors to reduce their possessions of ETF. While the price of gold fell below a number of important technical positions in a row, it in fact opened the round of callbacks space. The Fed's FOMC meeting will be held next week. Please pay attention to our programme "Daily Market Comments", the title of this forecast is "Gold fell below important support that might usher in a deeper correction".

Like (1)/Repost (374)/Collect/Comment (3) BOC 13092013 14:49 from Weibo

Extract 60: 哪一张让你深有同感，请不要吝啬，点个赞哦～ (图片来自网络)

贊 (109)|轉發 (86)|收藏|評論 (20) BOC 24122013 22:16 來自专业版微博|舉報

Extract 60: Which one of them touches you the most, please click like with no hesitation.

Like (109)/Repost (86)/Collect/Comment (20) BOC 24122013 22:16

Extract 61: #双节要和谐# 就在明天，2014 年的情人节和元宵节即将 "狭路相逢"。 是选择浪漫的 "二人世界"，还是温馨的 "合家团圆"? 你是否正在为这个 2014 年的 "最大难题" 而苦恼呢? 快快分享一下你的节日计划吧，@中国银行 还有机会获得精美小礼品呦。

贊 (10)|轉發 (1121)|收藏|評論 (141) BOC 13022014 16:00 來自新浪微博|舉報

Extract 61: #Perfect match of Valentine's Day and the Lantern Festival# Tomorrow in 2014 we see a coincidence of the Western Valentine's Day and the Chinese Lantern Festival. Would you prefer to spend such a memorable day with your significant other or with your parents and families? Are you so worried about this "hardest choice" of 2014? Come quick to share your smart plans with us and win free presents by @ Bank of China. There are opportunities of winning small presents.

Like (10)/Repost (1121)/Comment (141) BOC 13022014 16:00

Like/Repost/Collect/Comment (4) BOC 14022014 18:31

Extract 62: #周年感恩#看到堆积如山的工作就崩溃,有木有! 跳跃错乱的放假模式让人晕菜抓狂，有木有!莫桑心! 小编带来喜大普奔 "强心剂"! @中国银行 官方微博一周年感恩大回馈! 三星手机、 iPad mini 等你拿! 抽个大奖过大节啰! 内什么，还不快来参加! http://t.cn/z8r84TU

贊 (23)|轉發 (908053)|收藏|評論 (303251) BOC 23092013 12:01 來自微活动-#周年感恩…|舉報

Extract 62: #Anniversary thanksgiving# Almost collapsed with piles of work, are you! Complicated vacation scheme drives you crazy, does it! Don't be heartbroken! I bring to you the most exciting "cardiac"! @Bank of China. Anniversary of the BOC corporate Weibo! We have gifts such as Samsung smartphones and iPad minis! Celebrate the festivals with our gifts! Well, what are you waiting for! http://t.cn/z8r84TU

Listeners' liking and reposting serve as a palpable indication of the followers' proactive willingness to establish a least challenging dialogic relationship with the enterprises. It is found that the BOC's likes and reposting rate fell far behind that of the CMB. Followers of the CMB express fairly more enthusiasm in liking and reposting the microblogging updates than those of the BOC. As can be observed, it is updates centering on online marketing activities and branding practices that generate maximum likes and reposting rates in firm-follower interaction. This is equally applicable to both banks, as indicated in Extract 55, 56 and 62 where the banks proudly present themselves as generous financial enterprises equipped with material stimulus 今天是 5 份 iPad Air (5 iPad Airs for today), 三星手机、 iPad mini 等你拿 (Samsung smart phones and iPad minis). Both banks have termed hashtagged columns in the marketing activity for attention attraction and follower participation, e.g., respectively #小招微感恩# (#CMB is grateful#) and #周年感恩# (#BOC's anniversary thanksgiving#).

Apart from the commonalities in terms of likes and reposting between the BOC and the CMB, it is also revealed that a hashtagged column named #中银视界# (BOC vision) achieved a considerable degree of consistent saliency with regard to the reposting rate, though its degree of likes seems to be rather less insignificant. Statistics show that the mean of reposting of the hashtagged column #中银视界# (BOC vision) amounts to 241.4/update, an extraordinary performance that excels from the reposting of unspecific corporate tweets. Listeners' enthusiasm for continuously reposting the #中银视界# (BOC vision) is certainly a sign of recognition and trust, which contributes to co-constructing the BOC's specialist corporate identity and results in the BOC's regularly posting of financial forecast and industry analysis.

The other two highly popular Weibo updates Extracts 55 and 56 identify the CMB as its followers' peer and companion, either kindly providing useful insider experiences and insights to job applicants or concerning about its followers' rights of vacation on the Chinese New Year's Eve. It is concluded that critical events and key timeslots as such, regarding to the followers' self-interest or interest of the general public, are able to trigger super Weibo topics and possess massive dialogic potentials. On the other hand, the followers' emotions, care and exceptional concerns as reflected through the highly favored microblogging contents direct the CMB's awareness and motivation of constructing an identity as the followers' peer and caring companion. This interrelated mechanism is also applicable to the explanation of the BOC's friend-like style and stance, as the Extract 61 exemplifies in greater details.

Notice that likes are accumulated in particularly superlarge numbers as soon as banks call for and invite followers' interaction, for instance in the BOC's appeal of 请不要吝啬, 点个赞哦 (please click like with no hesitation) in Extract 59 and the CMB's invitation 明天上班的童鞋请转个发, 明天放假的请点个赞, 看下比例吧 (repost it if you have to go to work tomorrow and click like if you do not have to. Let us see the ratio) in Extract 58 and 如果觉得小招的服务不错就点个赞吧 (if you feel that the CMB service is not so bad, click like for this post ~) #为小招点赞# (#Click Like for the CMB#) in Extract 56. This has demonstrated the enterprises' conscious and continuous efforts of user engagement, a feature of dialogic propinquity, the exceptionally satisfactory interaction outcome of which is unnoticed otherwise. As "dialogue is a complex and multifarious process" (Kent and Taylor 2002, p. 33), by and large, listeners' interaction in the form of likes and reposts are practices of the tenets of dialogic communication, such as mutuality, empathy, propinquity and commitment, with an overt sense of compliment, supportiveness and acknowledgment. As an effective means of feedback, listeners' interaction on corporate social media quantifies the degree of updates' popularity and plays an imperative role in co-constructing the bank's projected identity, as the interviews in Chap. 7 further affirmed.

6.2.3 Interlocutors

Interlocutors are those who considerably attached to banks in the non face-to-face dialogic interaction, devoting themselves to interact with corporations in the form of unobligated written comments. Unfortunately though, their comments on corporate Weibo can only be viewed with at least one extra click on the bottom of each item of update, and even two or more clicks in many cases if a great number of comments have been accumulated and compiled. Given the information overload at the Weibo interface, it is found that the technical inconvenience of checking interlocutors' comments might prevent possible disseminations of followers' criticism, malicious or ill-mannered comments, thus reducing the risk caused by unedited, real-time published, user-generated content on corporate social media and diminishing the impact of uncontrolled external corporate communication of the corporate public image. In this sense, it might be concluded that interlocutors' comments play less critical and defining roles in co-constructing the banks' identities, in comparison to those of active contributors and listeners.

Extract 63:

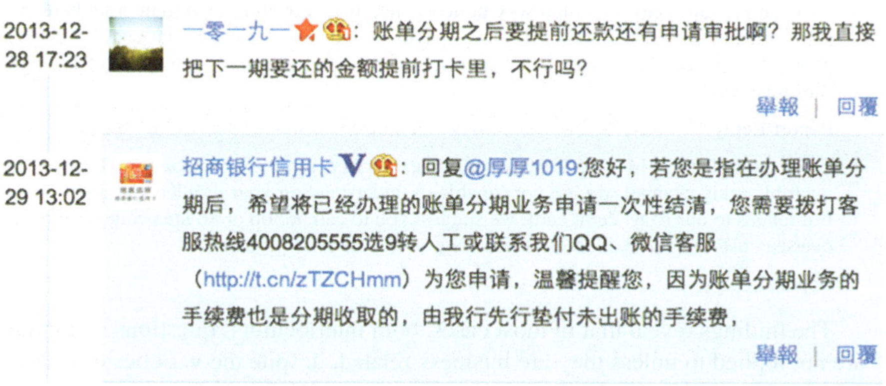

Extract 63: 28122013 17:23 一零一九一: In terms of the installment payment, do I have to apply for the CMB's approval in the case of prepayment? Can I just credit this month the amount of money due next month to my credit card?

Report/Reply

29122013 13:02 CMB credit card reply @ 一零一九一: Hello, if you sincerely wish to pay your loans back in a lump sum, given prior installment payment contract, you might need to make contact the CMB customer service hotline via 4008205555. Select 9 to connect to customer officer or contact our QQ and WeChat customer service (http://t.cn/zTZCHmm). A warm reminder to you that the service fee of your bill under installment is also charged by installment.

Report/Reply

Extract 64:

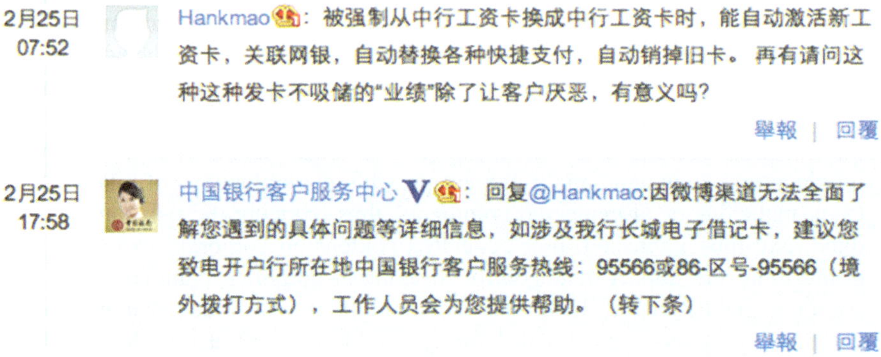

Extract 64:

25022014 07:52 Hankmao: As a compulsory user of the BOC salary card, I feel disgusted about BOC's all types of compulsory policies, automatically connected to internet banking, automatically prioritise all other means of payment and cancel the old salary card… Such a poor performance disgusts the BOC clients, how meaningful is this "new growth" of credit card business?

Report/Reply

Extract 64: 25022014 17:58 BOC: customer service reply @ Hankmao: Through the microblogging channel, we are not capable of understanding your problems in great detail. If it relates to our BOC debit card, we suggest you to call 95566 or 86 area code 95566 (for overseas users). Our staff shall be assisting you with your problems.

Report/Reply

The findings reveal that in most cases, both interlocutors' questions and inquiries are not replied to unless they are business-related, despite the varieties of followers' questions, comments and complaints on the banks' Weibo. In fact, the banks are not well versed and favourably disposed in addressing their followers with an individualised, conversational human voice. Consequently, the ascendancy of the authentic identity as a banking service purveyor of the CMB and the BOC may be viewed as a negative and even disruptive factor in the firm-follower interaction, although the dialogic types or adjacency pairs vary from extract to extract, as the inquiry/question-answer and criticism-follow-up/suggestion examples in the extracts show. From an interlocutor's inquiry 账单分期之后要提前还款还有申请审批啊 (In terms of the installment payment, do I have to apply for the CMB's approval in the case of prepayment?) in Extract 63 and the criticism on service quality in 请问这种发卡不吸储的"业绩"除了让客户厌恶，有意义吗? (such a poor performance disgusts the BOC clients, how meaningful is this "new growth" of credit card business?) in Extract 64, it is observed that the banks' responses remained homogeneous, and are characterised as formal, polite, cliché and formulaic call-center expressions, aimed at reinforcing its customer service image, with considerable use of honorifics—"您" in Chinese is a more respectful address form than "you" and "请" (please), as the contextualization cue for a businesslike relationship in corporate-follower dialogues. In fact, both corporate Weibo deployed a specialised customer service team to take complete care of the followers' comments, namely the CMB long-distance banking center and the BOC's customer service center. In so doing, banks take on a much more distant and official footing in relation to against their interlocutors. In response to the interlocutors, both the CMB and the BOC have taken off their "mask" and have their "real-life identities" entirely exposed (Androutsopoulos 2006b, p. 423). That is, the interlocutors' comments seem to be merely co-constructing the banks' real identities as no more than financial service purveyors, as many of their interpersonal orientated comments are primarily left unattended. As Kent and Taylor (2002) stated, there are two means of incorporating dialogue into public relations practice: building interpersonal relationships and building mediated dialogic relationships. Evidentially, the CMB and the BOC's performance in dealing with their interlocutors implies a lack of interpersonal orientation, notwithstanding the over-arching principles of dialogue, including mutuality, propinquity, commitment and empathy might be applicable too (see Kent and Taylor 2002), but without any traces of a conversational human voice (Keller and Miller 2006).

6.2.4 Lurkers

Lurkers constitute the majority of the follower audience, yet they do not physically participate in any dialogues with corporations. Although invisible in interaction, they are a real audience for whom the presentation of corporate identity are rehearsed and performed. Nonetheless, as their activity on corporate Weibo can only be traced from Weibo internal statistics, lurkers' behaviors are beyond the scope of discussion in the present study. In regard to the considerable number of lurkers, their silent presence itself are motivations of corporate Weibo, as an in-depth interview has disclosed that the browsing of corporate Weibo as a unique, internalised interaction might be activated for dialogues with corporations at anytime, given the appropriate occasion and outlet.

6.3 Summary

Despite the limitation of dialogue turns, it is revealed that the two corporations dialogues with its followers not only in theory perfectly conforms to the tenets of dialogic communication of Kent and Taylor (2002) and Health et al. (2006), but also in practice resemble naturally occurring face-to-face conversations among good friends. Throughout the firm-follower dialogues in Extract 48–61, both the CMB and the BOC seek to establish some kind of an affinity between themselves and followers as the general public, echoing the TV presenters' strategies of "claiming common identity with audiences and intentional projection of an attractive personality" (Fairclough 1995b, p. 128).

In conclusion, on the corporate social media, the practices of dialogic communication not only may be located but also are prevalent in the timely firm-follower conversations, which are essentially two-way systematical communication instead of enterprises' one-way monologic persuasion and self-boasting. The embodiment of the characteristics of dialogic communication that can be specified in the BOC and the CMB's Weibo is inclusive of the linguistic style, tones, emoticons, the use of photos as well as other intertextual and hypertextual resources…, all functioning as contextualization cues to signal the egalitarianism, sincerity, open-mindedness, mutual benefit and interactivity that are pervasive in the firm-follower dialogues. For example, the motivation of followers' self-initiation in the interaction with enterprise, as represented in the Extract 49 and 53, is an excellent demonstration of the tenet of dialogic commitment to conversations and the tenet of mutuality. The firm-follower dialogues in the Extract 48–64 are indications of the fact that the atmosphere of corporate social media largely resembles the environment of offline, face-to-face interaction amongst acquaintances and friends, where listening, speaking, mind exchanging, information-sharing, emotion-sharing and solution-seeking are focused, invited, engaged and attended to.

Nevertheless, the other side of the coin is in instant need of special attentions as the tenet of dialogic risk also resides in the firm-follower social media dialogues. As Theunissen and Noordin (2012) pinpointed, a dialogue with the public might incur disagreement rather than the intended agreement and expose differences and the risk of dialogic communication entails the understanding of and the preparation for the "vulnerability, unanticipated consequences and the recognition of the strange otherness" (p.) The risk of dialogic communication on corporate social media, as represented in the uncontrollability of follower-generated questions, in the tart complaints of followers and the unsatisfactory reply of the enterprise in the Extract 63 as well as in the millions of followers' unreplied comments, might cast a shadow over the corporate identity construction and relationship building with the public.

In summary, both conversation analysis and the theory of dialogic communication offered powerful tools for examining followers' interaction that allows for the co-construction of corporate identity. There is evidence to support that dialogues with followers enabled the co-construction of corporate identities and that the co-construction process has witnessed a double-edged sword in dialogic communication. Having benefited from establishing a dialogic relationship with the followers in the corporate identity co-construction, the enterprises are also confronted with the Achille's heel of dialogic communication, namely the risk arising from such real-time firm-follower dialogues.

Although the CMB is much more dialogic than the BOC in the firm-follower integration, the undialogic, formal and rigid replies of both enterprise to their followers' comments in regard to banking business were detected as the biggest loophole of firm-follower interaction. It is also found that banks are in partial control of the followers' co-construction of corporate identity, as manifested in the reposting right and replies to the active followers' comments. While the CMB's companion identity and interpersonal relationship are substantially reinforced in the jesting style firm-follower dialogues, the BOC's authentic and industry specialist identity is also strengthened through the praise-acknowledgment interaction with its followers. Simultaneously, the CMB's authentic identity has also been brought into play in many cases of tease and jesting dialogues, leading to a hybridised presentation of the bank's identity, rather than a clear-cut split between the companion CMB versus the specialist BOC throughout the co-construction process of corporate identity. Listeners' interaction in the form of likes and reposting confirms that the CMB outweighs the BOC in favorable feedbacks of followers. Further, the banks' repetitive non-interpersonal dialogues with interlocutors display the weakest characteristics of dialogic communication, (e.g., in commitment) in both banks' cases calling for improvement in effectively dealing with the followers' comments. Finally, note that a follower might simultaneously take up more than one role in the dialogic communication with the enterprise, by both clicking like or reposting as a listener and leaving comments as an interlocutor. Apart from the tiny proportion of follower interaction that might be motivated for the purpose of materialistic gifts, followers undertake their unobligated free-will dialogic communication with the corporations that co-shape the corporate identity.

Chapter 7
Cross-Bank Variations in Corporate Identity Construction

7.1 Introduction

The current chapter has two major components. The variations of corporate identity construction between the state-owned BOC and the joint-equity CMB were examined in details. Second, first-hand, in-depth qualitative interviews with the media creators of corporate Weibo shed light on their original communicative intentions of their corporate identity.

7.2 Variations of Identity Construction Between the State-Owned BOC and the Joint-Equity CMB

A comparison of the corporate identities projected on the corporate Weibo of the state-owned BOC and the joint-equity CMB is summarised in the Table 7.1.

As Table 7.1 illustrated, parallels between the BOC and the CMB regarding their corporate identity on social media were clearly discovered that there were equally five major categories of identities present in each bank's Weibo updates: the authentic identity, the specialist identity, the companion identity, the journalist identity and the identity as a socially responsible bank. The two banks showed statistical difference in the overall identity types. Despite of parallels, one of the most striking variance lies in the percentage of the specialist identity: while the BOC considerably demonstrated a preference of the specialist identity with 40.1% of all Weibo updates (573 items), only 1.2% updates were characteristic of the specialist identity on the CMB's Weibo (16 items). Secondly, the CMB evinced a generally positive attitude towards the journalist identity with 20.9% or 290 items of updates, approximately 2.5 times the percentage of the BOC's journalist identity (123 items or 8.6%). Thirdly, the apparent centrality of social media self-presentation of the CMB was the sweeping percentage of the companion

W. Feng, *Discursive Constructions of Corporate Identities by Chinese Banks on Sina Weibo*, DOI 10.1007/978-981-10-4469-4_7

Table 7.1 Comparison of corporate identity between the CMB and the BOC

	CMB		BOC		Pearson Chi-square
Identity types	No. of updates	%	No. of updates	%	
Authentic identity	214	15.4	270	18.9	800.22[a]
Specialist identity	16	1.2	573	40.1	
Companion identity	825	59.5	368	25.8	
Journalist identity	290	20.9	123	8.6	
CSR identity	30	2.2	83	5.8	

[a] $p < 0.01$

Note The corporate identity No. 2 and No. 4 have been converged to the specialist identity in this table

identity amongst the five identity types (59.5%), which doubled that of the BOC's (25.8%). In other words, the findings suggested a saliency between the corporate identities of the two banks, namely the BOC's construction of an authoritative identity versus the CMB's construction of a companion identity.

The investigations also highlighted that the heterogeneous identities of the two Chinese banks do not necessarily corroborate with Men and Tsai's (2012) claim that many Chinese companies have adopted the single tone of a caring friend in their SNS (social networking site) communications and a prior study suggesting that Turkish banks empolyed the single "casual fun tone" on social media (Ozdora-Aksak and Atakan-Duman 2015, p. 126). Despite the corporate identity as a caring friend is indeed overwhelmingly evidenced on the corporate social media, other corporate identities, e.g. the specialist corporate identity and the journalistic identity, that are carefully presented should not be ignored. A further exploration of Men and Tsai (2012), the present study confirmed the complexity of the degree of 'caring', which might dramatically vary between the two selected banking corporations (e.g. 25.8% for the BOC versus 59.5% for the CMB). It is argued that one important reason for such variations may be attributed to the economic ownership, company history and industry status, i.e., the BOC's long-standing state-owned status as industry giant versus the CMB's status as the first joint-equity bank with a two-decade history.

It is worth noting that the BOC has long established its fame and status as one of the earliest and world-class banks in China since 1912, specialising in foreign exchange. The century-old history of the BOC and its historical role of the nation's central bank have a significant impact on the market positioning and brand strategy of the present-day BOC, reflected through the concise and consistent advertising slogan 百年中行，全球服务 (century-old Bank of China, global service). Established on 5th Feb., 1912, one month after the foundation of the Republic of China on 1st Jan., 1912, the state-owned BOC shouldered a triparitite structure of responsibilities: as the central bank of China, the bank of foreign exchange and the bank of international trading. In the 1920s, the BOC commenced its ambitious target of operating on the global markets, focusing on the overseas remittance and exchange business, leading to its international debut, i.e. the establishment of the BOC's London office in 1929. As the fifth largest bank in the world by market capitalisation value, as of 2015, the BOC had operated business in its 11368 branches located in the Chinese mainland and 644 branches located in 46 nations and regions and had cooperative partner relations with over 1500 international banks. The overseas share of assets and profitability accounted for over 22% in totality, a percentage much more higher than the average level in the nation's banking sector. At present, the BOC's immense profitability relies on its long-standing international brand strategy, aiming at both the MNC (multinational corporations) customers in the developed worlds, e.g., the Europe, the United States and Japan as well as Chinese corporations as investors in the world's developing nations and regions.

The BOC's exclusive high-end identities were delivered daily or every two days through its regular hashtagged columns such as 中银动态 (News of BOC), 中银视界 (BOC Vision), 黄金市场 (Gold market) and 每日汇评 (Comments on the daily foreign exchange), updating its followers with in-depth professional analysis and financial forecasts. It is the BOC's specialism in foreign exchange that gives rise to the abovementioned hashtagged columns that contribute to the BOC's exclusive identities as a long-standing, worldwide and best-performing authoritative financial specialist. Noticeably, the linguistic style, which accords with the BOC's high-end identities (specialist and journalist identity), by no means involves the "playing cuteness", the sweeping conversational style on the CMB's corporate Weibo. On the contrary, a reporting, official linguistic style, full of financial jargons and long noun phrases, is allied with the BOC's identities as a financial specialist and long-standing, worldwide and best-performing bank.

The reason why the CMB downplayed the specialist identity on the social media may be attributed to the fact that the CMB is self-positioned in the market as the innovative e-bank and retail bank targeting at the nation's emerging high-income group. Founded in 1987, it is the first share-holding commercial bank wholly owned by corporate legal entities in China, rather than owned by the government of China as in the case of the BOC. The inadequacy of the CMB's non-virtual branch is supplemented by the availability of its powerful Internet banking service "Free Net Phone" (一网通 in Chinese) and mobile phone banking service. As of 2015, the CMB had topped all joint-equity banks in the nation (e.g., the China Mingsheng Bank, the Citic Bank of China etc.) in terms of offline branch size with 1770 branches in China's 120 cities and 5 cities overseas, a scale far from adequacy and less than 10% as compared to that of the BOC. According to the CMB statistics, over 93% retail banking transactions are conducted over self-service channels, inclusive of the Internet banking, mobile phone banking and ATM, leaving the 7% business transactions taking place in the over 1770 branches and sub-branches. The CMB's marketing strategy of e-banking and VIP retail bank echoed its service-based values and advertising slogan 因您而变 (We are here just for you). Taking full consideration of the emotional appeal of its mainstream customers, the CMB laid emphasis on the companionship of its brand persona on the corporate social media.

The CMB's companion identity was primarily manifested in the chicken-soup-for-the-soul updates. Chicken soup for the soul, originally a thumbs-up book series published in the U.S.A. in the 1990s, roughly refers to the warm, philosophical, touching and usually inspiring and encouraging (though sentimental) stories or style of writing. An operational definition of it for the present study is the microblogging updates that are characterised as inspirational, emotion-stirring philosophical remarks on life, love, and career. The meaning of life, happiness, and pressure release were discovered to be "eternal" topics of chicken-soup-for-the-soul updates on the CMB.

Extract 65: 一个人真正富足的状态应该是: 见多识广朋友多, 不缺吃穿不缺钱。会被一件漂亮的衣服让自己开心, 会因为吃到可口的美食而一扫阴霾, 不大惊小怪, 却仍会为每一种细碎的美好感动, 做最快乐的自己。 晚安!

贊 (38)|轉發 (268)|收藏|評論 (40) CMB 09012014 23:09 來自新浪微博|舉報

Extract 65: A person's true state of abundance should be: well-informed and with a large circle of friends, no shortage of clothes and money. Satisfaction can be realised by owning an item of pretty clothes. A blue mood may be ameliorated by a delicious gourmet meal. Be used to not making a fuss any more, yet will still be moved by fragments of goodness. Be the happiest you can be. Good night!

Like (38)/Repost (268)/Collect/Comments (40) CMB 09012014 23:09 from Sina Weibo

Extract 66: 孩子, 我要求你读书用功, 不是因为我要你跟别人比成绩, 而是因为, 我希望你将来会拥有选择的权利, 选择有意义、有时间的工作, 而不是被迫谋生。当你的工作在你心中有意义, 你就有成就感。当你的工作给你时间, 不剥夺你的生活, 你就有尊严。成就感和尊严, 给你快乐。(龙应台) 晚安!

贊 (66)|轉發 (523)|收藏|評論 (40) CMB 09122013 23:00 來自 iPhone 客户端|舉報

Extract 66: My child, my request for you to study hard has nothing to do with comparing your grades with others, but rather, I wish that you are entitled with a variety of choices of yourself for a meaningful job that allows you plenty of time, instead of being expelled to make a living for survival. You will be entitled with a sense of achievement if your job triggers meaning in your life. When your job offers you time to achieve, rather than stealing your time away, you will own enough dignity. A sense of achievement and dignity are accompanied by a joy of life. (by Long Yingtai) Good night!

Like (66)/Repost (523)/Collect/Comment (40) CMB 09012014 23:00 from iPhone app.

Extract 67: 人生需要"归零"。 每过一段时间, 都要将过去 "清零", 让自己重新开始。不要让过去成为现在的包袱, 轻装上阵才能走得更远。 删除心灵的垃圾, 每天刷新自己, 这样才能重获新生。 晚安～

贊 (43)|轉發 (169)|收藏|評論 (47) CMB 05012014 23:03 來自 iPhone 客户端|舉報

Extract 67: Life needs to be "zeroed". From time to time, we have to make our past "zeroed" in order to let ourselves restart. Do not permit the past to become a burden on your present life. Travelling light enables the journey further. Delete trashes of soul and refresh yourself each day, in an attempt for rebirth. Good night～

Like (43)/Repost (169)/Collect/Comment (47) CMB 05012014 23:03 from iPhone app.

Excerpt 65 introduced an innovative definition of wealthiness: "being well-informed and having a large circle of friends, no shortage of food, clothes and money", which is apparently in stark contrast to the take-for-granted, worldly assumptions of materialistic success and abundance. This definition is then illustrated with two instances: 会被一件漂亮的衣服让自己开心，会因为吃到可口的美食而一扫阴霾 (Satisfaction can be realised by owning an item of pretty clothes. A blue mood may be ameliorated by a delicious gourmet meal). It was also found that the CMB irregularly quotes writer's words of wisdom in their updates, conforming to the style of chicken-soup-for-the-soul, as typified in Excerpt 66. Dr. Long Yingtai, the renowned Taiwanese scholar and writer, is widely respected and appreciated for her unique, inspiring perceptions on life, love and culture. To cite Dr. Long's philosophy of parenting, in a tongue not as a writer but as a mother, the CMB stirs the maximum consensus from its followers with the initial suggestion 孩子，我要求你读书用功，不是因为我要你跟别人比成绩，而是因为，我希望你将来会拥有选择的权利， 选择有意义、有时间的工作， 而不是被迫谋生 (my child, my request for you to study hard has nothing to do with comparing your grades with others, but rather, I wish that you are entitled with a variety of choices of yourself for a meaningful job that allows you plenty of time, instead of being expelled to make a living for survival) and the conclusion 成就感和尊严，给你快乐 (sense of achievement and dignity are accompanied with a joy of life). Extract 67 is a piece of advice illuminating how the pressures of life should be released, metaphorically using computer science terms for a key of fashion in the communication effect, such as 删除心灵的垃圾，每天刷新自己 (delete trashes of soul and refresh yourself each day).

In contemporary China where middle-class individuals are pressurised for material success and increasingly prominent social status, their children are faced with even more accelerating peer pressures incurred by the complex of elite education, the CMB's "therapy" in Extract 66 offered the understanding, inspiration, warmth and companionship, all of which are ideal qualities one eagerly expects from a friendship. Notice the time of the Extract 65, 66 and 67, which was consistently around 11 pm. As Wu and Feng (2015) observed, emotional branding on social media is presented in many forms, one salient feature being the transition of targeting the market to targeting the moment. In the midst of the tide of emotional branding, social media followers' emotions are triggered synchronically with the corporations' real-time reference to current events on issues of general interest or with reference to simply a special time slot, such as each morning or an ongoing wave of a sports event fanaticism (e.g., the FIFA World Cup). The findings have verified their assertions that the CMB tactfully seized the time slot of going to bed and greet its followers "good night" each day, with caring and philosophical remarks in the extracts 65–67. By targeting at 23:09 pm, a rather private moment, away from work and perhaps with some reading on hand, the CMB's "good night" branded chicken soup is an excellent manifestation of targeting the critical moment of self-reflection at night for the spiritual inspiration and satisfaction. In summary, the chicken-soup-for-the-soul updates enabled the CMB to outperform the BOC in constructing a companion and soul mate-like identity that emotionally hooks tight the followers.

7.3 Interview Insights of Corporate Identity Construction: Insider Stories

7.3.1 The Interview with the BOC

7.3.1.1 Two Critical Identities the BOC Wishes to Construct

A senior manager in charge of the BOC Weibo (hereinafter Mr. S) and a front-line content creator and editor of the CMB corporate Weibo (hereinafter Miss Z) participated in separate interviews for the present study in order to release some insider stories.

Mr. S confirmed frankly that the most critical identity of the BOC on its corporate Weibo should be its real identity, presumably as a financial products seller, and the key identity as a financial specialist, these two roles being the most authentic and realistic in the social media environment. Mr. S confessed: "other identities that may emerge, such as the companion identity, as you call it, and the identity as a socially responsible bank in the minds of followers are in fact the ideal and objectives for us to work for, which are hard to be realised. The two identities I talked about just now are at the heart of the BOC corporate Weibo: the authentic and the specialist identity." In perfect conformity to the BOC's century-old history is the specialist identity, anything associated with which might be critical resources for the BOC on its corporate Weibo, as Mr. S added.

A paradox of the BOC's social media identities is interestingly unveiled as Mr. S attempted to manage his strand of thoughts. At one level, Mr. S admitted that the companion identity is more like an ideal that each corporation strives to achieve in the self-presentation and firm-follower dialogues, although it seems to be a necessary element of a corporate identity. That is, it is unrealistic and far from possible if a companion identity is placed ahead of any other identities. On the other hand, however, Mr. S corrected himself and stated that they wished to achieve a companion relationship with followers, aspiring for the BOC not only to be accepted but also to accumulate new followers on the Weibo. The cruxes of the BOC, as was inferred in the interview, is no more than a weigh-in between a realistic self and an ideal self, grounded in a full-ranged objective self-reflection. Nonetheless, Mr. S made a comparison of the firm-follower relationship to be "lifelong partner relations", focusing on the service role of a bank that runs throughout an individual's entire life, from the cradle to the grave. Hence, a true service provider is nothing but meaningful to the BOC staff. Concerning the constitution of updates, except for the specialist financial columns reported by the BOC analysts, other non-business related contents, as Mr. S named, belong to "garnish updates", including life experience sharing updates. This implied that the finance-related specialist contents as their main course otherwise, as he added, the contents might be too "hard" to digest. In the end, Mr. S confessed to the confoundedness of his team in posing for playing cuteness, as a means to construct a companion identity in the context of Weibo. Although the media creators of the BOC might wish to play cuteness on corporate social media, in practice they are confronted with difficulties in achieving it, e.g., in his own words "倒是想萌，萌不起来啊" (indeed playing cuteness is desirable but cuteness is hard to play). In brief, the interviewed indicated that the glorious history and specialism of the BOC preset a tune of seriousness, formality and professionalism, to some degree hurdling the penetration and success of the image of a cute companion. In the conclusion, Mr. S reasserted the predominance of the specialist identity: "the specialist identity has to be prominent, otherwise who would trust you?" To comply with such a specialist identity, a key of authoritativeness of the BOC has to be adopted in the media creation process on the Weibo. In sum, while the media creators of the BOC strengthened its specialist identity, they did not relinquish the easygoing companion identity, though the BOC had difficulty in playing cuteness in order to accomplish the companion identity construction.

7.3.1.2 Corporate Identity Co-construction of the BOC Followers

The in-depth interviews of the BOC's Mr. S have indeed suggested that followers' interactions do play a key role in co-shaping corporate identity through the corporations' creation of microblogging contents, as identities can be dependent on the nature and varieties of media contents. Mr. S of the BOC affirmed that followers' interactions provide "rather useful feedback and hints" to their selection and creation of Weibo contents, by which corporate identities are constructed anyway. He said their usual practice of "pondering over the reason why the followers show a preference of certain updates over others" enabled the BOC to trace followers' behavioral habits and ultimately their thinking habits. The updates with a large number of likes and reposts indeed play a recognition role, to indicate followers' attention and reading interest. In the process of researching followers reading behaviors, not only Weibo contents but also the linguistic style of contents are taken into consideration. Mr. S explicated the procedures in this way: "we conduct a small-scale analysis of our own updates and user feedbacks every month and a large-scale analysis every three months. Roughly, we have categorised our updates into three areas: business information, marketing activities and non-business information, such as current events or interesting stuff." By business information he meant Weibo updates that entail soft marketing contents. Afterwards, Mr. S and his team members were actively engaged in evaluating which type of contents proved to be more attractive than others. For example, in terms of marketing activities, through which the authentic identity as a banking corporation was constructed, conclusions were drawn from scratch, indicated by the number of likes, reposts and sometimes comments. Meanwhile Mr. S conveyed his concern and bothersome experience of checking each comment of followers, which could be endless and irrelevant to the posted items of updates. But likes and reposts could be much easier to grasp than comments, which are shown in their numerical forms only.

In the face-to-face interview, Mr. S further explained that: "we would reflect and think about from time to time why an interactive marketing activity on the BOC's Weibo turn to be popular or unpopular among our followers. If it is unattractive to followers, is it because this activity is hard to participate in or because the material benefits and awards are not good enough. Or is it simply because the design of the marketing activity is hard to understand and so cannot attract followers' attention and interest, as those with a higher reposting rate must have gained more attention and be of more interest." In addition to the design, he said language use was subject to their reflection too. He summarised that there are a few numbers worth noting: likes, reposts, comments and increase of followers. As was disclosed by Mr. S, Weibo updates that are characterised with marketing activities are found to have a determining impact on the expansion of followers. Based upon their regular analysis, Mr. S and his team surveyed on this causality and discovered surprisingly that a single marketing activity could contribute the BOC Weibo a sum of new followers from 20,000 to tens of thousands. It is implied that the dèbut of the BOC's impression management as a generous bank must be one of the main reasons. In summary of Mr. S's remarks, the followers' interaction served as the propellant of the optimisation of their corporate identity performance, and while unfortunately it was hard to be precise with such an optimisation, as "the firm-follower interaction is still a water-testing process for us".

7.3.2 *The Interview with the CMB*

7.3.2.1 Brand Personality of the CMB

An interview with the CMB was conducted for ethnography-like data collection. One of the CMB's front-editors, Miss Z, started the interview with a remembrance of the CMB's identity transition on Sina Weibo. She reported that on the whole, the initial self-presentation of the CMB was a man of career success in his mid-30s, which has transformed to the present twenty-something vivacious, lovely and urban girl over the years. The delicate change was manifested both in the language use and in the contents. In terms of the language choice, Miss Z admitted that they intentionally play cuteness on its corporate Weibo with an emphasis on the most fashionable netspeak expressions, for the CMB precisely presents itself as twenty-something vivacious, lovely and urban girl.

This interview revealed that the companion identity serves as the most critical one that the CMB aspired to, ahead of the journalistic identity and others, with a specialist identity being the weakest in terms of desirability on its corporate social media. Miss Z elaborated that a prime concern for the construction of a companion identity was largely derived from the relaxing and youthful nature of Weibo in general, while the CMB does have other channels to cater for the communication needs of senior clients. Furthermore, a companion identity accords with the CMB's innovative and youthful corporate culture and image, an intangible possession of the CMB brand widely known to both insiders and laymen. Miss Z exemplified the companion identity through updates of the chicken-soup-for-the-soul style. While they once considered cancelling the column of such a style, their own research found that it in fact considerably helped to form its followers' habit of reading of the CMB updates. For the sake of companion relationship building, chicken–soup-for-the-soul updates were well retained and developed, and have now become its followers' "rigid demand" of checking the CMB Weibo in Miss Z's words. The CMB followers' consistent reposts and comments towards chicken-soup-for-the-soul updates are the best confirmation of its heart-touching effect.

7.3.2.2 Dialogic Communication with the CMB Followers

Likewise, the CMB has taken initiatives to adapt itself to the interaction with followers, as Miss Z stated: "we make our changes in accordance with the changes of our followers". She argued that the co-shaping of corporate identity was a two-sided coin. On the one hand, the CMB presumes and predicts the interest of followers before the issuance of Weibo updates and conducts the post hoc analysis for improvement and optimisation to find out "what can be added and what else can be reduced and deleted". On the other hand, Miss Z discovered that the CMB's new media creators are very aware of the cultivation of the loyalty of its followers. The CMB's media creators have their own observations as regards to the various means of interactivity. While pinpointing the transition of corporate Weibo, as noted earlier, Miss Z stressed the transformation of follower interactivity. At the advent of Weibo in 2010, people were thrilled with its interesting contents, thus leading to "an exceptional rate of reposting and comments" over a short time span. As time went on, consumer behaviors altered to be increasingly inclined to a simple click of "like", and followers were much less active in reposting and commenting. Miss Z even alleged that it was not realistic to make judgments of interactivity based on the numbers of reposts and comments, since a large proportion of followers do nothing on the corporate Weibo besides browsing. Unless there is a public event triggering resonance, followers' reposting and commenting behaviors would soar correspondingly, such as during the Olympic games.

The interview with Miss Z discovered that in firm-follower relationships, a dialogic communication had been realised in practice over the past four years of development of the CMB Weibo. At the very beginning, when Weibo was initially launched, the CMB took great caution in replying to followers' comments, primarily in formulaic and polite clichés, and the standard tone of customer service, such as "how can I help you?" and "hello and you" in their honorifics in Chinese. Looking back, Miss Z stated that in those early days it was not firm-follower interaction in the true sense. Later on, as mutual understanding deepened, Miss Z and her team members were less prudent in their responses to follower's comments, and began to take an equal stance when addressing them, in other words, "which is interaction in the true sense".

A prerequisite of dialogic communication, as Miss Z summarised, resided in the attitude of communication: 招行接地气、不端着 (the CMB is down-to-earth and has long got off from her high horse)". According to Miss Z, the CMB's dialogic attitude was manifested in ways as specified below. First, the youthful and lively nature of her team, exposed to similar waves of up-to-date flows of information on social media, made it possible to fall into social media conversations with the CMB's followers. Second, continuous interaction experience taught her team that friend-like dialogues with followers are preferred over any other means of interactive forms. She described the commonality between themselves and their followers as "they and us essentially belong to the same age group. We are peers and have no difficulty in interaction". Third, the characteristics of social media fit into a dialogic communication between the CMB and its followers. Miss Z added that other channels of corporate communication might be suitable for presenting an authoritative image for the deference of others (e.g. press conference), but definitely not through the CMB's social media. Meanwhile she admitted that they learned a lot and kept learning from other enterprises' firm-follower interaction on their corporate Weibo on how to create dialogues and respond to followers. Up to now, the interaction with followers has developed into a quite natural and everyday component of Miss Z and her colleagues' workload.

7.4 The Link Between the Textual Evidence and the Interviews

The interviews affirmed and supported the textual findings in a number of ways. First, the interviews disclosed the variations of image projection between the two selected banks with distinctive ownership difference. While Mr. S admitted that the century-old history of the BOC somehow hurdled the identity of a cute companion, the Miss Z of the CMB stressed the significance of establishing an equal, friend-like companionship on social media, which she regarded as a breakthrough and innovation in the corporate communication via social media.

Second, the textual evidence paved the way for interviews, as both interviewees demonstrated no explicit objection towards the textual findings, i.e., the multiple identities specified from their social media updates. Mr. S explicitly conceded the existence of their specialist, authentic, companion and CSR identity, based on which the first two identities were what he prioritised for the communicative intensions on the social media interaction with followers. Similarly, the brand personality delineated by Miss Z of the CMB, which is a twenty-something vivacious, lovely and urban girl, perfectly suits the dominant companion identity located in the textual findings. Furthermore, the confession of Miss Z's intentional playing cuteness clearly indicated their orientation and construction of the companion identity.

7.5 Summary

All and all, the much-needed interviews have sustained the present study with sufficient, situated and contextual information that the findings of the research questions may be accurately grounded on. In summary, on the basis of both the textual and interview findings, this chapter examined the corporate identity variations lying between the selected banks: the BOC and the CMB. The most noteworthy interbank difference in corporate identity construction is found in the existence of a primacy in the CMB's corporate Weibo-the companion identity-but not in the BOC's Weibo, where the specialist identity plays a more significant part than the compaion identity and the authentic identity. In-depth interviews shed new light on the rationale for the banks' construction of corporate identities. However, as differently projected on social media, both corporations intentionally conveyed their strengths and avoided their own weaknesses, in the communication of 'who they are' with their followers. It is also implied through the interviews that the construction of the desired corporate identities is consistent with the respective market positioning of the two banks. To conclude, a complete hybrid, the state-owned heritage brand BOC takes pride in projecting its status as the industry specialist and giant, whereas the joint-equity brand CMB is more skillfully adjusted to the overall 'playing cuteness' atmosphere of social media and has successfully created an intimate companion identity to target followers of the younger generation.

Chapter 8
Conclusion

8.1 Introduction

The final chapter consists of three sections. First, this chapter concludes the research with a summary of the main findings, namely the answers to each research questions under scrutiny. Second, based on the present findings, the relevant discussion has been expanded to include broader realms of corporate identity research and research of public relations on social media. Ultimately, the research ended with a report of the research limitations and implications for future research.

8.2 Summary of the Main Findings

This section summarises the key findings of the present study, i.e., the answers to the four research questions raised in Chap. 3.

RQ1: By means of corporate Weibo updates, what identities have the two Chinese banks constructed?

Except for the authentic identity as a financial institution, a number of humanised identities were identified on the corporate Weibo of the BOC and the CMB. Specifically, approximately 60% (59.5%, 825 items) of the joint-equity CMB's updates seek to present the bank as primarily a companion (an intimate, witty and caring friend), followed by the journalistic identity realised in almost one fifth of the updates (20.9%, 290 items). The third most prominent identity is the authentic identity as a financial product seller or a financial institution, actualised in about 15% (15.4%, 214 items) amongst the total updates. The remaining two identities are weak enough, as the CSR identity and the specialist identity account for merely 2.2% (30 items) and 1.2% (16 items) respectively on the CMB's corporate Weibo.

W. Feng, *Discursive Constructions of Corporate Identities by Chinese Banks on Sina Weibo*, DOI 10.1007/978-981-10-4469-4_8

By contrast, the state-ownd BOC has laid differentiated emphasis in the self-presentation on social media. The most noticeable identity, represented by 573 items or 40.1% of the entire updates, falls into the specialist identity, inclusive of the identity as an authoritative financial specialist and as a long-standing, world-wide, best-performing bank. Secondly, the companion identity of the BOC as an intimate, witty and caring friend of the followers is projected through 368 items, taking up 25.8% of the BOC tweets. Thirdly, the unmarked authentic identity of the BOC is related to 270 items or 18.9% of the total contents. The fourth journalist identity, informing the CMB's followers of informative news reports, especially relating to financial and economic domains, accounts for 8.60% in proportion. The weakest CSR identity is reflected through merely 83 tweets, a slightest coverage of 5.8% amongst the BOC contents.

It is worth noting that on social media, the authentic identity of both banks as a financial institution has been significantly downplayed to account for approximately 20% of the total updates, which entails that brand communication on social media is substantially oriented to the long-term relationship building, rather than a short-time sales pitch. By means of a wide variety of interpersonal contents on the corporate social media such as news items, prose and chicken-soup-for-the-soul remarks, the 'fake' identities of corporations, e.g. the companion identity and specialist identity of Chinese banks, are actualised in the follower's habitual daily browsing of their personal social media accounts where the followers' real-world friends' updates and virtual humanised corporate updates are mingled together. This is the true-life picture and process of how corporations disguise themselves on social media in order to psychologically hook and groom their followers for a long-term relationship of faithfulness.

RQ2: What impression management strategies have the two Chinese banks employed in the management of their identities and images?

There is sufficient evidence that both the BOC and the CMB have employed two overarching impression management strategies: humanising and popularising the corporate self and persuading followers into trusting (and eventually trading with) the corporate self. Unsurprisingly, both of them belong to the acquisitive impression management strategies, specifically ingratiation and self-promotion (Rosenfeld et al. 2002). Sub-strategies of both banks' impression management are also noted and extracted, such as a 'playing cuteness' conversational style, face-work (greetings; expressing gratitude; the raillery of followers and self-ridicule), offer of free material benefits to followers, the change of footing along posts: establishing power or solidarity, devoting themselves to follow-up and interaction and detailing company awards and benefits of promotions or product launch.

RQ3: What are the dialogic patterns/types in the firm-follower interaction? In what ways did the followers play a role in the co-construction of corporate identities on the corporate Weibo?

There is evidence that followers co-construct the corporations' corporate identities, primarily through forms of dialogues as active contributors who @ the banks, as listeners who like and repost corporate Weibo contents or as interlocutors who comment on the corporate Weibo contents. Overall the CMB is much more dialogic than the BOC in both dialogic frequency and dialogic degree/quality, as evidenced by the number of dialogic patterns/types in firm (active contributor)-follower communication and the degree of reposting and liking. Specifically, there are five dialogic patterns/types on the CMB's Weibo: question-raillery; storytelling/praise-acknowledgement; question-answer; raillery-counter-raillery; and storytelling-raillery, whilst only two dialogic patterns/types at the BOC's Weibo interface: storytelling/praise-acknowledgement and question-raillery. It is also revealed that the features of the dialogic theory (mutuality, propinquity, empathy, risk and commitment) (Kent and Taylor 2002, pp. 25–30) are pervasive in the firm-follower interaction.

RQ4: Are there any variations between the state-owned bank and the non-state-owned bank in their corporate identity construction? If yes, how differently do they present themselves on the Weibo interface?

The constitution and communication of corporate identity witnessed significant variations between the BOC and the CMB. Thematic analyses identified that both the CMB and the BOC projected heterogeneous identities on their corporate Weibo, although the constitutions might vary substantially. As results of RQ1 indicate that while the CMB exhibits its particular preference for its warm and intimate companion identity, the BOC is 'paradoxical' in both demonstrating a companion identity and seeking "deference" (Goffman 1967, p. 47) and power from its followers with its intentional construction of the bank as an industry specialist. There is powerful linguistic evidence illustrating such variations. For instance first, playing cuteness as a conversational style is much more evident on the CMB's corporate Weibo than on the BOC's Weibo for constructing the companion identity of youthfulness, playfulness and companionship. The overwhelming use of overdone face-work or overdone linguistic intimacy has revealed the CMB's persistent effort in closing firm-follower distance. Second, the great number of the chicken-soup-for-the-soul updates on the CMB's corporate Weibo is noticeable. Third, the CMB's Weibo is more dialogic than the BOC's Weibo, a realisation of the CMB's companionship to its followers. On the other hand, although the BOC has also intentionally built up its companion identity, the BOC's distinctive high-end identity as an authoritative industry specialist has been especially highlighted in many aspects, from address forms to contents design.

In-depth interviews affirmed the textual findings as regards the corporations' communicative intensions of corporate identities. The companion identity indeed serves as the most critical one the CMB wishes to build up on its corporate Weibo, topping journalist identity and others, with a specialist identity the least desirable to be constructed on social media. Reasons of intentions as such, as Miss Z of the CMB suggested, are mostly derived from the playing cuteness, relaxing and playful nature of social media platforms. In other words, the corporate self-presentation on the social media is designed especially for younger stakeholders, for the CMB is equipped with other channels of communication to target the senior and mature customers. In Miss Z's own words, the CMB's corporate persona on the Sina Weibo is a twenty-something vivacious and lovely girl. By contrast, the interview of the Mr. S. of the BOC revealed that the BOC's most valued corporate identities are its authentic identity as a financial institution and the industry specialist identity. The companion identity in Mr. S's view is no more than an ideal that the BOC strives hard to achieve.

8.3 Discussion and Conclusion

8.3.1 The Multiplicity of Corporate Identities on Social Media

As one of the major findings, the present research conceptualised a theoretical framework: a two-way dialogic construction of corporate identity on social media, consisting of two pairs of discourse initiations and responses driven by both corporations and their social media followers. While the company's self-initiated updates are considered as the impression management of its corporate identity, the followers' initiation and responses make up the co-construction of the corporate identity. It is unveiled that the corporate identities on social media are essentially forms of "pragmatic identity", communication-dependent, temporary, dynamic, variable, resourceful, subjective and purposeful, (Chen 2013, p. 4). In other words, the corporate identities specified on social media are the conscious, voluntary selection of speaker identity in an attempt to well adjust to the social media context and generate desirable communicative outcomes of follower engagement.

The findings have supplied empirical evidence that corporate identity construction on social media similarly complies with the rhetorical or symbolic interactionist view of corporate identity communication, in which signs, symbols and linguistic resources employed by a company do not merely designate social practice but also constitute it (Cheney 1991; Cornelissen and Harris 2001). Although the analogy of human identities in corporate identities has been long argued and the corporate personality was even claimed as the nature of corporate identity (Olins 1978), corporate identity, enabled by both internal organisational behavior and external societal and market imperatives, is tested far more than a sole expression of one corporate personality (Cornelissen and Harris 2001). This argument resonates with Balmer's (1998, p. 975) stance that the analogy between the corporate and human personality should not be excessively stressed, as "unlike human personality, the corporate personality is capable of a greater degree of control of its own make-up." The findings contribute to this rhetorical or symbolic interactionist view of corporate identity by expanding the arguments to the social media setting, where the multiple traits of human identities are specified and communicated as the entire expression of the company.

The finding of a multiplicity of corporate identity, somehow replicating the human identities, has evidently expanded the assertions that Chinese corporations acted as "a caring friend" of their social media followers (Men and Tsai, 2012, p. 729) and Turkish banks employed the single "casual fun tone" on social media (Ozdora-Aksak and Atakan-Duman 2015, p. 126). Prior to the advent of social media, Balmer (2001) claimed that corporate identity was characterised as multi-faceted and multi-dimensional in nature. The present finding of a multiplicity of corporate identities in both banks' SNS has not only empirically corroborated with but also expanded his research claim. The findings implied that while corporate identity as an elusive and multi-faceted concept and the process of corporate identity and its content being complex (Melewar 2008; Allori and Garzone 2010), the objective of corporate identity construction on social media is for long-term rapport management (Spencer-Oatey 2002) and relationship building with stakeholders. This is fundamentally different from the construction of corporate identity in the traditional media, where the value of corporate identity lies in the marketing practice, as emphasised by scholars (Balmer 2001; He and Balmer 2013), which is somehow shorter-term oriented. In other words, in face of the social media challenges, the construction of corporate identity on SNS is by no means designed for immediate revenues, but for the youthful and cool corporate image, indicating that the corporation is indeed "keeping up with the tide" in public relations, in the BOC interviewee Mr. S's words.

Although corporate identities might be invented by and under the control of corporations (Topalian 1984), the findings revealed that on social media corporate identities are prone to be constrained by the corporations' industry status and market positioning in reality. Or rather, corporate identity on social media is a social construct, instead of something pre-given, complying with the non-essentialist view of the third phrase of identity construction: "identity as practice" (Dyer 2007, p. 105). Further, the construction of a multiplicity of corporate identity on social media is substantially situated and contextualised to cater for the social media traits, e.g., interactive, synchronic and many-to-many (Herring 2007, 2013) and the massive use of netspeak (Crystal 2001). This finding is consistent with Cornelissen and Elving's (2003) assertion that both media and message are crucial dimensions of managing the corporate identity.

Nevertheless, as the findings indicated, although corporations are playing their cuteness from time to time, they are not merely passive recipients of the social media context, but rather businesses have actively adjusted to the context without compromising their own traits. Furthermore, other contextual factors such as the Chinese youth culture and Internet culture from which the playing cuteness and certain culture-specific jokes (e.g. weight-loss) arise should not be neglected. It has to be noted that perhaps the playing cuteness conversational style is most salient and peculiar only to the construction of corporate identities of Chinese corporations. Although the conversational style as such is high-involved (Tannen 2005) and engaging, corporations might not seem equally appealing to followers from other cultural backgrounds where for example the playing cuteness may be a taboo. In the American social media of Facebook, Tannen (2013) examined the conversational style of interpersonal interaction and located a number of discursive strategies for a high-involvement style, such as capitalisation, repetition of words and brevity of text messages, but nothing relating to "playing cuteness".

8.3.2 Impression Management on Social Media

Both the BOC and the CMB have basically adopted similar impression management strategies–humanising and popularising the corporate self and persuading followers into trusting (and eventually trading with) the corporate self, presenting themselves with humanised identity to their followers, although slight differences in sub-strategies might arise, such as the way face and politeness are handled in interacting with their followers. The findings of the impression management strategies corporations employed on social media are also orientated to rapport management and customer relationship building, which are tied in with Men and Tsai (2012, 2013), Hou and Zhu's (2012) stress in the significance of attaining harmony with customers in the public relations practice of China.

Impression management is in fact an integral part of the process of corporate identity construction, as "managing corporate identity is about identifying the right image for an organisation, and communicating it effectively" (Wood 2004, p. 95). The Chinese corporations' entire effort of impression management is found to be tailor-made for the construction of their desirable corporate identities. The findings imply that an emerging trend of impression management is the dissolution of the authentic corporate identity and the humanisation of corporate identity, realised in the corporations' "conversational human voice" (Kelleher and Miller 2006, p. 395) in addressing their followers. Thus, the impression management on corporate social media is a typified on-stage performance (Goffman 1959), eliciting more intensified customer interaction as compared to the traditional media contexts. The artful change of footing is mostly noted in the corporations' impression management practice to construct power and/or solidarity. The humanising, popularising and persuading elements in the impression management strategies identified in the present study not only corroborated with but also expanded and advanced Lillqvist and Louhiala-Salminen's (2014) findings of corporations' impression management strategies on the Facebook fanpage: upholding corporations' acceptability and promoting their credibility. Furthermore, the examination of corporations' face and politeness strategies on social media indicated that although complexities of impression management are present in both studies, the findings located a number of new, culture-specific and industry-specific characteristics, including the overdone linguistic intimacy (unconventional face-work) in language use, the playing cuteness conversational style, the humanised self-ridicule and the light-hearted tease of followers' weight and financial situations as well as regular material stimulus for follower interaction. In addition, money matters is understandably a recurrent issue to be concerned, discussed and joked about on the banks' corporate social media.

As one of the sub impression management strategies, it is found that face-work on corporate social media has been apparently ‘overdone’, in a desperate exchange for attention, involvement, solidarity and linguistic intimacy, as shown in greeting, thanking and climaxing in the corporations’ raillery of followers and self-ridicule. It is concluded that the unwavering, all-embracing face-work and the delicate face game of the Chinese banks on social media, represented by the speech act of greeting, appreciation and the raillery of followers and self-ridicule, could be well compared to play-acting and hybridised to have incorporated both “playing safe” in the orthodox norm of respect tribute and the creative form of “overdone acting”, climaxing in the raillery of followers and self-ridicule. In the age of conversationalisation and interpersonal discourses’ colonisation in the public domains (Fairclough 1989, 1992), the findings further argue that corporations’ playing safe and overdone acting of face-work cooperatively mingle with each other on social media. The findings are in line with West and Trester’s (2013) study on face-work on the Facebook that large amounts of positive face strategies are intentionally employed to adorn messages in a just-kidding manner, in an attempt to offset the drawbacks caused by a faceless voice in the interpersonal social media communication. Although the findings does not perfectly corroborate Hwang’s (1987) assertion that face-work is precisely weighed and effected in terms of participants’ guanxi in between and Gu’s (1990) sincerity principle of politeness, they do echo Hwang’s (1987) argument that the exploitation of face-work in social interactions is driven by the underlying motivation of resources pursuit. To this end, the dual division of face-work on the corporate social media is directed, rehearsed and enacted to appeal to potential resources generated either from the followers’ attention or from the continuous accumulation of followers. In this sense, overdone face-work is the creative, masked and virtual form of positive politeness strategy.

8.3.3 The Co-construction of Corporate Identity

Corporate identity is a two-way traffic, rather than “one-way traffic” (Peverelli 2006, p. 2). The present research is very likely to be the first empirical study that examines the co-construction of corporate identity on social media through dialogues with the followers in the Chinese context, subsequent to the pilot study of and the call for the dialogic co-creating corporate identity proposed by Theunissen (2014). Firm-follower dialogues, as suggested in the findings, do facilitate the co-construction of corporate identities, entailing that corporations are no longer in the sole control of their corporate identities. The more dialogic the corporation is, the more interactive their followers will become. The fact that the CMB is more dialogic than the BOC in follower interaction and is more responsive to followers leads to the virtuous circle of interaction, generating waves of followers’ participation in the co-construction of corporate identity on the CMB’s corporate Weibo. Nevertheless, there is always room for improvement, as the embarrassment of corporations' "undialogic" communication arising from their rather limited responsiveness to some followers' comments (e.g. complaints).

Although corporate identities resemble personal identities in many ways (Hatch and Schulz 2002; Johansson 2007), the interview findings revealed that the construction of corporate identity can be far less stable than the formation of personal identity. The findings also imply that virtual interaction and dialogues as co-construction forces of corporate identity might lead to an enduring fluid state of corporate identity (i.e., one that is in constant flux). This finding of social media application is in line with Balmer's (2001) argument that corporate identity is characterised as variability (they are immutable but evolutionary) and Albert and Whetten's (1985) claim that corporate identity is the central distinct and enduring dimensions of a company. Hence, the changes of corporations' marketing positioning and other socio-economic factors underlying corporate identity might incur substantial adjustments of corporations' corporate identity.

The dialogic patterns identified in Table 6.3 in firm-follower interaction cover a wide variety, such as question-answer, storytelling-praise/acknowledgment, question-raillery and raillery-counter-raillery, all of which are manifestations of the tenets of dialogic communication: mutuality, propinquity, empathy and commitment (Kent and Taylor 2002). The dialogic patterns as such precisely illustrate the definition of dialogic communication—"negotiated exchanges of ideas and opinions in public relations" (Kent and Taylor 1998, p. 325).

8.4 New Contributions

The present study bears a few new contributions to the extant body of literature. First and foremost, the theoretical dialogic analytical framework of corporate identity construction on social media (Fig. 3.1) is brand-new, sense-making and applicable, sorting out the interaction mechanism in both the company's construction and followers' co-construction of corporate identities. Figure 3.1 not only clearly manifested the two-pair two-way dialogic communication of corporate identity construction, but also paved the way for the further updates of the institutionalised interaction model of Initiation-Response-Feedback (Sinclair and Coulthard 1975).

Second of all, methodologically, an integrated sociolinguistics approach helps to shed light on corporate identity construction on social media. As the title of the present research indicated, the study attempted and has accomplished the untangling of the research questions by employing three sets of sociolinguistics-related methods of analysis: thematic analysis, interactional analysis and in-depth interviews. By responding to the dearth of discourse-centered online ethnography in the extant literature (Androutsopoulos 2008), the ethnographic interviews have sufficiently assisted and verified the textual findings generated by the researcher, leading to a comprehensively grounded and contextualised understanding of the communicative process and mechanism where corporate identities are being (co-)constructed and negotiated.

Thirdly, the new constructions of the research reside in the key findings and their implications. Although the extant literature has already noted the company's impression management strategies (e.g. Lillqvist and Louhiala-Salminen 2014) and the followers' co-construction of corporate identity on social media (Theunissen 2014), there is a significant void of the empirical dialogic patterns/types in company-customer interaction on social media. As one strand of the findings of the present study, the dialogic patterns/types as such has managed in extending the current body of research. While extant literature has almost neglected the ownership as a critical factor in determining corporate identity online, except for Ozdora-Aksak and Atakan-Duman (2015) in the Turkish setting, another strand of the research findings provides timely and empirical insights into the state-owned and non-state-owned enterprises' variations of their image projection on social media. In terms of the findings of the impression management strategies identified, some localised/globalised features (e.g. the playing cuteness conversational style and the overdone face-work) of the generalised ingratiation impression management strategy have broadened the existing research scope and horizons [e.g., the embodiments of the "situated politeness" by Davies et al. (2011, p. 1)] to take into consideration of more contextualised factors of impression management that uphold and underpin the communication practice.

8.5 Research Implications and Limitations

In terms of implications for the upcoming research, the present findings affirmed Feng and Goodman's (2010) claim that managing and improving corporate image is more emphasised than the marketing and publicity needs in the age of social media and Ngai and Ng's (2013) claim that PR practitioners in Greater China have acknowledged the importance of using social media to enhance communication with young stakeholders. While participants in their study (Ngai and Ng 2013) were doubtful about the effectiveness of social media across fields, the present study authenticated that the banking industry is apparently one of the sectors suitable for corporate communication with younger customers on social media. Therefore, future research is encouraged to examine social media's empirical role in enhancing corporate image and reputation in sectors other than banking.

Methodologically, future studies are expected, in addition to the call for a larger-scale cross-industry and cross-cultural examination, to apply a multimodal analysis for a more comprehensive and contextualised understanding of the social media updates and its all-round communication mechanism. It is sincerely hoped that the present research builds a bridge across which thorough insights towards the dialogic and interactive nature of corporate identity construction in new media context can be inspired.

Identity construction prevails in all human communication. In the process of realising diverse personal identities and corporate identities, communication contexts matter considerably. It should be noted that the playful Weibo context dramatically mediates the hierarchical and censored ideology of China's mass media practice with its interactive mechanism and fun-nature media content enacted through a handful of amicable identities. As one of the directors of the BOC Weibo Mr. S. emphasised, it is their aspiration to 'play cuteness' in their corporate Weibo practice, a goal that was unimaginable just a decade ago in public relations practice of China. Hence, future research is advised to make comparisons of a single corporation's corporate identity construction and impression management strategies between new and traditional media contexts.

In regards to the research limitations, the leading demerit of the research lies in the representativeness of the textual data that is inevitably brought about by its case-study nature. Likewise, there is limited key informant interview data to cater for the case study. Another limitation of the study, due to the constraints of technology and time and difficulty of accessibility, might be the lack of interviews with banks' followers for their motivation of communicative participation and their views towards corporate identities as well as their own contribution in the dialogic process. Finally, the study might be the most accurate if the coding software Nvivo 10.0 had been utilised, an effective means to eliminate the subjectivity arising from the manual coding.

Appendix

Interview questions in Chinese

1. 贵行发布新浪微博的目的与预期目标何在？ 是否有长期目标和短期目标之分"？
2. 贵行发布新浪微博的指导方针是什么？有什么具体策略或禁忌？
3. 公司网站中的银行身份与形象和微博中的身份与形象有何不同？ 为什么会产生这些差异？
4. 在语言使用策略上，贵行是否特别留意在微博上使用特定的语言？或不使用特定的语言？
5. 微博使用的语言与公司网页或电视广告有区别吗？区别在哪里？
6. 贵行在新浪微博中与几百万粉丝互动的原则是什么？有何策略与经验？
7. 贵行的新浪微博在公共关系中的角色与作用是怎样的？
8. 您认为贵行在新浪微博中通过话语使用试图建构出怎样的身份？ 这样的身份是否与传统媒体中银行试图建构的身份是否一致？如果不一致，有何差异？
9. 贵行是否关注粉丝的互动，粉丝的点赞，转发与评论对贵行在微博的身份与形象是否有影响？
10. 对贵行而言，粉丝的点赞，转发与评论哪个最重要？你们是否一一回复评论，怎样回复？
11. 粉丝的互动对以后的微博内容选择有何种程度的影响？能否举例说明.
12. 您认为微博平台对贵行公共关系的意义有多大？
13. 有哪些具体措施提高新浪微博粉丝的互动性？
14. 贵行的所有制结构对贵行采用的公共关系策略是否有影响？
15. 贵行在新媒体公共关系沟通中的最大障碍是什么？
16. 作为老牌四大国有银行之一，在公共关系上面临的竞争压力是否巨大？
17. 国家的金融政策对贵行在公共关系维护上又哪些倾斜性政策？

W. Feng, *Discursive Constructions of Corporate Identities by Chinese Banks on Sina Weibo*, DOI 10.1007/978-981-10-4469-4

Bibliography

Abdullah, Z., Nordin, S. M., & Yuhanis, A. A. (2013). Building a unique online corporate identity. *Marketing Intelligence & Planning, 31*(5), 451–471.

Akgun, A. E., Kocoglu, I., & Imamoglu, S. Z. (2013). An emerging consumer experience: Emotional branding. *Procedia-Social and Behavioral Sciences, 99,* 503–508.

Albert, S., & Whetten, D. A. (1985). Organizational identity. *Research in Organizational Behavior, 7,* 263–295.

Allen, M. W., & Calliouet, R. H. (1994). Legitimation endeavors: Impression Management strategies used by an organization in crisis. *Communication Monographs, 61,* 44–62.

Allori, P. E., & Garzone, G. (2010). Identities, discourse and genres in corporate communication: an introduction. In P. E. Allori & G. Garzone (Eds.), *Discourse, identities and genres in corporate communication.* Berlin: Peter Lang.

Allori, P. E. (2010). Corporate identity and image promotion through sponsoring international sports events: A view from the Web. In P. E. Allori & G. Garzone (Eds.), *Discourse, identities and genres in corporate communication.* Berlin: Peter Lang.

Androutsopoulos, J. (2006a). Multilingualism, diaspora, and the Internet: Codes and identities on German-based diaspora websites. *Journal of Sociolinguistics, 10*(4), 439–450.

Androutsopoulos, J. (2006b). Introduction: Sociolinguistics and computer-mediated communication. *Journal of Sociolinguistics, 10*(4), 419–438.

Androutsopoulos, J. (2008). Discourse-centered online ethnography. In J. Androutsopouls & M. Beibwenger (Eds.), *Data and methods in computer mediated discourse analysis*. Special issue, Language@Internet 5.

Androutsopoulos, J. (2010). Localising the global on the participatory web. In N. Coupland (Ed.), *Handbook of language and globalization* (pp. 203–231). Oxford: Oxford University Press.

Androutsopoulos, J. (2011). Language change and digital media: A review of conceptions and evidence. In T. Kristiansen & N. Coupland (Eds.), *Standard languages and language standards in a change Europe* (pp. 145–161). Oslo: Novus.

Anis, J. (Ed.). (1998). *Internet, Communication et Langue Fran, caise.* Paris: Hermes.

Arkin, R. (1981). Self-presentation styles. In J. T. Tedeschi (Ed.), *Impression management in the organization* (pp. 311–333). New York: Academic Press.

Arundale, R. B. (2006). Face as relational and interactional: A communication framework for research on face, facework and politeness. *Journal of Politeness Research, 2,* 193–216.

Balmer, J. M. T. (1998). Corporate identity and the advent of corporate marketing. *Journal of Marketing Management, 14*(8), 963–996.

Balmer, J. M. T. (2001). Corporate identity, corporate branding and corporate marketing: Seeing through the fog. *European Journal of Marketing, 35*(3/4), 248–291.

Balmer, J. M. T. (2008). Identity based views of the corporation: Insights from corporate identity, organizational identity, social identity, visual identity, corporate brand identity and corporate image. *European Journal of Marketing, 42*(9/10), 879–906.

W. Feng, *Discursive Constructions of Corporate Identities by Chinese Banks on Sina Weibo*, DOI 10.1007/978-981-10-4469-4

Bargiela-Chiappini, F. (2003). Face and politeness: New (insights) for old (concepts). *Journal of Pragmatics, 35,* 1453–1469.

Baym, K. N. (1995). The performance of humor in computer-mediated communication. *Journal of Computer-Mediated Communication, 1,* 2.

Beißwenger, M. (Ed.). (2001). *Chat-Kommunikation.* Stuttgart, Germany: Ibidem.

Bell, A. (1984). Language style as audience design. In N. Coupland & A. Jaworski (Eds.), *Sociolinguistics: A reader and coursebook* (pp. 240–250). New York: St Mattin's Press Inc.

Bhatia, V. K. (2004). *Worlds of written discourse: A genre-based view.* London and New York: Continuum.

Bhatia, V. K. (1993). *Analyzing genre: Language use in professional settings.* Harlow: Longman.

Biber, D. (1988). *Variation across speech and writing.* Cambridge: Cambridge University Press.

Biber, D. (1995). *Dimensions of register variation: A cross-linguistic comparison.* Cambridge: Cambridge University Press.

Belal, A. R. (2008). *Corporate social responsibility in developing countries: The case of Bangladesh.* Aldershot, England and Burlington, VT: Ashgate.

Boggio, C. (2010). Automobile advertising for cultural elites: A multimodal analysis. In P. E. Allori & G. Garzone (Eds.), *Discourse, identities and genres in corporate communication* (pp. 145–162). Berlin: Peter Lang.

Bortree, D. S., & Seltzer, T. (2009). Dialogic strategies and outcomes: An analysis of environmental advocacy groups' Facebook profiles. *Public Relations Review, 35,* 317–319.

Bourdieu, P. (1986). The forms of capital. In J. G. Richardson (Ed.), *Handboook of theory and research for sociology of education* (pp. 241–258). New York: Greenwood Press.

Boxer, D. (2002). *Applying sociolinguistics: Domains and face-to-face interaction.* Amsterdam/Philadelphia: John Benjamins.

Boyatzis, R. E. (1998). *Transforming qualitative information.* Thousand Oaks, CA: Sage.

Boyd, D., Golder, S., & Lotan, G. (2010). Tweet, tweet, retweet: Conversational aspects of retweeting on Twitter. In *Proceedings of the 43rd Hawaii International Conference on Social Systems (HICSS).* IEEE.

Briones, R. L., Kuch, B., Liu, B. F., & Yan, J. (2011). Keeping up with the digital age: How the American Red Cross uses social media to build relationships. *Public Relations Review, 37*(1), 37–43.

Brown, P., & Levinson, S. (1987). *Politeness: Some universals in language use.* Cambridge: Cambridge University Press.

Brown, R., & Gilman, A. (1960). *The pronouns of power and solidarity.* New York: Bobbs-Merrill.

Buber, M. (1970). *I and thou.* New York: Scribner.

Buchholtz, A. K., & Carroll, A. B. (2008). *Business and society: Ethics and stakeholder management* (7th ed.). Mason, OH: Southwestern Cengage Learning.

Butler, J. (1990). *Gender trouble: Geminism and the subversion of identity.* New York: Routledge.

Bury, R. (2005). *Cyberspaces of their own: Female fandoms online.* New York: Peter Lang.

Cameron, D., & Panovic, I. (2014). *Working with written discourse.* London: Sage.

Camerson, D. (1990). Demythologizing sociolinguistics: Why language does not reflect society. In J. E. Joseph & T. J. Taylor (Eds.), *Ideologies of language* . London: Routledge.

Capriotti, P., & Pardo Kuklinski, H. (2012). Assessing dialogic communication through the Internet in Spanish museums. *Public Relations Review, 38*(4), 619–626.

Carroll, A. B. (1991). The pyramid of corporate social responsibility: Toward the moral management of organizational stakeholders'. *Business Horizon, 34*(4), 39–48.

Cheong, P. H., Martin, J. N., & Macfadyen, L. P. (2012). Introduction: mediated intercultural communication matters: Understanding new media, dialectics and social change. In P. H. Cheong, J. N. Martin, & L. P. Macfadyen (Eds.), *New media and intercultural communication: Identity, community and politics.* New York: Peter Lang.

Chen, R. (2001). Self-politeness: A proposal. *Journal of Pragmatics, 33,* 87–106.

Chen, G. M. (2011). Tweet this: A uses and gratifications perspective on how active Twitter use gratifies a need to connect with others. *Computers in Human Behavior, 27*(2), 755–762.

Chen, X. (2013). Pragmatic identity: Dynamic choice and discursive construction. *Foreign Language Reserach, 140*(4), 27–32.

Cheng, W. (2003). *Intercultural conversation.* Amsterdam and Philadelphia: John Benjamins.

Cheney, G. (1991). *Rhetoric in an organizatoinal society: Managing multiple identities.* Columbia, SC: University of South Carolina Press.

Cho, S., & Huh, J. (2010). Content analysis of corporate blogs as a relationship management tool. *Corporate Communications: An International Journal, 15*(1), 30–48.

Cinar, E. M., & Tang, A. Y. (2003). *Privatization in the Chinese banking industry.* Presentation at USCPFA National Convention in Chicago.

Cissna, K. N., & Anderson, R. (1998). Theorizing about dialogic moments: The Buber-Rogers position and postmodern themes. *Communication Theory, 1,* 63–104.

Conway, B. A., Kenski, K., & Wang, D. (2013). Twitter use by presidential primary candidates during the 2012 campaign. *American Behavioral Scientist, 57*(11), 1596–1610.

Cormode, G., & Krishnamurthy, B. (2008, June). Key differences between Web 1.0 and Web 2.0. *First Monday, 13*(6), 2. Retrieved April 4, 2014 from http://firstmonday.org/

Cornelissen, J. P., & Elving, W. J. L. (2003). Managing corporate identity: An integrative framework. *Corporate Communication: An International Journal, 8*(2), 114–120.

Cornelissen, J. P., & Harris, P. (2001). The corporate metaphor: Perspectives, problems and prospects. *Journal of Marketing Management, 17*(1–2), 49–71.

Crystal, D. (1987). *The Cambridge encyclopedia of language.* Cambridge: Cambridge University Press.

Crystal, D. (1988). *The English language.* Harmondsworth: Penguin.

Crystal, D. (2001). *Language and the Internet* (2nd ed.). Cambridge: Cambridge University Press.

Dabrowska, M. (2013). *Variation in English: Faces of Facebook English.* Frankfurt, Germany: Peter Lang.

Davies, B. L., Haugh, M., & Merrison, A. J. (Eds.). (2011). *Situated politeness.* London and New York: Continuum.

DiStaso, M. W., McCorkindale, T., & Wright, D. K. (2011). How public relations executives perceive and measure the impact of social media in their organizations. *Public Relations Review, 37*(3), 325–328.

De Fina, A., Schiffrin, D., & Bamberg, M. G. W. (Eds.). (2006). *Discourse and identity.* Cambridge: Cambridge University Press.

Degano, C. (2009). Marketing identities on Nestle's websites. In G. Garzone & P. Catenaccio (Eds.), *Identities across media and modes: Discursive perspectives.* Bern: Peter Lang.

Degano, C. (2010). Linguistic perspectives on image construction and moral identity: The case of banks. In P. E. Allori & G. Garzone (Eds.), *Discourse, identities and genres in corporate communication.* Peter Lang.

DeGeorge, R. T. (2010). *Business ethics* (7th ed.). Upper Saddle River: Pearson Education.

Dubrin, A. J. (2011). *Essentials of Management* (9th ed.). Boston, USA: Cengage Learning.

Dubrin, A. J. (2011). *Impression management in the workplace: Research, theory, and practice.* New York: Routledge.

Dyer, J. (2007). Language and identity. In C. Llamas, L. Mullany, & P. Stockwell (Eds.), *The Routledge companion to sociolinguistics.* London and New York: Routledge.

Eckert, P. (2000). *Linguistic variation as social practice: The linguistic construction of identity.* Belten High, MA: Blackwell Publishers.

Elliott, A. (Ed.). (2011). *Routledge handbook of identity studies.* London and New York: Routledge.

Elliott, A. (2001). *Concepts of the self.* Cambridge: Polity Press.

Erikson, E. H. (1964). *Insight and responsibility.* New York: Norton.

Erikson, E. H. (1968). *Identity: Youth and crisis.* New York: Norton.

Erjavec, K. (2004). Beyond advertising and journalism: Hybrid promotional news discourse. *Discourse & Society, 15*, 553–578.

Fairclough, N. (1989). *Language and power*. New York: Longman.

Fairclough, N. (1992). *Discourse and social change*. Cambridge: Polity Press.

Fairclough, N. (1995). *Critical discourse analysis: The critical study of language*. Harlow, England: Longman.

Fairclough, N. (1995). *Media discourse*. London: Edward Arnold.

Fairclough, N. (1996). Technologisation of discourse. In C. R. Caldas-Coulthard & M. Coulthard (Eds.), *Text and practices: Readings in critical discourse analysis*. London and New York: Routledge.

Feng, J. (2008). *Advertising discourses and social changes in China: an investigation of the changing advertising discourses in "Yangchen Evening News" and "Nanfang Daily" from 1980 to 2002*. Ph.D. dissertation, The Hong Kong Polytechnic University.

Feng, J., & Goodman, M. B. (2010). Corporate communication practices and trends: A China study. In *Conference of Corporate Communication International at Baruch College/CUNY, New York, NY*.

Feng, J., & Wu, D. (2009). Changing ideologies and advertising discourses in China: A case study of Nanfang Daily. *Journal of Asian Pacific Communication., 19*(2), 218–238.

Feng, W., & Wang, L. (2017). New media english: New linguistic features and its value to EFL. *Journal of Xi'an International Studies University*, 25(2), 131–136.

Fischer, E., & Reuber, A. R. (2011). Social interaction via new social media: (How) can interactions on Twitter affect effectual thinking and behavior? *Journal of Business Venturing, 26*(1), 1–18.

Franklin, A., Qian, J., & Qian, M. (2008). China's financial system: Past, present and future. In L. Brandt & T. G. Rawski (Eds.), *China's great economic transformation*. Cambridge: Cambridge University Press.

Friedman, T. (2006). *The world is flat: A brief history of the twenty first century*. New York: Farrar, Straus and Giroux.

Gao, G. (2009). Face and self in Chinese communication. In Francesca Bargiela-Chiappini & Michael Haugh (Eds.), *Face, communication and social interaction*. London and Oakville: Equinox.

Gao, L. (2004). *Chinese internet language: A study of identity construction*. Ph.D. dissertation, University of Illinois at Urbana-Champaign.

Gao, L. (2006). Language contact and convergence in computer-mediated communication. *World Englishes, 25*(2), 299–308.

Gao, L. (2012). Synchronic variation or diachronic change: A sociolinguistic study of Chinese Internet language. In Jin Liu & Hongyin Tao (Eds.), *Chinese under Globalization: Emerging trends in language use in China*. Singapore City: World Scientific.

Garnaut, R., Song, L., & Yao, Y. (2006). Impact and significance of state-owned enterprise restructuring in China. *China Journal, 55*, 35–63.

Garnaut, R., & Song, L. (2004). *China's third economic transformation: The rise of the private economy*. London and New York: Routledge.

Garzone, G., & Catenaccio, P. (2009). Discursive perspectives on identities across media and modes: An introduction. In G. Garzone & P. Catenaccio (Eds.), *Identities across media and modes: Discursive perspectives*. Bern: Peter Lang.

Garzone, G. (2010). Actors, identities and roles in professional and academic discourse: An introduction. In Giuliana Garzone & James Archibald (Eds.), *Discourse, identities and roles in specialized communication*. Bern: Peter Lang.

Garzone, G., & Archibald, J. (Eds.). (2010). *Discourse, identities and roles in specialized communication*. Bern: Peter Lang.

Gergen, K. J. (1994). *Realities and relationships, soundings in social construction*. Cambridge, MA: Harvard University Press.

Gergen, K. J. (1999). *An invitation to social construction*. London: Sage Publication.

Giacalone, R. A., & Rosenfeld, P. (1989). *Impression management in the organization*. Hillsdale, NJ: Lawrence Erlbaum.

Gilmore, F., & Dumont, S. (2003). *Brand warriors China: Creating sustainable brand capital*. London: Profile Books.

Gioia, D. A. (1998). From individual to organizational identity. In D. A. Whetten & P. C. Godfrey (Eds.), *Identity in organizations: Building theory through conversations*. Thousand Oaks, CA: Sage Publications.

Gobe, M. (2001). *Emotional branding: The new paradigm for connecting brands to people*. New York: Allworth Press.

Gobe, M. (2007, Winter). Let's brandjam to humanize our brands. *Design Management Review, 18*, 68–75.

Gobe, M. (2009). *Emotional branding: The new paradigm for connecting brands to people (revised edition)*. New York: Allworth Press.

Goffman, E. (1959). *The presentation of self in everyday life*. Garden City, NY: Doubleday.

Goffman, E. (1967). *Interaction ritual: Essays in face-to-face behavior*. Harmondsworth and Ringwood: Penguin Books.

Goffman, E. (1974). *Frame analysis: An essay on the organization of experience*. New York: Harper & Row.

Goffman, E. (1976). Replies and responses. *Language in Society, 5*(3), 257–313.

Goffman, E. (1981). *Forms of talk*. Oxford: Basil Blackwell.

Goodwin, M. H. (1996). Shifting frame. In D. I. Slobin, J. Gerhardt, A. Kyratzis, & J. Guo (Eds.), *Social interaction, social context and language*. Mahwah, New Jersey: Lawrence Erlbaum Associates.

Gordon, C. (2011). Gumperz and interactional sociolinguistics. In R. Wodak, B. Johnstone, & P. Kerswill (Eds.), *The Sage handbook of sociolinguistics*. London: Sage.

Gu, Y. G. (1990). Politeness phenomena in modern Chinese. *Journal of Pragmatics, 14*, 237–257.

Gu, X., & Li, Y. (2007). Language and identity construction: Literature review. *Foreign Language Research, 139*(6), 101–108.

Guest, G. (2012). Introduction to thematic analysis. In K. M. MacQueen & E. E. Namey (Eds.), *Applied thematic analysis*. Thousand Oaks, CA: Sage.

Gumperz, J. (1982). *Discourse strategies*. Cambridge: Cambridge University Press.

Gumperz, J. (Ed.). (1982). *Discourse and social identity*. Cambridge: Cambridge University Press.

Gumperz, J. (1974). The linguistic anthropology in society. *American Anthropologist, 76*, 785–798.

Gumperz, J. (1971). *Language in social groups*. Stanford: Stanford University Press.

Guth, S., & Helm, F. (2012). Developing multiliteracies in ELF through telecollaboration. *ELT Journal, 66*(1), 42–51.

Hatch, M. J., & Schultz, M. (2002). The dynamics of organizational identity. In M. J. Hatch & M. Schultz (Eds.), *Organizational identity*. Oxford: Oxford University Press.

Hatim, B., & Mason, I. (1990). *Discourse and the Translator*. London: Longman.

Habermas, J. (1984). *The theory of communicative action* (Vol. 1). Heinemann.

Harlow, R. F. (1976). Building a public relations definition. *Public Relations Review, 2*, 16–36.

He, H., & Chen, X. (2015). A pragmatic account on the construction of online shop owners' relational identities. *Modern Foreign Languages (Bimonthly), 38*(3), 347–356.

He, H.-W., & Balmer, J. M. T. (2013). A grounded theory of the corporate identity and corporate strategy dynamic: A corporate marketing perspective. *European Journal of Marketing, 47*(3/4), 401–430.

He, Z., & Ren, W. (2016). Current address behaviors in China. *East Asian Pragmatics, 1*(2).

He, M., & Zhang, S. (2011). Re-conceptualizing the Chinese concept of face from a face-sensitive perspective: A case study of a modern Chinese TV drama. *Journal of Pragmatics, 43*, 2360–2372.

Health, R. L., Pearce, W. B., Shotter, J., Taylor, J. R., Kersten, A., & Zorn, T. (2006, February). The processes of dialogue. *Management Communication Quarterly, 19*(3), 341–345.

Herring, S. (1996). *Computer-mediated communication: Linguistics, social and cross-cultural Perspective*. Amsterdam: John Benjamins.

Herring, S. (2004). Computer-mediated discourse analysis: An approach to researching online behavior. In Barab A. Sasha, Rob Kling, & Gary H. James (Eds.), *Designing for virtual communities in the service of learning*. Cambridge: Cambridge University Press.

Herring, S. (2007). A faceted classification scheme for computer-mediated discourse, *language@Internet*.www.languageinternet.org/articles/2007/761

Herring, S. (2013). Discourse in Web 2.0: Familiar, reconfigured and emergent. In D. Tannen & A. M. Trester (Eds.), *Discourse 2.0: Language and new media*. Washington D.C.: Georgetown University Press.

Ho, D. Y. (1976). On the concept of face. *American Journal of Sociology, 81*(4), 867–884.

Hofstede, G. (1983). Culture's consequences: International differences in work-related values. *Administrative Science Quarterly, 28*(4), 625–629.

Holtgraves, T. M. (2002). *Language as social action*. Mahwah, New Jersey: Lawrence Erlbaum Associates.

Honeycutt, C., & Herring, S. C. (2009). Beyond microblogging: Conversation and collaboration via Twitter. In *Proceedings of the Forty-Second Hawaii International Conference on System Sciences (HICSS-42)*. Los Alamitos, CA: IEEE Press.

Hopkins, L. (2009). *Social media: The new business communication landscape*. North Sydney, London and Peoria: Ark Group.

Hou, J. W. (2011). Economic reforms of China: Causes and effects. *The Social Science Journal, 48* (3), 419–434.

Hou, Z., & Zhu, Y. (2012). An institutional perspective of public relations practices in the Chinese cultural contexts. *Public Relations Review, 38*, 916–925.

Hu, H. C. (1944). The Chinese concept of face. *American Anthropologist, 46*(1), 45–64.

Hwang, K. K. (1987). Face and favor: The Chinese power game. *American Journal of Sociology, 92*(4), 944–974.

Hwang, K. K. (1995). *Knowledge and action: A socio-psychological interpretation of Chinese cultural tradition*. Taipei: Sin-Li (In Chinese).

Hwang, K. K. (1997). Guanxi and mientze: Conflict resolution in Chinese society. *Intercultural Communication Studies, VII*(I), 17–37.

Hwang, K. K. (2004). Hua Ren She Hui Zhong de Lian Mian Yu Gou Tong Xing Wei (Communicating behaviors of face in Chinese societies). In G. Chen (Eds.), *Zhong Hua Chuan Bo Li Lun Yu Yuan Ze (Theories and principles of Chinese mass communication)*. Taipei: Wu-Nan Culture Enterprise.

Hu, H. C. (1944). The Chinese concept of face. *American Anthropologist, 46*(1), 45–64.

Hymes, D. (1974). *Foundations in sociolinguistics: An ethnographic approach*. Philadelphia: University of Pennsylvania Press.

Hynes, G. E., & Janson, M. (2010) Using semiotic analysis to determine effectiveness of advertising in Internet marketing. In P. E. Allori & G. Garzone (Eds.), *Discourse, identities and genres in corporate communication*. Berlin: Peter Lang.

Irwin, A. (2011). Social constructionism. In R. Wodak, B. Johnstone, & P. Kerswill (Eds.), *The Sage handbook of sociolinguistics*. London: Sage.

Ivanov, V. (2001). Heteroglossia. In A. Duranti (Ed.), *Key terms in language and culture* (pp. 95–97). Malden, MA: Blackwell.

James, K. V., & Melewar, T. C. (2008). Explicating the relationship between identity and culture: A multi-perspective conceptual model. In T. C. Melewar (Ed.), *Facets of corporate identity, communication and reputation* (pp. 3–34). London and New York: Routledge.

Johansson, C. (2007). Goffman's sociology: An inspiring resource for developing public relations theory. *Public Relations Review, 33*, 275–280.

Jones, E. E. (1990). *Interpersonal perception*. New York: W. H. Freeman & Company.

Kaplan, A. M., & Haenlein, M. (2010). Users of the world, unite! The challenges and opportunities of social media. *Business Horizons, 53*(1), 61.

Kasper, G. (1990). Linguistic politeness: Current research issues. *Journal of Pragmatics, 14,* 193–217.

Kelleher, T., & Miller, B. M. (2006). Organizational blogs and the human voice: Relational strategies and relational outcomes. *Journal of Computer-Mediated Communication, 11,* 395–414.

Kelleher, T. (2009). Conversational voice, communicated commitment and public relations outcomes in interactive online communication. *Journal of Computer-Mediated Communication, 59,* 172–188.

Kelly, K. (2016). *The inevitable. Understanding the 12 technological forces that will shape our future*. New York: Penguin Publishing Group.

Kent, M. L. (2013). Using social media dialogically: Public relations role in reviving democracy. *Public Relations Review, 39,* 337–345.

Kent, M. L., & Taylor, M. (2002). Toward a dialogic theory of public relations. *Public Relations Review, 28,* 21–37.

Kent, M. L., & Taylor, M. (1998). Building dialogic relationships through the World Wide Web. *Public Relations Review, 24*(3), 321–334.

Kent, M. L., Taylor, M., & White, W. J. (2003). The relationship between Web site design and organizational responsiveness to stakeholders. *Public Relations Review, 29*(1), 63–77.

Kotler, P., & Lee, N. (2004). Marketing good behavior. *Standford Innovation Review, 1*(4), 14–23.

Labov, W. (1972). *Sociolinguistic patterns*. Philadelphia: University of Pennsylvania Press.

Labov, W. (1980). *Locating language in time and space*. New York: Academic Press.

Lakoff, R. (1975). *Language and woman's place*. New York: Harper & Row.

Larsson, A. O., & Moe, H. (2012). Studying political microblogging: Twitter users in the 2010 Swedish election campaign. *New Media & Society, 14*(5), 729–747.

Leary, M. R. (1996). *Self-presentation: Impression management and interpersonal behavior*. Boulder, CO: Westview Press.

Lee, K. M. C. (2011). Micro-blogging and status updates on Facebook: Texts and practices. In C. Thurlow & K. Mroczek (Eds.), *Digital discourse: Language in the new media*. New York: Oxford University Press.

Lee, K. M. C. (2013). My English is so poor… so I take photos: metalinguistic discourses about English on Flickr. In D. Tannen, & A. M. Trester (Eds.), *Discourse 2.0: Language and new media*. Washington D.C.: Georgetown University Press.

Laforet, S., & Li, X. (2005). Consumers' attitudes towards online and mobile banking in China. *International Journal of Bank Marketing., 23*(5), 362–380.

Leech, G. (1983). *Principles of pragmatics*. London: Longman.

Liddicoat, A. J. (2011). *An introduction to conversational analysis*. London and New York: Continuum.

Lee-Wong, S. M. (2000). *Politeness and face in Chinese culture*. Frankfurt: Peter Lang.

Li, C., & Wu, D. (2016). Relational acts in corporate social media. *Chinese Journal of ESP*, 7(2), 30–40.

Li, T., Berens, G., & de Maertelaere, M. (2014). Corporate twitter channels: The impacts of engagement informedness on corporate reputation. *International Journal of Electronic Commerce, 18*(2), 97–125.

Lillqvist, E., & Louhiala-Salminen, L. (2014). Facing Facebook: impression management strategies in company-consumer interactions. *Journal of Business and Technical Communication, 28*(1), 3–30.

Lin, T. C. W. (2010). Too big to fail, too blind to see. *Mississippi Law Journal, 80,* 355–365.

Lin, Y. (1935). *My country and my people*. New York: Reynal & Hitchcock.

Lippincott, J. G., & Margulies, W. P. (1957). The corporate look: A problem in design. *Public Relations Journal, 13,* 27.

Liu, J., & Tao, H. (Eds.). (2012). *Chinese under globalization: Emerging trends in language use in China*. Singapore City: World Scientific.

Liu, M., & Wu, D. (2015). Discursive construction of corporate identity on the web: A glocalization perspective. *Intercultural communication studies*, 24(1), 50–65.

Liu, X., Jia, S., & Li, F. (2011). Corporate social responsibility as a legitimate concern for Chinese enterprises: an analysis of media depictions. *Public Relations Review, 37,* 207–216.

Liu, Y., Cheng, W. C., & Mu, H. S. (2009). *Industrial organization of Chinese banking*. Shanghai: Shanghai Finance and Economics University Press.

Locher, M. A., & Watts, R. J. (2005). Politeness theory and relational work. *Journal of Politeness Research, 1,* 9–33.

Lomicka, L., & Lord, G. (2012). A tale of tweets: analyzing microblogging among language learners. *System, 40,* 48–63.

Luoma-aho, V., & Vos, M. (2010). Towards a more dynamic stakeholder model: Acknowledging multiple issue arenas. *Corporate Communications: An International Journal, 15*(3), 315–331.

Maat, H. P. (2007). How promotional language in press releases is dealt with by journalists: Genre-mixing or genre conflict. *Journal of Business Communication, 44,* 59–95.

Madichie, N. O., & Hinson, R. (2014). A critical analysis of the "dialogic communications" potential of sub-Saharan African police service websites. *Public Relations Review, 40,* 338–350.

Maignan, I., & Ferrell, O. C. (2004). Corporate social responsibility and marketing: An integrative framework. *Journal of the Academy of Marketing Science, 32*(1), 3–19.

Mantzopoulos, V., & Shen, R. (2011). *The political economy of China's systemic transformation: 1979 to the present*. New York: Palgrave Macmillan.

Marcia, J. E. (1966). Development and validation of ego identity status. *Journal of Personality and Social Psychology, 3,* 551–558.

Markus, H. R., & Kitayama, S. (1991). Culture and the self: Implications for cognition, emotion, and motivation. *Psychological Review, 98*(2), 224–253.

McCall, G. J., & Simons, J. L. (1966). *Identities and interactions*. New York: The Free Press.

McCorkindale, T., & Morgoch, M. (2013). An analysis of the mobile readiness and dialogic principles on Fortune 500 mobile websites. *Public Relations Review, 39,* 193–197.

McKinlay, A., & McVittie, C. (2011). *Identities in context: Individuals and discourse in action*. Oxford: Wiley-Blackwell.

Melewar, T. C. (2003). Determinants of the corporate identity construct: A review of the literature. *Journal of Marketing Communications, 9,* 195–220.

Melewar, T. C. (Ed.). (2008). *Facets of corporate identity*. London and New York: Routledge.

Melewar, T. C., & Jenkins, E. (2002). Defining the corporate identity concept. *Corporate Reputation Review, 1*(1), 76–94.

Melewar, T. C., & Karaosmanoglu, E. (2005). Seven dimensions of corporate identity: A categorization from the practitioners' perspectives. *European Journal of Marketing, 40*(7/8), 846–869.

Melewar, T. C., & Wooldridge, A. (2001). The dynamics of corporate identity. *Journal of Communication Management: An International Journal, 5*(4), 327–340.

Melewar, T. C., & Navalekar, A. (2002). Leveraging corporate identity in the digital age. *Marketing Intelligence & Planning, 20*(2), 96–103.

Men, L. R., & Tsai, W. S. (2012). How companies cultivate relationships with publics on social network sites: Evidence from China and the United States. *Public Relations Review, 38*(5), 723–730.

Men, L. R., & Tsai, W. H. S. (2013). Beyond liking or following: Understanding public engagement on social networking sites in China. *Public Relations Review, 39,* 13–22.

Mersham, G., Theuissen, P., & Peart, J. (2009). *Public relations and communication management: An Aotearoa/New Zealand perspective*. North Shaore, NZ: Pearson.

The Education Ministry of China. (2012). *Language situation in China*. Beijing: The Commerical Press.

Moingeon, B., & Ramanantsoa, B. (1997). Understanding corporate identity: The French school of thought. *European Journal of Marketing, 31*(5/6), 383–395.

Morrison, S., & Crane, F. G. (2007). Building the service brand by creating and managing an emotional brand experience. *Brand Management, 14*(5), 410–421.

Myers, G. (2010). *Discourse of blogs and wikis*. New York and London: Continuum.
Nao, M. (2011). The pragmatic realization of the native speaking English teacher as monolingual ideal. *Journal of Pragmatics, 43*(15), 3370–3781.
Ngai, C. S. B., & Ng, P. P. K. (2013). Transforming into the new era: Public relations industry in Hong Kong and China. *Public Relations Review, 39,* 575–577.
Olins, W. (1978). *The corporate personality: An inquiry into the nature of corporate identity*. London: Design Council.
Ozdora-Aksak, E., & Atakan-Duman, S. (2015). The online presence of Turkish banks: Communicating the softer side of corporate identity. *Public Relations Review, 41,* 119–128.
Pacea, O. (2011). CorpTweet: Brands, language and identity in Web. 2.0. *Annals of Ovidius University Constanta-Philogy, 22*(2), 157–168.
Packer, M. J. (2011). *The science of qualitative research*. New York: Cambridge University Press.
Page, R. (2012). The linguistics of self-branding and micro-celebrity in Twitter: The role of hashtags. *Discourse & Communication, 6*(2), 181–201.
Palmer, R. J., Walker, R. B., Campbell, T. L., & Magner, N. R. (2001). Examining the impression management orientation of managers. *Journal of Managerial Psychology, 16,* 35–49.
Pan, Y., & Kadar, D. (2011). Historical vs. contemporary Chinese linguistic politeness. *Journal of Pragmatics, 43,* 1525–1539.
Perez, A., & del Bosque, I. R. (2012). The role of CSR in the corporate identity of banking service providers. *Journal of Business Ethics, 108,* 145–166.
Planken, B., Sahu, S., & Nickerson, C. (2010). Corporate social responsibility communication in the Indian context. *Journal of Indian Business Research, 2*(1), 10–22.
Pearson, R. (1989). *A theory of public relations ethics*. Ph.D. dissertation, Ohio University.
Peng, Y. (2007). *The Chinese banking industry: Lessons from history for today's challenges*. London and New York: Routledge.
Peverelli, P. J. (2006). *Chinese corporate identity*. London and New York: Routledge.
Pieczka, M. (2011). Public relations as dialogic expertise? *Journal of Communication Management, 15*(2), 108–124.
Pomering, A., & Johnson, L. W. (2009). Advertising corporate social responsibility initiatives to communicate corporate image: Inhibiting skepticism to enhance persuasion. *Corporate Communications: An International Journal, 14*(4), 420–439.
Pollach, I. (2005). Corporate self-presentation on the WWW: Strategies for enhancing usability, credibility and utility. *Corporate Communications: A n International Journal, 10*(4), 285–301.
Pullen, A., & Linstead, S. (Eds.). (2005). *Organization and identity*. London: Routledge.
Rieber, R. W., & Carton, A. S. (1987). *The collected works of L.S. Vygotsky*. New York and London: Plenum Press.
Ren, S. (2014). Three banks to buy. *Barron's., 94*(50), M6.
Rosenfeld, P., Giacalone, R. A., & Riordan, C. A. (2002). *Impression management: Building and enhancing reputations at work*. London: Thomson Learning.
Rossiter, J., & Bellman, S. (2012). Emotional branding pays off: How brands meet share of requirements through bonding, companionship and love. *Journal of Advertising Research, 52* (3), 291–296.
Rosenfeld, P. R., Giacalone, R. A., & Riordan, C. A. (1995). *Impression management in organizations: Theory, measurement, and practice*. New York, NY: Routledge.
Rybalko, S., & Seltzer, T. (2010). Dialogic communication in 140 characters or less: How Fortune 500 companies engage stakeholders using Twitter. *Public Relations Review, 36,* 336–341.
Sacks, H., Schegloff, E. A., & Jefferson, G. (1974). A simplest systematics for the organization of turn-taking for conversation. *Language, 50,* 696–735.
Sacks, H. (1987). On the preferences for agreement and contiguity in sequences in conversation. In G. Button & J. R. E. Lee (Eds.), *Talk and social organization* (pp. 54–69). Clevedon, Avon: Multilingual Matters.
Saville-Troike, M. (1982). *The ethnography of communication: An introduction*. Malden, USA: Blackwell Publishing.

Saville-Troike, M. (2003). *The ethnography of communication: An introduction* (3rd ed.). Malden, USA: Blackwell Publishing.

Schiffrin, D. (1994). *Approaches to discourse*. Cambridge: Blackwell.

Schlenker, B. R. (1980). *Impression management: The self-concept, social identity, and interpersonal relations*. Montery: Brooks/Cole Publishing Company.

Schegloff, E. A., & Sacks, H. (1973). Opening up closings. *Semiotica, 7,* 289–327.

Schegloff, E. A. (1968). Sequencing in conversational openings. *American Anthropology, 70*(6), 1075–1095.

Schegloff, E. A., Sacks, H., & Jefferson, J. (1977). The preference for self-correction in the organization of repair in conversation. *Language, 53,* 361–382.

Schwartz, S. J., Luyckx, K., & Vignoles, V. L. (Eds.). (2011). *Handbook of identity theory and research*. New York: Springer.

Scollon, R., & Scollon, S. W. (1995). *Intercultural communication: A discourse approach*. Oxford: Blackwell Publishers.

Scollon, R., & Scollon, S. W. (2001). *Intercultural communication: A discourse approach* (2nd ed.). Oxford: Blackwell Publishers.

Sennett, R. (2006). *The culture of the new capitalism*. Yale: Yale University Press.

Searls, D., & Weinberger, D. (2001). *The Cluetrain Manifesto: The end of business as usual*. New York: Perseus Publishing.

Shi-xu, Kienpointner, M., & Servaes, J. (eds.). (2005). *Read the cultural other: Forms of otherness in the discourses of Hong Kong's decolonisation*. Berlin: Mouton DeGruyter.

Shi-xu. (2010). *Cultural discourse studies*. Beijing: Peking University Press.

Shi-xu. (2012). Expand methodologies of discourse research. *Journal of Multicultural Discourses, 7*(3), 209–211.

Sinclair, J., & Coulthard, R. M. (1975). *Towards an analysis of discourse: The English used by teachers and pupils*. London: Oxford University Press.

Soffer, O. (2012). Liquid language? On the personalization of discourse in the digital era. *New Media & Society, 14*(7), 1092–1110.

Stivers, T., & Sidnell, J. (2013). Introduction. In Jack Sidnell & Tanya Stivers (Eds.), *The handbook of conversation analysis*. Chichester: Wiley-Blackwell.

Spencer-Oatey, H. (2002). Managing rapport in talk: Using rapport sensitive incidents to explore the motivational concerns underlying the management of relations. *Journal of Pragmatics, 34,* 529–545.

Spencer-Oatey, H. (2007). Theories of identity and the analysis of face. *Journal of Pragmatics, 39,* 639–656.

Stoker, K. L., & Tusinski, K. A. (2006). Reconsider public relations' infatuation with dialogue: Why engagement and reconciliation can be more ethical than symmetry and reciprocity. *Journal of Mass Media, 27*(2–3), 156–176.

Streissguth, T. (2008). *China in the 21st century: A new world power*. Berkeley Heights, NJ: Enslow Publishers.

Su, H. (2009). Coding-switching in managing a face-threatening communicative task: Footing and ambiguity in conversational interaction in Taiwan. *Journal of Pragmatics, 41,* 372–392.

Tajfel, H., & Turner, J. C. (1979). An integrative theory of inter-group conflict. In W. G. Austin & S. Worchel (Eds.), *The social psychology of intergroup relations* (pp. 94–109). Monterey, CA: Brooks-Cole.

Tajfel, H. (1981). *Human groups and social categories*. Cambridge: Cambridge University Press.

Tan, Y. (2014). *Performance, risk and competition in the Chinese banking industry*. Kidlington, Oxford: Chandos Publishing.

Tang, L. (2012). Media discourse of corporate social responsibility in China: A content analysis of newspapers. *Asian Journal of Communication, 22*(3), 270–288.

Tannen, D. (1984). *Conversational style: Analyzing talk among friends*. Norwood, New Jersey: Ablex Publishing Corporation.

Tannen, D. (1989). *Talking voices: Repetition, dialogue, and imagery in conversational discourse*. Cambridge: Cambridge University Press.
Tannen, D. (1990). *You just don't understand: Women and men in conversation*. New York: Morrow.
Tannen, D. (1992). Interactional sociolinguistics. In Willaim Bright (Ed.), *Oxford international encyclopaedia of linguistics* (Vol. 4, pp. 9–12). New York: Oxford University Press.
Tannen, D. (1996). *Gender and discourse*. Oxford: Oxford University Press.
Tannen, D. (2005). *Conversational style: Analyzing talk among friends (new edition)*. New York: Oxford University Press.
Tannen, D. (2006). Language and culture. In R. W. Fasold & J. Connor Linton (Eds.), *An introduction to language and linguistics* (pp. 343–372). Cambridge: Cambridge University Press.
Tannen, D. (2009). Framing and face: The relevance of the presentation of self to linguistic discourse analysis. *Social Psychology Quarterly, 72*, 300–305.
Tannen, D., & Trester, A. M. (Eds.). (2013). *Discourse 2.0: Language and new media*. Washington D.C.: Georgetown University Press.
Theaker, A. (2004). *The public relations handbook* (2nd ed.). Abingdon: Routledge.
Theunissen, P. (2014). Co-creating corporate identity through dialogue: A pilot study. *Public Relations Review, 40*, 612–614.
Theunissen, P., & Wan Noordin, N. W. (2012). Revisiting the concept "dialogue" in public relations. *Public Relations Review, 38*, 5–13.
Thompson, C. J., Rindfleisch, A., & Zeynep, A. (2006). Emotional branding and the strategic value of the Dopelganger brand image. *Journal of Marketing, 70*(1), 50–64.
Thurlow, C., & Mroczek, K. (Eds.). (2011). *Digital discourse: Language in the new media*. Oxford: Oxford University Press.
Topalian, A. (2003). Experienced reality: The development of corporate identity in the digital era. *European Journal of Marketing, 37*(7/8), 1119–1132.
Topalian, A. (1984). Corporate identity: Beyond the visual overstatements. *International Journal of Advertising, 3*, 55–62.
Tracy, K., & Robles, J. S. (2013). *Everyday talk: Building and reflecting identities*. New York: The Guilford Press.
Tracy, K. (2002). *Everyday talk: Building and reflecting identities*. New York: Guilford Press.
Trusov, M., Bucklin, R. E., & Pauwels, K. (2009). Effects of word-of-mouth versus traditional marketing: Findings from an Internet social networking site. *Journal of Marketing, 73*(5), 90–102.
Tsai, W. S., & Men, L. R. (2012). *Motivations and antecedents of public engagement on corporate social networking sites*. Paper presented at the 96th Annual Convention of Association for Education in Journalism and Mass Communication, Chicago, United States of America.
Vaccari, C. (2010). "Technology is a commodity": The Internet in the 2008 United States presidential election. *Journal of Information Technology & Politics, 7*(4), 318–339.
van Dijk, T. (1988). *News analysis: Case studies of international and national news in the press*. Hillsdale, NJ: Lawrence Erlbaum Associates.
van Riel, C. M. B. (1995). *Principles of corporate communications*. London: Pentice-Hall.
Verschueren, J. (1999). *Understanding pragmatics*. London and New York: Arnold Publishers.
Vignoles, V. L., Schwartz, S. J., & Luyckx, K. (2011). Introduction: Toward an integrative view of identity. In S. J. Schwartz, K. Luyckx, & V. L. Vignoles (Eds.), *Handbook of identity theory and research*. New York: Springer.
Wang, L., & Chen, Z. T. (2006). Practical and theoretical research on instrumental variety of language-the perspective from Internet language. *Yu Yan Wen Zi Ying Yong (Applied linguistics)*, 3.
Watkins, B., & Lewis, R. (2014). Initiating dialogue on social media: An investigation of athletes' use of dialogic principles and structural features of Twitter. *Public Relations Review, 40*(5), 853–855.
Waters, R. D., & Jamal, J. Y. (2011). Tweet, tweet, tweet: A content analysis of nonprofit organizations' twitter updates. *Public Relations Review, 37*, 321–324.

Werner, M., & Chung, A. (2010). *Chinese banking: A primer on the market*. New York, NY: Bernstein Global Wealth Management.

West, L., & Trester, A. M. (2013). Face-work on facebook: Conversations on social media. In D. Tannen & A. M. Trester (Eds.), *Discourse 2.0: Language and new media*. Washington D.C.: Georgetown University Press.

Wood, D. (1991). Corporate social performance revisited. *The Academy of Management Review, 16*(4), 691–718.

Wood, E. (2004). Corporate identity. In A. Theaker (Ed.), *The public relations handbook* (2nd ed.). London and New York: Routledge.

Wood, E., & Somerville, I. (2008). Public relations and corporate communication. In A. Theaker (Ed.), *The public relations handbook* (3rd ed.). London and New York: Routledge.

Wortham, S. E. F. (1996). Mapping participant deictics: A technique for discovering speakers' footing. *Journal of Pragmatics, 25,* 331–348.

Wouter, C. (1986). Formalization and informalization: Changing tension balances in civilizing processes. *Theory, Culture & Society, 3*(2), 1–19.

Wu, D. D. (Ed.). (2008). *Discourses of cultural China in the globalizing age*. Hong Kong: Hong Kong University Press.

Wu, D., & Chan, K. (2007). Multilingual mix in Hong Kong advertising pre- and post-1997. *Asian Journal of Communication, 17*(3), 301–317.

Wu, D. D., & Feng, W. (2015). Pragmatist, evangelist, or sensualist? Emotional branding discourse on Sina Weibo. In C. Ngai & P. Ng (Eds.), *Role of language and corporate communication in Greater China: From academic to practitioner perspectives* (pp. 225–239). Berlin: Springer.

Wu, D., & Hui, H. M. (1997). Personage description in Hong Kong versus Mainland Chinese entertainment news discourse. *Text, 17*(4), 517–542.

Wu, D., & Ng, P. (2011). Becoming global, remaining local: The discourses of international news reporting by CCTV-4 and Phoenix TV Hong Kong. *Critical Arts, 25*(1), 73–87.

Wu, D., Li, C., & Feng, J. (2016). Sociolinguistic studies of new media: Review and prospect. *Contemporary Linguistics*, 18(4), 514–531.

Wu, D., & Lin, M. (2017 forthcoming). Relational acts and facework by Chinese celebrities on Weibo. In Chen, X. (Eds). *Politeness phenomena across Chinese genres*. London: Equinox.

Yin, J., Feng, J. & Wang, Y. (2015). Social media and multinational corporations' corporate social responsibility in china: The case of conocophillips oil spill incident. IEEE Transactions on Professional Communication, 58(2), 135–153.

Yu, G. (2010). Building solidarity in radio phone-in consultation in China: A case study. *Journal of Asian Pacific Communication, 20*(2), 226–242.

Yu, G., & Wu, Y. (2015). Managing awkward, sensitive, or delicate topics in (chinese) radio medical consultations. *Discourse Process*, 52(3), 201–225.

Yu, G., & Wu, Y. (2017 forthcoming). Anticipating the likelihood of success: Inviting in mandarin. *Journal of Pragmatics*.

Yu, G., Xiong, Z., Liu, H., Sun, S., & Zhang, L. (2001). *Survey of the internet language*. Beijing: China Economy Publishing House.

Yuan, Z. (2011). *An empirical study of medical consultants' pragmatic identity construction from the adaptationist perspective*. Ph.D. dissertation, Nanjing University, China.

Yuan, Z., & Chen, X. (2013). A study of pragmatic identity construction from the perspective of linguistic adaptation theory—A case study of medical consultations. *Foreign Language Teaching and Research, 4,* 518–530.

Yoo, C., & MacInnis, D. (2005). The brand attitude formation process of emotional and informational ads. *Journal of Business Research, 58,* 1397–1406.

Zeng, J. (2013). *State-led privatization in China: The politics of economic reform*. Abingdon, Oxon: Routledge.

Zhu, Y., & Hildebrandt, H. W. (2013). Effective persuasion of international business sales letters: An emic-etic perspective. *Management International Review, 53,* 391–418.

The manufacturer's authorised representative in the EU is Springer Nature Customer Service Centre GmbH, Europaplatz 3, 69115 Heidelberg, Germany. If you have any concerns regarding our products, please contact ProductSafety@springernature.com

Printed and bound by CPI Group (UK) Ltd, Croydon, CR0 4YY
30/09/2026
02225465-0014